Seasons of Preaching

Seasons of Preaching

◆

160 Best Sermons from the Preaching Resource, *Word & Witness*

Edited by
John Michael Rottman &
Paul Scott Wilson

Liturgical Publications Inc.
New Berlin, WI

Liturgical Publications, Inc.
New Berlin, Wisconsin
1-800-876-4574
email: lpi@execpc.com

160 Best Sermons from the Preaching Resource, *Word & Witness*
Edited by John Michael Rottman and Paul Scott Wilson.

ISBN: 0-940169-12-6

First Printing: March 1996

Table of Contents

List of Contributors

Doug Adams
Ronald Allen
Philip Apol
Alice Babin
David E. Babin
Douglas Bacon
Raymond Bailey
James Ball
Bonnie Benda
Judith Beyler
Harold Brack
Sally Brown
Daniel Bryan
David Buttrick
Ronald Cadmus
Ernest T. Campbell
William Carl III
Donald Chatfield
James Chatham
Jana Childers
Linda Clader
Charlotte Cleghorn
Ralph Clingan
Evans Crawford
Richard Cushman
Jill Edens
J. Richard Edens
Donald Edwards
Neil Engle
Joanne Enquist
Clyde E. Fant
Stephen Farris
Deryl Fleming
R. Benjamin Garrison

David M. Greenhaw
Paul Grosjean
Robert G. Hall
Larry Henning
Kim Henning
Terry Immel
David Schnasa Jacobsen
Philip Jones
Franklyn Jostt
James Kay
Jeffrey Kisner
Erik Kutzli
William Lawrence
Karen Engle Layman
Richard Lischer
Thomas G. Long
Craig A. Loscalzo
Barbara Martin
J. Allan McIntoch
Linda Mckieran-Allen
Frank Meadows
Duane Morford
Sue Ann Steffey Morrow
Mary Alice Mulligan
Errol Narain
Norman Neaves
Morris J. Niedenthal
Sam Portaro
Neta Pringle
David J. Randolph
David Reynolds
Charles L. Rice
Eduard R. Riegert
John Michael Rottman

Cynthia Ruud
Fleming Rutledge
Alan Salmon
David J. Schlafer
Cynthia Scott
J. Paul Seltzer
Dwight Shellaway
Robert Drew Simpson
Jerry Sisson
Lara Smit
Robert F. Smith
Michael Stewart
Lawrence H. Stookey
Richard L. Thulin
Thomas H. Troeger
Mary Donovan Turner
Suzanne Vanderlugt
Earl Vorpagel III
Norman Wall
Robert A. Wallace
Cheryl Jane Walter
Jon M. Walton
Peter Weaver
Earl Whepley
W. James White
Steve Willey
William H. Willimon
Patrick J. Willson
Deanna Wilson
Paul Scott Wilson
Eugene Winkler
Harry Winters
Peter Wyatt
Robert Young

PREFACE

Most preachers lament their lack of opportunity to hear good biblical preaching—other than their own! In a preaching class in seminary or in continuing education, we learn from hearing colleagues render God's Word in a faithful manner, even as we are sustained by that Word. One additional advantage of hearing others preach is stimulation of our own imagination. While we cannot have others prepare sermons for us, we nonetheless gather insights to biblical texts, theology, and a wide range of human experience and expression. One purpose of this anthology is to provide preachers the opportunity of hearing many sermons and homilies based on the lectionary and linked to seasons of the church year.

Not all readers will be preachers serving churches, however. Students in preaching classes will find here a large number of sermon samples. Other readers will be lay people and study groups, and they will find this to be a strong biblical and theological resource. It provides understanding of the church year and offers challenging insight to many personal, regional, and world issues.

Word and Witness is a lectionary-based journal that began publication in September 1976, the first major ecumenical journal of its kind. The sermons represent only one quarter of the publication. For each Sunday and holy day of the year there is: biblical commentary; suggestions for the worship service; a section on images and ideas; and a short sermon. The journal is a unique contemporary offering and over the years has become a resource for practical homiletical research. In celebration of twenty years of publication, we have selected these sermons from over 1,100 fine possibilities.

This collection is designed for use by the preacher, student, and lay person, and has several strengths:
(1) These sermons are of excellent quality. They were chosen according to a range of criteria, including enduring interest, biblical interpretation, stories, clarity, theological insight, focus on God's action, completeness, imagination, as well as other factors having to do with numbers and sections.
(2) They were originally designed to be short and move quickly to their purpose, thus readers may find help quickly.
(3) Many approaches and models are used.
(4) Large pages have been used to allow teachers and students to see entire sermons for easy analysis and discussion.
(5) There are 160 sermons, arranged according to the church season and special day.
(6) No other contemporary preaching resource offers as wide a range of seasonal sermons. Where a particular text is not present, seasonal concerns are nonetheless addressed. An index of biblical texts is provided.
(7) Over the years, preachers from many denominations have written contributions and many of the names here are well-known in preaching circles. An index of authors is also provided.

The lectionary has evolved during the life of our journal. Its roots lie in the Roman *Lectionary for Mass* that appeared in 1969. An ecumenical version appeared first as the *COCU Lectionary* (Consultation on Church Union, 1974), then later as the *Common Lectionary* (1983), that later became *The Revised Common Lectionary*[1] (1992).

Word & Witness is in a unique position to offer a strong collection of lectionary-based sermons. Yet the lectionary revisions also point to limitations here. Sermons in all sections, for example, the Seasons of Advent or Lent, are arranged chronologically through the 20 years of *Word and Witness* from 1976. The Sundays of the church year for which sermons were originally written are provided, but in some cases prior to 1992 and the current lectionary, they may no longer correspond to current readings. Use of the biblical index will help to facilitate finding specific texts.

There was merit in reproducing the sermons essentially as they originally appeared, with three exceptions: in the interest of uniformity, the sermons that had titles have had them dropped. In the interest of simplicity, only the biblical text(s) upon which the sermon is based is listed. In the interest of inclusivity, exclusive language has been altered.

Thanks are due to a number of people: Professor Charles L. Rice, who teaches homiletics at Drew University was the gracious editor of *Word and Witness* from 1977-1991, and first edited many of the pieces included here. We are grateful also to Professor Donald Macleod of Princeton Seminary, who was the founding editor in 1976. Vicki Kingsbury Flanagan and her staff at Liturgical Publications Inc., in New Berlin, Wisconsin, publish *Word and Witness* and were enthusiastic about this project from the start. They made smooth its path. Gratitude is owing to the many writers who have contributed to *Word and Witness* over the years, including those whose sermons could not be included here for reasons of space. We have lost touch with some contributors and others have now died, thus we have identified authors simply by their designations at the time of initial writing.

Finally we wish to thank the journal's subscribers around the world. The gifts of many people support the best labors we each bring to the privilege of proclaiming the gospel of Jesus Christ through the seasons of the years.

John Michael Rottman
Paul Scott Wilson
Editors, *Word and Witness*

---

[1] *The Revised Common Lectionary* is produced by an ecumenical gathering of nineteen churches or church agencies called The Consultation on Common Texts (CCT), based in Washington, D.C., and is published by Abingdon Press, Nashville, 1992. Our use of it is by permission of CCT.

Season of Advent

JOHN 1:6-8, 19-28

THE THIRD SUNDAY OF ADVENT
DECEMBER 17, 1978

In his book, *Frontiers for the Church Today*, Robert McAfee Brown remembers a New Yorker cartoon he once saw: "A cleric is seated before a typewriter late at night. There is a blank sheet of paper in his typewriter and an equally blank expression on his face. The topic to which he is devoting his energies is 'The Role of the Church in a Changing World'" (p. xi).

There is not only confusion about the role of the Church today, there is also despair—despair that the Church seems so weak, so idle, so ingrown, so outnumbered. Where there used to be anger at the Church, there is now often only pity. People "leave the Church," writes Robert Barrat, "on tiptoe." Even in this Christmas season, which seems by rights to belong to the Church, the tinny jangle of pre-taped Christmas carols blended with the ring of cash registers at the shopping malls erases all illusions about who really holds the power in society.

Perhaps, however, our despair over a limited, weak, insufficient Church is misplaced. *we used to —* In the gospel lesson for the day we are given a glimpse of what the Church, as the witnessing community, is all about, and the picture that emerges is one of a servant people, bound and limited, lacking authority and status, always pointing beyond itself to God who comes in Christ.

Our passage is surrounded with soaring poetry about Christ: "The Word was with God, and the Word was God.... The Light shines in the darkness.... The Word became flesh and dwelt among us, full of grace and truth." Suddenly—even abruptly—our text brings us thudding back to earth by introducing John the Baptist and by bending over backward to let us know that "he was *not* the light." He was *not* the Christ—not even Elijah or the prophet. He had no status of his own. In response to the question "Who are you?" he could only point to the vision beyond the horizon and say, "I am the voice of one crying in the wilderness, 'Prepare to meet the One who comes.'"

The Church finds itself in the same position as John the Baptist. It, too, is "not the light," but it, too, has "come to bear witness to the light." How can the Church do this? *← By hearing God's voice*

By being a servant people. Whenever the Church tries to re-establish Christendom, to build for itself an institutional base of power, authority, and status, it cuts itself off from God and from the world. By seeking itself to be the light, it thereby fails to bear witness to the light in Christ.

By acknowledging its limitations. *In Man's Need and God's Action*, Reuel Howe relates the experience of a discussion group of young parents. They were increasingly guilty and frustrated over their failures to be able to love their children completely and perfectly. Finally, notes Howe, they were able to see that their attempts to be "perfectionists in love" were really attempts to "play God," to usurp God's position. They came to understand that God used the limited nature of their love to point beyond them to God's love, and to prepare them to receive the love only God can give. Even so with the Church. The love of the Church, limited and sinful, prepares the world for the fulfilling love of God in Christ.

By *remaining faithful, even in the darkness, to the light of the vision of Christ*. Ernest T. Campbell tells the story of Samuel Zwemer, pioneer missionary to Arabia. To use the Christmas images of Bethlehem, he worked always in life's stables, but he kept his eye on the vision of the star. "Far, far away from home," writes Campbell, "he lost his four-year-old daughter Ruth, and his seven-year-old daughter, Katharina, within a span of eight days. Their bodies were laid to rest in a grave on Bahrein Island in the Persian Gulf. One headstone served both, one inscription, 'Worthy is the lamb that was slain to receive riches' " (Rev. 5:12). "A vision is not a sedative," Campbell goes on, "it is a stimulant. The man with a star in his soul can take a stable in his stride." The Church, in all its weakness, is a voice in the wilderness assuring a broken world that the God who binds up the brokenhearted is indeed coming. The Church is a signpost, pointing beyond itself and its own insufficient life, to the vision of the light—the all-sufficient Christ who comes to save.

Thomas G. Long, a minister in the Associate Reformed Presbyterian Church, in 1978 was Professor of Preaching and Worship at Columbia Theological Seminary, Decatur, Georgia.

MARK 1:1-8

THE SECOND SUNDAY OF ADVENT
DECEMBER 10, 1978

"I can't look! Tell me when it's over." "I can see it coming!" "I knew this would happen!" "I told you so!" How we want to believe it's all predictable (usually disastrously so!). *Why* we want to believe it is another question. So dull, so boring; life and the universe ticking down toward doom like a bomb mailed us by a monster. Books claiming to extract this message from the Bible, and knowing the day and the hour, sell in the millions. Why? Perhaps there's a kind of dour security, believing in predictability. (And who needs God then? We know what's going to happen.)

But if we think of the flux of life and the world, we know we're wrong. How varied it all is! We have been misled by loose talk of "natural law" and by neat charts of the physical elements and the genus-and species-groupings of life. But the wind shifts, and mocks all forecasts; the rocks on the beach are infinite in their solidity and variation; no two plants or puppies seek sun or supper in just the same way.

And we must not be misled by a Bible with a fixed table of contents into thinking of a God we can see coming. The Christian year comes 'round again, the same characters pose before us; like the same kids in the same Christmas pageant? Not at all! A whole wing of angels muster to sing: for shepherds ("To shepherds, Lord? If you say so."). Barren old Elizabeth suddenly gets pregnant, and her son grows to wander the ringing Judaean emptiness, bug-eyed at the wonder of God, dimly seeing Someone coming. An artisan's fiancee bears a babe in a barn; oriental astrologers come and kneel.

And doesn't it seem that the unexpectedness of God is finally more often on the side of mercy and reprieve than of judgment? Israel is carried off into Babylon; there faith grows, the synagogues develop, the early books of the Bible find their flowering, Psalms of depth are written ("By the waters of Babylon, there we sat down and wept," Psalm 137:1), heights of prophecy are reached (Ezekiel, the second Isaiah). John the Baptizer comes, threatening fire from an apocalyptic figure hard at his heels; and behold a preacher and healer, who submits to John's baptism, and breathes on his disciples to give them the Holy Spirit. The first Christians look for a quick, catastrophic end; gradually the realization dawns that God is waiting so that more and yet more will have a chance to enter a new life.

Christmas coming again, and the same old card list and the same old routine. But how many changed addresses and paths of life? How many braces on, or off? How many gone to glory, or born to enchant us? Who would have predicted, last year, where this Advent would find us? Without God, we must look desperately into our chances and changes for some fixity, some predictability. We want a pattern we can depend on; the alternative too fearsome.

But with God, the changes and chances bring always more mercy (even in judgment or disaster). The dependability is not in the events, but in the unexpected ways God finds to move into our lives again and ever again.

Donald F. Chatfield, a minister of the United Presbyterian Church in the U.S.A., in 1978 was professor of preaching, Garrett-Evangelical Theological Seminary, Evanston, Illinois.

LUKE 1:39-49

FOURTH SUNDAY IN ADVENT
DECEMBER 23, 1979

When Mary and Elizabeth met, it was like a comic opera. Here they were, big-bellied women, pregnant beyond a doubt, meeting in the back hills of Palestine. Like two plump divas they sing back and forth their separate arias. Put the picture in mind and it's almost ridiculous. But take a second look, and you'll discover they are acting out a drama, a drama of God-with-us.

One thing sure: Mary and Elizabeth were ordinary women. Elizabeth was an angular clergy's wife, while Mary was an adolescent peasant girl: scarcely heroic figures. They would fit in our world. Some years ago an artist put out a book of paintings, portraits of biblical people in modern dress. In his book, Mary came off as an open-faced, not too bright, blond with a scarf around her hair. Underline the fact, the two women were unremarkable. They were ordinary people.

But look, God chose to work through them, through their humanity. God always elects our ordinary lives. He chooses flesh! Oh, we expect 3-D spectaculars strung from the stars, trumpeting angels, disco whirls of lightening to signal God's activity; but God comes modestly—a bulge of flesh, a wet baby, a helplessness. He embraces our "low estate." God wandered into our world "incognito," as a poor child of a peasant mother from a hick town in a hick land. Think of a God who chooses to work through our humanness!

What matters is that we believe God is at work. Mary did. "Blessed is she who believed...." We must believe God is working the impossible in our too prosaic world. For, listen, if the coming of Christ tells us anything, it says that when human energies are down and out, and human wisdom dim, God is still working out our salvation—through us! Who in bleak, broke, over-run Israel would have "magnified the Lord" over a pregnant peasant girl? Nevertheless, God had entered his world with saving power. If the story of Christ tells us anything, it tells us to trust God. We must trust and, like sweet Mary, believe!

Of course, Mary did more: she offered herself to the purposes of God. She offered her body. Taken by the Lord, she still gave to the Lord. Believing isn't mere mental conjuring, it's bodily commitment. Though chosen, we must still choose—bodily. Some years ago there was a book with an odd title, *Ideas Have Legs*. Well, faith has legs, and lips and hands and, in Mary's case, a tummy, not to mention patience and love. Yes, the Lord will work his will through human ways, but faith cooperates. Mary offered herself bodily to the Lord.

Well, no wonder a baby John the Baptist leapt for joy! Hope turns to dancing when it catches sight of the Lord coming true! Revolutions feed on hope, but soon eat it away. Politics survives on hope, but endlessly betrays it. All our dreams go to dust, except God. God alone saves. So catch sight of God's grace in flesh fulfilling promises and you too will leap for joy. A mountain folk hymn matches the mood: "Clap hands, here comes Jesus!" Jesus is witness to God's word in flesh working among us, still working, still through flesh. Not hope, but joy. Sure joy!

Advent is a celebration of God and flesh. Even as we worship, God is working in our world, unseen, unrecognized, disguised in our humanity. He chooses us, and all flesh is "blessed."

David G. Buttrick, a minister of the United Presbyterian Church, in 1979 was Professor of Homiletics at The St. Meinrad School of Theology.

MATTHEW 11:2-11

THIRD SUNDAY IN ADVENT
DECEMBER 14, 1980

On the evening of June 3, 1980, as I rode my bike home from the church, the sky was growing unnaturally dark and a cloud the color of used motor oil was thickening in the northwest. The air seemed to grow heavy enough to resist the bike as I peddled forward. Only a few blocks from home, the storm siren began its eerie wail.

This happens so often that while my heart skipped a beat, there seemed to be no reason for undue concern. As I walked into the basement, the radio announcer rasped that all in our corner of the city should take cover, "In your basement or in a closet; in either place covered by something like a mattress." After what seemed like forever (but was in fact ten minutes) the radio reported that a tornado had ripped through a suburb three miles away and that another funnel had been sighted moving along the north edge of the city. Before midnight, seven tornadoes had left nearly 1,000 families homeless or with homes severely damaged.

Called out to use our church bus, it was an awesome experience to drive down what, only three hours before, had been the major commercial center, and to have the beam of the headlights pass across places where businesses— and friends — stood. And the beam continued into the darkness because there was nothing left standing for six or eight blocks on either side of the major street to reflect the light.

Nine families in our congregation came up out of the basements to the windy sky. Everything was gone. While none was literally blind, lame, leprous or dead, they were devastated. Some could not see a future. Some could hardly walk among the ruins. Some felt almost as sick as if they had an incurable disease. Others had literally become poor. The elderly and others on fixed income (and, consequently, inadequate insurance) desperately needed Good News.

It felt like a savage, hostile force had raked its claws across the face of our community.

Phone calls quickly formed work crews from the church who went directly to the devastated homes. The first response was nearly always simply to stand in silence. Young, old, male, female joined together under the naked sun to move watersoaked furniture, to pick up bricks and boards, to pack whatever family things could be saved. Money, food, clothing, began to pour in. Where nothing else could be given, a hug was shared. A long-range plan to provide emotional support was initiated for the time when the euphoria of the clean up drained away. It was a layperson who led a comprehensive program of support and advocacy for the poor while the Mayor's Council wrung its hands over the lost tax dollars of the businesses.

It wasn't "miraculous" in anything except a metaphorical sense. But the looks on the faces of the homeless, the surprise that so many cared, the feeling of support that would continue through the church after the clean-up crews left, surely exemplify something of what they felt who, in Jesus' day, once were blind but then could see.

Perhaps this experience will enlarge our vision to see that in the third world and in pockets of poverty all across our land, there are people who wake up every day to the kind of devastation and lifelessness to which we came out of our homes on June 4.

When John's disciples came to Jesus, they asked if Jesus would be the one to begin the Messianic age. He replied that they should look at the results of his ministry and make their own answer on the basis of what they saw.

Sometimes I wonder about our church's ministry—whether we are really witnesses to the dawning of the Messianic Age. Sometimes it seems that we spend a lot of time blowing our noses and washing our hands. But once, at least, I have seen something more than a reed shaking in the wind.

Ronald Allen, a minister of the Christian Church (Disciples of Christ) in 1980 was co-minister with his spouse of First Christian Church, Grand Island, Nebraska.

ISAIAH 40:1-11

THE SECOND SUNDAY IN ADVENT
DECEMBER 6, 1981

From what I observe of myself and others, it's not the unexpected surprises which make life difficult—it's the expected, humdrum, sameness which makes life so deadly. I heard a psychologist say it the other day; "The average person's back is breaking under an oppressive weight of tedium, drudgery, and boredom induced by constant attention to the trivial and inconsequential."

How is it for you?

"I go to work, punch in at 8:30, sit down at my desk, and wait for it to happen—but it hardly ever happens," I was told by someone recently. The same dragging out of bed, the same newspaper with the same bad news, the same glass of juice and the same soggy cornflakes, same family, same petty bickering, same bills, same arguments, same hassles, same life. And how is it for you?

Your days may be filled with change and challenge, you may bounce out of bed each morning filled with eagerness for the freshness of a new day. If that's you, fine. But if you're like most of us, I suppose it's more often than not the same. The thus-and-so-ness of it all is what gets us.

But no matter how it is for you, what about the world? How does the world look outside your door? Soaring crime rate, population explosion, threats of war and more than threats. I read the morning newspaper. The bad news, the bad tidings and gloom definitely have the upper hand. We humans—tooth-claw-and-nail, inching ever closer to the brink of disaster, taking two steps backward for every step forward, trapped in the sameness of our human cruelty, frailty, and stupidity—and what hope is there for us?

I am a preacher. What should I preach in the midst of such gloom, "What shall I cry?" the prophet asks. The words of despair come easily,

All flesh is grass,

and all its beauty is like the flower of the field.

The grass withers, the flower fades,

when the breath of the LORD

blows upon it;

surely the people is grass. (Isaiah 40:6-7)

And there you have it, the fading, withering, humdrum, expected death of it all. Monday morning at the office, standing at the kitchen sink, on the edge of nuclear holocaust, increasing shortages of food and too many people. There you have it.

But what if? What if there were another word to speak? What if it was a word to Israel languishing in Babylonian exile (our Old Testament setting), a word to Judea crushed under the heel of the Roman overlords (the gospel setting), a word to a despondent church grown weary from waiting for the Second Coming (today's epistle)? What if we're seeing the "facts of life" all wrong? What if the news of the newspaper is not the real news? What if our actions or lack of action is not the only action in our world? What if things are breaking forth, breaking up the boring, orderly, progression of things? What if God…(Read Isaiah 40:3-5).

Stranger, more surprising things have happened before, you know. In fact, the Bible could be read as one long record of all the surprising, strange, unexpected ways God has intervened to take a hand in our world. The exile from Egypt, the freedom from Babylonia, the words of the prophets, the birth of Christ—all showing that God takes a hand, often when we throw up our hands. In the night, the words thunder forth: (Read Isaiah 40:9).

Imagine yourself in the days of the first advent, living in some hot, dusty, insignificant little backwater town in Judea, some Bethlehem of a place. What if you heard the words, "Prepare the way of the Lord?"

What difference would it make if you heard that? If you believed that? If you acted upon that? What if?

And there you are, with that lump in the throat the doctor says might be malignant, with a marriage more masquerade than marriage, with children slipping away from you, with a job more drudgery than vocation, with a world gone bad and getting worse all the time—What if?

What if, in the midst of all that, you came to church and got Good News rather than bad?

What if you were to see God Almighty stepping into your life, your world and taking hand? Would you be led to take a hand? Would you change to suit the change? What might you do differently tomorrow if you heard, really heard, that word today?

What if this letter, this word, were addressed to you, to our church in the twentieth century, not only their church in the second century. What if? (Read II Peter 3:8-14).

William H. Willimon in 1981 was pastor of Northside United Methodist Church in Greenville, South Carolina, and Adjunct Professor of Liturgy and Worship at Duke Divinity School, Durham N. C.

---

2 SAMUEL 7:1-5, 7-16

THE FOURTH SUNDAY IN ADVENT
DECEMBER 20, 1981

Nathan at first agreed. David lived in his house at rest from all his enemies. The old promises had come true. Only the last remained: to build the house for the Lord. Actually, it was almost embarrassing. David in his house of fine cedar, the best that Lebanon could supply, looking out over the tent of the Lord, much the worse for wear, even though it had been well taken care of. After all, a tent is a tent, even if it is a fine one. And tents just don't hold up. The sun rots the fabric. The wind tatters the edges. The dust becomes part of the cloth. It fades. It tears. Not at all a fitting place for the Lord of Lords and the King of Kings.

It was okay when they were travelling around, moving from place to place. But they were now settled in the land as God had promised. They had settled down. They were respectable. The tent was a disgrace. Besides, David had a few ideas about architecture that he wanted to try out. And Nathan had a few things he wanted in a temple, too.

The building committee had been appointed. They had done their feasibility studies. Money was not a problem. They had got this far (with God's help). Now they were going to do something great for God. They would build for God a house worthy of his name. One that would add some importance (and value) to the neighborhood, indeed, one that would be the center of the whole city, the whole nation, the whole world. O Almighty God, what we intend to do for you, you wouldn't believe!

That night, Nathan went home to sleep on it. To dream his dreams of grandeur, of hope, of promise. And God came to Nathan in that dream, and put things back into their proper perspective. "It is not what you will do for me," God said, "but what I will do for you. I will build you a house beyond your wildest dreams. David will not have only a house, he will have a dynasty. And my kingdom will be established forever. Tell *that* to David," God said.

It is not what you are going to do for God, but what God is doing for you. And it is far greater than you ever imagined. God has turned things completely around. God doesn't do things in our accustomed way. God is a surprise.

Probably no one was more surprised than Mary. "She considered in her mind what sort of greeting this might be" is the second greatest understatement in all of scripture, surpassed only by "How can this be, since I have no husband?" Surprise, Mary, you're pregnant! By the Holy Spirit! And he will be called the Son of the Most High. And of his kingdom there will be no end. And you thought Elizabeth was surprised to have a child in her old age.

It is not what we are doing for God; it is what God is doing for us. What do you do with a surprise like that? You receive it with joy, that's what. That's what Mary did, and David, and Hannah before them. Receive it with joy. It is God's gift, God's grace, God's surprise.

Sometimes we treat Advent too much as preparation, as if Christmas will come only if we properly prepare for it. We have to buy the presents (at the last minute), prepare the tree, ready the feast, sing the cantata, build the nativity. Then Christmas will come. Maybe, someday, if we, like Mary, were simply to let it be, Christmas might come in a new and surprising way. For the only real preparation for Christmas is receptivity, openness to the new and surprising thing God is doing for us, willingness to say "Yes" to the outrageous surprise of God.

It is not what we can do for God, but what God is doing for us. And that can surprise us beyond our wildest imaginings when we are willing to say "Yes." And, "Let it be."

Terry Immel in 1981 was a minister of the Christian Church (Disciples of Christ) serving Marana Community Christian Church of Marana, Arizona.

✦ ISAIAH 61:1-4; 8-11

THE THIRD SUNDAY IN ADVENT
DECEMBER 13, 1981

Our grandson wants an electric train for Christmas. The other day, he closed his eyes, squeezed himself, jumped up and down and said, "I'm hoping, I'm hoping, I'm hoping." I was struck by the fact that his was a vibrant, physically active form of "hoping." He was literally hopping with hope. Let's think about the meaning of Christian hope, its foundations and its implications.

The biblical words "hope" and "wait" are key words for this season, but they are not, as many think, passive words. Erich Fromm calls hope "the crouched tiger, which will jump when the moment for jumping has come" (*The Revolution of Hope*, Bantam, Toronto, 1968, p. 9). Ernest Campbell likewise describes the biblical word "wait." The biblical word is *apokaradokia*. Campbell tells of friends who named their cat Apokaradokia. Why? Because the biblical notion of "waiting" is like a cat crouching—still and silent, it has every muscle bunched, ready, "poised to press into new and unknown places." "Forget the word," says Campbell, "Forget the cat. But remember the posture." That is the posture of spirit that belongs to Christian waiting and to Christian hope (*Locked In a Room With Open Doors*, Word, 1974).

Christian hope rests on two foundations. First, God's promise of presence, "Arise, shine, for your light has come. Unto us a child is born. One shall come after me..." and second, "The Lord has anointed me to bring good tidings." All these wondrous words celebrate the season of hope.

The other foundation stone is found in John's preaching. "Repent, for the Kingdom of God is at hand." And in Peter's— "Repent...and you will receive...for the promise is to you and your children." Repentance is not a very cheerful word for this joyful season but hope is, and human hope begins with repentance. For repentance says that we are capable of change. There is dignity and responsibility in that. And out of these comes hope.
Now the implication: our hope is for ourselves, but for others also. It would be much easier if we could just ignore justice issues for December, especially these last two weeks, but if we take the Christmas story seriously we will have to remember that it has two dimensions. The wise men, shepherds, and holy family represent one side of the story. The mothers of Bethlehem, Herod, and the Roman soldiers stand on the other side of the Christmas stage.

While we celebrate the coming of light, we recall also the reality of darkness. That darkness that will overwhelm many this Christmas. Yet the opposite of hope is not hopelessness, (that simply is an absence of hope) but cynicism, that subtle sin that nibbles at our souls until they are tattered and diminished. Hope is the mental ingredient of life and growth. It presses forward with determination and confidence. The prophet announces the coming of a wondrous commander, but that commander will rally his forces to march for peace and justice.

Deliverance comes before Decalogue, but one surely follows the other. Christmas comes before the Sermon on the Mount, but one cannot be separated from the other. Jesus was not born into a gentle world, and his mother's meditation was shot through with grim reality. "He has exalted the humble and meek." Hope tells us that God himself will not ultimately fall victim to our stupidity and greed and violence, and that His presence empowers the meek to dare and to die to self, that a world may have fresh hope.

Robert A. Wallace, a minister of the United Church of Canada, in 1981 was senior minister at Rosedale Church, Toronto, Ontario

---

ISAIAH 7:10-17

THE FOURTH SUNDAY IN ADVENT
DECEMBER 18, 1983

The cartoon strip *Peanuts* is filled with anxiety-stricken characters constantly searching for assurance that life will be okay. Charlie Brown stands on the pitcher's mound, checking the weather, the opposition and his own players for some sign that his team might win one game. Linus nervously crouches in the garden, hunting for a sign that the Great Pumpkin will arrive. Even Lucy is often found at the foot of the piano, waiting for some sign, however far-fetched, that Schroeder loves her.

We, too, constantly seem to be looking for signs. Every day, many of us examine our personal lives for evidence that we are loved and accepted by our families and friends. It is true of our physical health also. Day by day, signs of recovery are anxiously monitored. Most of us seek signs that we are succeeding in our professions. Much of our energy as a country lately has been spent looking for signs of economic recovery. More missiles, better armies, increased recruitment—for some, these are signs of national security. Even in our churches we examine the books each month for signs of growth.

Underlying all of this searching for signs is a need to feel secure, to attain a sense of well-being. We want to know that we will not be alone, that life will turn out OK. And the more we look, the more anxious we become. There is little peace of mind when we are continually having to seek reassurance. Security is never completely guaranteed for us by marriage, our jobs, the doctors, or the government.

Ahaz, the king of Judah, was plagued by anxiety. Assyria, a pagan nation, was expanding its empire, a threatening situation. Several of the small surrounding states were angry at Ahaz for not uniting with them to oppose Assyria. What should he do? He looked around in panic for some sign that Judah would not be completely devastated. Perhaps he should make an alliance with Assyria? Isaiah counseled Ahaz to forget military pacts and look to God for security. "God will even give you a sign of his continuing protection. A young woman shall conceive a son, and his name will be called Emmanuel, God with us." But Ahaz ignored this sign and faithlessly sold out to Assyria.

Advent is supposedly a time of joyous expectation. Yet, here we are, just like Ahaz, anxious about what will become of us. Is it possible that we too are looking in the wrong place for signs of security? Maybe Advent is just what we need, for it is a preparation to celebrate the most important sign ever given to humanity, the sign of God's presence with us, the Word made flesh. We are reminded by the sign of a babe lying in a manger that the Savior, our assurance, has already entered our lives. "Jesus is the sign raised among the nations, demonstrating the love of God for humanity" (Worgul).

Once this sign of God's presence manifested in the man Jesus was gone, a new sign emerged. The Church as the Body of Christ, became the concrete reality of God's being with the world. The Church, in its best moments, continues making the Word flesh as it cares for the poor, confronts the comfortable and witnesses to the good news. As individuals encounter the Church, they encounter God.

The sacraments, as offered by the Church, unfold the loving aspects of Jesus' ministry as "outward and visible signs of an inward and spiritual grace." They parallel the great moments and needs in human life, and thus are signs of God's presence at all stages of birth, growth and death. "Through the Christian sacraments, self-giving, of which the supreme example is the Incarnation, finds another and continuous expression by entering into the everyday lives of humans."

We also find signs of God's presence within ourselves, if we look closely. As with Mary and Joseph, God can come to us in dreams and visions. Meditation images, fantasies, thoughts which come to us in prayer may be God's communication to us from the unconscious. We are not even alone in the core of our beings.

To the extent that Jesus the Christ is incarnated in our own words and actions, we ourselves also become signs of God's presence. When we give comfort, work for justice and pursue peace, we become, in the words of Paul, "saints" continuing the mission of Jesus.

During Advent, we are called to open our eyes to the signs of the incarnation, which will provide real security for our anxiety-torn lives and world. O come, O come, Emmanuel!

Bonnie L. Benda, an ordained minister of the United Methodist Church, in 1983 was the teacher of preaching at St. Thomas Seminary, Denver, Colorado, and a pastor of Evergreen United Methodist Church in Evergreen, Colorado.

LUKE 21:25-36

THE FIRST SUNDAY IN ADVENT
DECEMBER 1, 1985

The world doesn't turn out the way we'd like it to. We can recite a litany of loss and catastrophe from history and from today's news; we can add, each one of us, disasters both minor and major through which we have lived, from the death of a pet when we were small to the terror of nuclear annihilation which faces and challenges us today. Even Christmas never quite turns out the way we want; for some of us it is an annual emotional disaster. "Well," we finally are tempted to say, "that's just the way it is. The world's a cheat; nothing good can last; hope is the doorway to an aching heart."

But Jesus, having told his disciples that there will be cataclysms even worse than the shattering destruction of Jerusalem and its temple, having foretold the dissolving of the heavens, monstrous tidal waves, and people fainting dead away from the terror of it all, says, "when these things begin to take place, look up and raise your heads, because your redemption is drawing near" (Luke 21:28). Someone once wonderfully parodied a verse from Kipling: "If you can keep your head when all about you are losing theirs…you don't understand the situation!" And we've known that often enough to laugh ruefully in recognition.

But Jesus tells us more than the parody, and more even than Kipling originally did. It's the *others*, he tells us, who don't understand the situation. It's those who hear of economic collapse and step out of windows, or of death camps and despair of life, or of mortal illness and become morose, or of nuclear war and give up on life and hope…it is those people, it is us when we give way to such despair, who don't understand the situation.

The truth is, says Jesus, that the approach of doom heralds my entry into the field, my appearance in the desperate situation. Disaster is not identical with the will of God; but it is a sign to the Christian to be up and looking for his or her Lord and Savior. For example: A sentence of death is also the sound of the door opening into unending life. A bereavement is also a challenge to find God's mercy in greater depths around us. The birth of a damaged child is also a time when God gives waves of love. A divorce is also a chance to get help in dealing with people in a new and more healthful way, a way more in line with God's intentions for us. A loss of a part of our body is also a chance to reach out to others in a similar condition. A disaster brought on by alcohol abuse is also an opening to surrender, in the company of others, to a power higher than ourselves. Economic catastrophe is also a challenge to see what our good is, when our goods are drastically reduced.

Alzheimer's disease, famine, cancer, tornados, poverty, cystic fibrosis, war, accidental death and maiming—all these and so many more afflict and threaten our poor, inadequate definitions of what life and happiness are all about. But in Advent the church says, in the midst of all of this comes the Christ, just as he came to two refugees in a stable in an occupied country, just as he has come in the midst of oppression and disaster and martyrdom for a great company of Christians of all places and times, just as he will come in and through and triumphing over the thunder of the end of time. The world is not a cheat, he tells us; but when you feel it shaking, look up! There's more to it than what you see, and better—and it's on the way!

Donald F. Chatfield, a minister of the Presbyterian Church U.S.A., in 1985 was professor of preaching and worship, Garrett-Evangelical Theological Seminary, Evanston, Illinois

MATTHEW 11:2-11

THE THIRD SUNDAY OF ADVENT
DECEMBER 17, 1989

A holiday commercial of several seasons ago pictured a young couple exchanging gifts. The woman's face lights up as her husband hands her what is obviously a box containing a wristwatch. The womans face falls, however, when she studies the contents of the box, and she barely gets off a less than-heartfelt "thank you." When asked what the problem is, she answers, "Well, I was hoping for a Longines."

Besides being an image of shallow ingratitude (which, I'm sure, the commercial makers did not intend), the commercial urges us to wish for and expect the best. And we're disappointed if we don't receive it.

On a larger scale, unmet expectations not only disappoint and frustrate us—they can sour and skew our view of life. As a member of the "Baby Boomer" generation growing up in the fifties and sixties, I was led to expect that the "American Dream" of peace and economic prosperity would always be mine, if I just worked at it. However, economic excesses, an unwinnable war which fractured the nation, and the reality of limited resources on all fronts have burst the balloon of the "American Dream" for many. In the area in which I live, the young can't afford housing, the elderly can't afford to keep their homes, and families with two incomes can't make ends meet. The number of homeless grows. The heady optimism of the fifties and sixties has given way to the greedy, grabbing cynicism of the eighties. We'll elect any "messiah" who promises to help us keep what is "ours." And if that messiah has clay feet, well that's just part of the game. "Don't expect much, and you won't be disappointed."

It was within such an atmosphere of "great expectations" and deep disappointments that the imprisoned John the Baptist sent his disciples to Jesus with the query, "Are you he who is to come, or shall we look for another?" Messianic expectations were at a fever pitch, and John himself had helped to fuel the fire with his incendiary denunciations of the current religious leadership and his apocalyptic warnings to repent and prepare for the avenger who was to come. The expected Messiah would be a first century "Rambo," wiping out the Roman oppressors and setting up his kingdom, like that of David in the "good old days."

John had thought he had seen these qualities in Jesus at Jesus' baptism, but now, imprisoned and facing death, he began to wonder. This Jesus certainly didn't behave as expected.[1] Had John "put his money on the wrong horse?"

Jesus doesn't answer John directly. His reply does, however, raise an alternate vision of the Messiah—one stretching back hundreds of years, deep into Israel's prophetic roots. This is a Messiah who does not destroy, but builds up, who does not hurt, but heals. This is a Messiah who more than meets the expectations of his people. This Messiah is a true giver of "Shalom"—a wholeness, wellness, completeness—not just physical, but emotional and spiritual—all that God intends for his people.

Jesus' reply puts the ball squarely back into John's court. "What were you expecting? Look at the record, and decide for yourself." "And blessed is he who takes no offense at me" is a challenge to faith for John—and for us.

Just what are we expecting as the days of Advent slip by and the "big day" is only a week and a day away? A cute little baby, wrapped in swaddling clothes and misty nostalgia who will help us escape, at least for a little while, from the realities of life? A "therapeutic counselor"[2] who will make us feel good about ourselves and bless our aspirations for "success?" A "cosmic politician" who can be called upon to sanction our economic policies and nationalistic ambitions as a "Christian" nation?

Jesus offers an alternative vision. The One who comes is a healer and restorer. He looks past the veneer of our wants and addresses our deep-set needs. He sees us as we are—sin-broken, sin-crippled people, groping in our blindness for answers to the meaning of our lives, limping along on the crutches of egoism, racism, nationalism, pragmatism, militarism, or whatever other "ism" promises to give us fulfillment.

And he heals. He heals our brokenness by himself being broken on the cross. He salves our wounds with the ointment of his own blood, shed for our redemption. He tastes death so that eternal death will not devour us. He rises, scarred but victorious, so that "by his wounds we are healed." He offers to us Shalom—the wellness, wholeness, completeness only he can grant.

The old Rolling Stone's song says, "You can't always get what you want...but sometimes you get what you need." The One whom we await may not fulfill our wants and expectations, but he does fulfill our needs by giving us himself. That is his promise. That is our hope. And that hope will never be disappointed.

Notes:

[1] In a longer sermon format, this might be a good place to quote Buechner's contrast of John's and Jesus' ministries—"Peculiar Treasures," p. 70, Harper & Row Pub.

[2] For a critique of preaching that presents Jesus in this manner, see David G. Buttrick's "Preaching Jesus Christ," Fortress Press.

Dwight D. Shellaway in 1989 was pastor of Holy Trinity Lutheran Church, Hasbrouck Heights, New Jersey.

MARK 13:32-37

THE FIRST SUNDAY OF ADVENT
DECEMBER 2, 1990

Advent has on occasion been referred to as a "little Lent," a time when as Christians we subject ourselves to a kind of spiritual examination. Our passage today from the gospel of Mark helps us to do exactly that. There Jesus warns us to make certain we are awake and alert. This passage gives us a chance to splash a little cold water on our faces. It gives us opportunity to make certain that we are wide awake and ready for Advent, the coming of our Lord.

Wakefulness does not come naturally to us. You may remember how in The Wizard of Oz, Dorothy and her fellow travelers stray from the yellow brick road and fall into danger among the poppies. As she lingers among the beautiful poppies she very nearly reaches a premature end to her journey home. Unbeknownst to her the seemingly harmless poppies lull her to into a deep and potentially deadly sleep.

Like those poppies, our world is full of attractions which threaten to lull us to sleep and turn us from our spiritual journeys. Not all of those distractions are ugly or obviously evil either. Any number of things can lull and dull our sensibilities to the coming of our Lord. An over fascination with sports and recreation, business success, or our quest for the perfect home are a few of the many things which can distract our attention from the advent of our Lord. Jesus seems to recognize the dangers. He warns us to stay awake. Take an inventory. Watch how you are spending your money. Watch how you are spending your time. Watch. You don't want to be caught napping.

But then how can ordinary Christians like ourselves expect to stay awake? We all know how easy it is to get caught and lulled to sleep by all the various distractions in our world. What are the chances that we will be awake when the master returns for us? We need help.

For several years I worked the night shift on the nursing staff in a psychiatric hospital. The shift ran from 11 pm to 7 am and employees were cautioned against falling asleep at the cost of losing their jobs. But staying awake when everyone else was sleeping was often a real battle, especially after a long weekend of late nights and little sleep. Sometimes I would guzzle coffee and at other times splash myself with cold water. On those nights I lived in mortal fear of falling asleep only to be awakened by the supervisor's cold touch and to hear her announce that I would be looking for another job.

And then one night it happened. I had had an especially exhausting weekend and toward five in the morning, try as I might to stave it off, I fell asleep. Sometime later I felt a surge of panic as someone called my name and tapped me on the shoulder. John, wake up. But as I turned to face the supervisor, I saw the face of the nurse who worked on the unit down the hall. I saw the supervisor's car coming, she informed me. I knew how sleepy you were earlier, so I came to make sure you were awake.

The good news of the gospel today is that in a similar way those of us who belong to Jesus Christ do not watch alone. Just as in the Garden of Gethsemane, Jesus still stands beside his drowsy disciples. Our spiritual well being does not depend upon fearful, heroic, watching. No, Jesus watches with us and for us. He stands ready to wake us up if we become drowsy. And so we have confidence that we will not be sleeping at the crucial moment because he watches with us.

John Rottman in 1990 was the pastor of the First Christian Reformed Church of Toronto, Ontario.

LUKE 1:26-38

THE FOURTH SUNDAY OF ADVENT
DECEMBER 23, 1990

It's just after dawn in the Ethiopian province of Eritrea. The sun's rays are just beginning to streak up over the Eastern horizon. The only sound I hear is hungry children, scratching for kernels of wheat in the dry cracked land. It's just after dawn and a voice whispers to an ordinary refugee: "Do not be afraid. I've come to take you to a new land. How quickly can you be ready?"

Two thousand years earlier it's midnight in the town of Nazareth. A light shines in the darkness and a voice says to a poor peasant girl: "Hail, O favored one. God is very near to you."

My name is Mary and I have a story to tell. I am betrothed to a man named Joseph. Today I have received startling news. Come along with me and I'll tell you as I'm telling Joseph.

"Yes, Joseph, I know it's the middle of the night. And I know that we're not supposed to be alone together now. But I cannot wait to tell you.

I was sitting in my bedroom weaving a piece of red cloth for the rabbi. I love to weave. It relaxes me. I think a lot about you, Joseph, when I'm weaving. I think about the future. Will we have children? And what will it be like for our children?

Just when I was weaving the last strand of gold into the bright red cloth, the threads began to glisten in a way they never have before. It was strange but I didn't think much about it.

Besides I was getting sleepy, so I blew out the candle and got into bed. But just as I was settling down my eye caught a strange light. The gold threads on the cloth seemed to be dancing in the light. I had the feeling I wasn't alone in the room. It was then I heard the voice say: "Mary, you are God's favored one. God is with you. You are not alone."

I sat bolt upright in bed. The light on the gold threads disappeared. I was both excited and frightened. And the startling words kept echoing through my mind: "Mary, you are God's favored one. God is with you." Me! Ordinary Mary!
It embarrasses me to even think about being called God's favored one. Why would God single me out? No one's ever paid any attention to me except you, Joseph. I'm just a handmaid.

The voice continued. "Do not be afraid, Mary, God loves you dearly. You will become pregnant and give birth to a child and you will name him Jesus. He will be great and will be known as the Son of the Most High. His reign shall never end."

You can imagine my utter shock and disbelief at that. I could hardly take such news sitting down. "A baby! I'm not married. Can't you see the scandal this will create? This is too much!"

Joseph, I couldn't blame you if you didn't believe me. Why should you? You don't even have to say anything. I can see by your eyes that you're hurt. Yes, I've thought about all those things, too. What will the neighbors think? Can't you just feel the whispers and gossip.

It frightens me to think of the terrible things Joseph could do. What if he doesn't believe me. He could save himself by making me the scapegoat of the town. My God! I could be stoned to death.

But the messenger still wasn't finished: "The Holy Spirit will come upon you, the power of the Most High will cover you with its shadow. Your child will therefore be called Holy—the Son of God."

When I heard that I could scarcely contain myself. And my response seemed to be coming from somewhere else, though I was the one saying it: "Let it be to me according to your word."

Now, my friend, what would you do? Would you accept a gift like that? If you were in my shoes, would you want your child to break your heart in pieces while jealous leaders trump up little schemes? And could you stand and watch while soldiers toss dice and laugh and tell dirty jokes? Could you really say: "Let it be done to me according to your word?"

Believe me, I spend sleepless nights trying to make sense out of all of this. Over over again I ask myself, "Why me? How can I cope?" But no longer can I fight it disbelieve it.

I began this story as a village girl weaving a piece of ordinary cloth. Now I am a woman of faith conscious that the Spirit of God is alive in me. I came with a piece of tapestry that I was weaving. Now God chooses to weave me into God's own tapestry. I say "yes" to the angel and a song starts to sing in me and you and you....

Cynthia Scott is ordained in the United Church of Canada and in 1990 was minister of Victoria Village United Church, Toronto, Canada.

LUKE 1:26-38

FOURTH SUNDAY IN ADVENT
DECEMBER 19, 1993

"Are you ready for Christmas?" It's one of those conversation starters I find myself asking and being asked. How do most of us respond? With a groan? With a recital of all the things we have yet to do? With an honest "No!" By now, maybe even with a "Yes."

This is the time of year where we spend a lot of time and energy getting ready for Christmas, or rather, we spend a lot of time and energy getting ready for the festival. How much time and energy do we spend getting ready for the Christmas which is "Christ's mass", the birth of the child who lies at the heart of it all? Even if you are one of the organized ones who is ready for Christmas, are you ready for Jesus?

I wonder that about Mary. The angel came with his announcement. Surely she was surprised: who wouldn't be? I doubt if she was any more used to seeing angels than you or me. But somehow she was prepared.

The other day I got to thinking about the shepherds. If Luke was right about a host of singing angels, then surely there must have been other folk within sight and sound. Why didn't they see? What was it about the shepherds that prepared them to respond?

"Watch", says Jesus, "for you do not know when I will come." What is also clear from the Christmas story is we don't know how he will come. There were so many who missed him. We don't want that to happen to us.

The festivities of Christmas are fun: the food, the family, the presents, the tree, the sense of expectancy. They are great fun, but if that's all there is, then it's empty. It passes and we are left with left overs and a messy house - and a cranky disposition! How do we prepare ourselves for that child who comes to us and stays with us, through the festivals and the pain?

It's a pregnant time of year. Pregnancy is a time of waiting, of watching, of getting ready. It's a good image for us today. I suspect that's not an image that most of you men have thought about claiming for yourselves. Try it. Play with it.

Pregnancy has to do with letting the child grow within us. It's part of us, yet at the same time it comes from beyond. Our job is simply to be attentive to it, and cherish it, be ready so that when it's born it has a place in our lives. Can you let this child grow within you? Can you prepare a place for him in your life?

How do we do that? Partly it is just a matter of being receptive. There are so many ways in which the child comes to us. Simple things. Think of all the Christmas carols that blare over loudspeakers, sing from car radios, invite us to sing along. Do we even hear the words anymore? What if we really listened? What if, like Mary, we pondered them in our hearts? How many Christmas scenes do we pass by with hardly a glance? There's one on the lawn at Village Hall, a hundred varieties that come on the Christmas cards. Pause for just a moment. Put yourself into the scene. Kneel with the shepherds. Offer your gift like the Magi. Tend him like Mary and Joseph. Find your own ways: a prayer while you bake cookies, a time of meditation as you drive, family worship at the dinner table. Let the presence of that child grow in your life.

Jesus says another way we prepare is to watch. Nowadays we have satellites in the sky to do our watching for us. In Jesus' day cities posted watchers on the city walls who scanned the horizon for signs of danger or of promise. If you've ever done a lot of watching, then you know that if you stare hard enough you begin to see what you are looking for. Even if it's not there. The danger is that you won't see what is there. Staring straight ahead doesn't work. You have to be able to see out of the corners of your eyes. Peripheral vision is more likely to catch the movement of something coming. A good watcher must continually scan the horizon, looking in more than one place, keeping the eyes moving.

Do you think Christmas can only come to you in one way? Do you know for sure how Jesus will come to you this year? You might see what you are looking for—and miss the reality. Being prepared means keeping your eyes—and your heart—open for however he might come.

Preparation is a kind of pregnancy, it's a time of watching, even more it is a willingness to respond. "Let it happen to me as you have said," says Mary. Did she know what she was getting into? Was she really prepared? How could she? Yet she was willing.

What does Jesus call you to do? It may seem foolish, or exciting, or quite impossible. You may not be prepared, but are willing to give it a try? If you are willing to respond, then you will discover that whatever you bring to the adventure, God will use, God will empower. God is prepared.

The Rev. Neta Pringle in 1993 was Pastor of Concord Presbyterian Church,
Wilmington, Delaware

LUKE 21:25-36

FIRST SUNDAY OF ADVENT
NOVEMBER 27, 1994

It's tempting for me to apologize to you every year at the beginning of Advent. To apologize for God. After all, it happens the same way every year. Just as the Christmas lights are strung and lit, and the shop windows are being dressed with gentle scenes of the gospel, God's Word, broadcasts violence. Just when we are thinking up annual greetings to faraway friends, the gospel disturbs our peace with threat and thunder. "Nation will rise against nation.... There will be great earthquakes, famines and pestilences...signs in the sun, moon and stars. On the earth nations will be in anguish and perplexity at the roaring of the sea. Men will faint from terror...." And we all murmur to ourselves, "not at my Christmas party, please!"

Suddenly our silent nights are not so certain anymore. Why must Advent begin this way every year, or be this way at all? If we don't hear the doom from Luke, we hear it from Matthew or Mark. St. John—the only one who could spare us—we don't hear from the first Sunday in Advent. Are we supposed to burn the stockings, forget the tree? Instead of the Advent calendars, should we count down the days with the four horsemen of the Apocalypse, a few plagues, and an earthquake or two?

Today the church year begins once again. We come out of so-called "ordinary time" into so-called "holy time," a special season celebrating God's intense activity. God may act in every moment, but in some moments God acts extraordinarily. Advent is the first of those seasons in the church year, and the contrasts are stark, the tones black and white, not gray. Before the news is good, it is bad.

God seems to revel in situations like this, when the news is bad before it is good. The time of Noah, when a good man was hard to find; God only found one. The situation of Abraham and Sarah, a couple barren and hopeless, without a child to carry on their name. A people in Israel's predicament after 450 years in Egypt; they came as guests, but ended up slaves. Now they are stuck, with the one who can deliver them on Pharaoh's ten-most-wanted list. God majors in these derailed moments in our lives and our world, when, as H. Richard Niebuhr said, "right is on the scaffold, and wrong is on the throne." The moment is stamped "impossible."

Living in the world Jesus describes in Luke 21 seems impossible. Jesus says it is a world a'comin. It is an unpredictable world: you feel you could roll off. A worn world, with seemingly little give left in its fabric. If you believed in a God who wound the world up like a clock at its beginning, you would call it a world wound down, to nearly nothing. It is a world of "nature red in tooth and claw," as the poet said. Not a peaceable kingdom, but a kingdom in pieces. A world we awaken to more and more of every morning, in our headlines; and for some of us in our lives. A world where it appears "the center cannot hold," or where there is no center.

In the lands of plenty we call home, there is less and less to go around. No longer can we tell our children they will have a higher standard of living than we do. We may not be able to maintain the lifestyle we have today. Violence, increasingly random, could stray from the neighborhoods where it's supposed to happen, drive by and hit us. Our earth, our air, our water—these essentials are draining with the runoff of our greed. And evil grows like weeds.

Research on human stress has demonstrated that one of the ways we deal with anxiety is by falling asleep. When things around and within us are winding tighter, just then when we need to pay attention, our bodies will want to shut down, tune out. I know of someone who lived under financial strain, trying to keep a family together by working day and night. She never got the sleep she needed. One morning at dawn, returning from her night job, she fell asleep at the wheel of her car. Her relatives believe, just for an instant. But it was a fatal instant; she struck a parked truck and was killed.

Jesus tells us in this passage that just when we will be most tempted to tune the world out, or may do it unawares, just then we must stay alert and awake. For once it is what we fail to do that endangers us. We fail Christ by omission, by passivity, not by bold transgression. In fact, it is a holy boldness Jesus calls us to in hard times! When life is more than we can take, things really are not as they seem. Behind the curtain of circumstances the Holy Observer is more than looking on. And our vigilance, determined, should also be confident. We are eager but not anxious. God is working beyond our view, preparing this earth for a new world order. The kingdom of our world will become the kingdom of our Lord and of the Christ; and he will reign forever. And he must not find us sleeping when he comes. Christ's second advent is not a holiday season for Christian believers.

This Christmas season builds toward a day, December 25, on which we celebrate Jesus' birthday. Our lives and time build towards a day too, not when a baby will be born, but when a new heaven and earth will be born. The contractions that announce both births grow worse as the good news approaches: God is about to do a new thing in Jesus Christ.

The most important work of God has already been accomplished in Jesus Christ, who has come. But our most important work is not done, until he returns. In parables, and here in Luke 21, Jesus waits to see what we will do in his absence, with the time when he is physically away, gone away to prepare a place for us. Will we listen to his instructions to pay attention, or fall asleep? Will we make the most of the time, even when the days are evil? Will we feel the firm footing of his promises beneath us, and take risks in his name turning one talent into five, or five into ten? Or will we "tax shelter" the talent we have, out of fear?

When those who lived through Hitler's Blitz on London were asked what were the happiest days of their lives, a surprising majority said, "the days of Hitler's Blitz on London." They felt a clear sense of purpose, remembered a stark difference between good and evil, and felt their own participation on the side of right. They felt alive; they persevered and prevailed.

May God give us the same grace in these last days.

Philip Apol in 1994 pastored the Christian Reformed Church in Silver Spring, Maryland, outside Washington, D. C.

LUKE 3:1-6

SECOND SUNDAY OF ADVENT
DECEMBER 4, 1994

He was an embarrassment to the good religious folk of his day. The wilderness was the appropriate setting for this wild man with his bizarre dress and manner and disturbing message. John made people uncomfortable. Many of those who came out to hear him surely only sought a diversion, an entertainment. Thank God John is not around to make us uncomfortable and embarrass us. We Christians have worked so hard to become sophisticated and socially acceptable. The trouble-makers who prick the public conscience on matters such as war and peace, hunger and the environment are outsiders. John would not receive many invitations to speak in our temples.

John's message would not be well received today. The salvation he proclaimed came with that disturbing provision - repentance. John did not say that "we are all okay just the way we are and that God's grace accepts us just the way we are." John said that God would make us obey in spite of ourselves. People today are not likely to flock to hear a call that they change. Our pleasure oriented culture does not long to hear of a "baptism of repentance for the forgiveness of sins" (Lk. 3:3). And yet Mark tells us that Jesus echoed John's call to repentance (1:15). It is not, however, a tune we hear often today. Saying "I'm sorry" does not seem to come easily to Americans. Modern history might be very different if Richard Nixon had admitted his errors with regard to Watergate and simply said, "I am sorry." A biographer of U.S. President Lyndon Johnson noted that Johnson said about U.S. action in Vietnam that he never "felt he had the luxury of reexamining my basic assumptions." (Mark Miller, *Lyndon: An Oral Biography*). God's breaking into our lives in Christ requires of each of us that we do exactly that - re-examine our basic assumptions.

Karl Rahner points out that the setting has changed only in form, "we keep discovering that we too are in the wilderness the wilderness of a great city, the wilderness of isolation, a wilderness that seems to have no center, a wilderness that we cannot feel at home in" (*The Great Church Year*, ed. by Albert Raffelt [New York: Crossroad, 1993] p. 30). John declared that the wilderness was the wilderness of the Spirit, the parched lifeless emptiness of our making. The beasts to be feared, then and now, are the beasts of selfcenteredness, avarice, the lust for power. What the urban wilderness needs is a church that will call the mockers to repentance.

John understood Advent. Someone was coming with something new and wonderful. "Every mountain and hill shall be brought low; and the crooked shall become straight." This new thing could be possessed only by those who are willing to turn loose of the old. Repentance means letting go of those things which have made us sick in order to be well. A woman reported to her therapist that she was mentally, emotionally and physically drained by her promiscuous lifestyle. By her own admission, she was the victim of the use of drugs, alcohol and illicit sex. The psychologist suggested that she simply change her lifestyle. Her reply, "You mean I really don't have to do what I want to do?" (Daniel Yankelovich, "New Rules in American Life: Searching for Self-fulfillment in a World Turned Upside Down," *Psychology Today* [April, 1981], p. 80.) The crookedness of our lives needs to be made straight.

Arthur Miller's post World War ll drama "All My Sons" tells the story of a family destroyed by the revelation that defective airplane engines built by the father resulted in the death of many airmen including one of his own sons. The climax comes as the surviving son confronts the father and to the father's confession responds, "being sorry is not enough, you have to change."

Christian repentance is not just turning from something; it is turning to something. Karl Barth said that it is what we are called "to" that frightens us. "Repentance is turning about to that which is nearest and which we always overlook; to the center of life which we always miss; to the simplest which is still too high and hard for us" (Karl Barth "Repentance," *The Protestant Pulpit*, compiled by Andrew Blackwood [Nashville: Abingdon, 1957], p. 173).

John's message told of the Advent of a new way of being in the world. He did not just introduce Jesus but the whole life of Jesus. The church sometimes misses the life which unfolded between cradle and cross. "Advent is about illusions about life and the disclosure of reality in Jesus. Advent is about being set free from fear in order to live "in holiness and righteousness before him" (Luke 1:74-75). John understood that Jesus revealed judgment and justice and that one is impossible without the other. Jesus' life was disrupting to life-as-usual in a fallen world. It still is.

When the church stops repenting and preaching repentance the meaning of Advent is lost. Following in the footsteps of John we must disturb and disrupt as we are instruments of the revelation of God in Jesus Christ. The church is called to demonstrate the new life possible in Christ. True repentance means a reorientation of human personality and of all relationships. Faith in Christ is faith in the new order he represented.

Raymond Bailey in 1994 was Professor of Preaching and Chair of the Department of Preaching at The Southern Baptist Theological Seminary in Louisville, Kentucky.

MATTHEW 3:1-12

SECOND SUNDAY OF ADVENT
DECEMBER 10, 1995

John the Baptist is a crazy kind of figure. Clearly he never read *How to Win Friends and Influence People*. Can you see him, standing on the river bank, hair all matted, dressed in bizarre garb—like some Rastafarian, but shouting an urgent plea for repentance before the wrath of God comes with a burning whirlwind? Yet, people flock to him, even proper religious folks and worship leaders. Something in his urgent cry touches the heart of them and drives them to their knees. The Messiah is coming. Prepare the way for the presence of God on earth.

Our world seems good enough to many of us. We live our lives fairly satisfied with the way things are. Most of us wake up every day and get ready to head out to school or work. We put in our 8 or 9 or 10 hours; come home satisfied that our hard work will one day get us our piece of the American pie. On weekends, we tinker around the house a little; we may even play a little racquetball. Sometime we'll fix ourselves a nice meal. Then, on Sunday mornings we find ourselves in church, trying to support good projects around the globe. We have to admit, ours is not a bad life. Even the predictability is comforting, like old shoes we slip into when we come in the front door. As one of our church leaders recently said, "I'm the champion of routine." We like our lives the way they are. Our world seems about good enough for most of us.

But God will have the world "right." God is bringing the world to the absolute way it's supposed to be. For a long time, people called the dawning of the new age the coming of the kingdom of God. "Kingdom" might be an outmoded word now. No one even calls England a monarchy anymore. Instead of kingdom, some people say the commonwealth of God; others, the realm of God, but what they mean is the world made right, according to the perfect ruling of God. Ancient prophets paint the vision of the realm with images of lions and lambs frolicking together, carnivores eating straw. To modern eyes, nature seems all topsy-turvy in the realm, but the vision is right-side up. The prophets report the way the world ought to be. God's perfect realm is the vision from which to gauge the rightness or wrongness of everything else. The prophet is like an ancient builder using a plumb line to make an entire building square. The realm is the plumb line for making the world right, where beggars have places set for them at the most aristocratic banquet anyone can imagine. The vision of the realm is the way the world is supposed to be. And God will make the world "right."

Even now, Christ is at hand The one who initiates the realm is within our reach. Celebrating Advent is like waiting on the steps outside in the freezing cold. We can't even see inside, but we've been told the hand is on the door and it will fling open at any moment We know the birth of the Anointed One is about to be celebrated. With Jesus, the realm of God comes crashing in to human history. All we have to to is think about the life of Jesus. Wherever he is, the realm breaks in. The lame wall, the blind see, and the mute shout praises for the mercy of God, wherever Jesus is. We can feel the little moments of divine perfection when Jesus acts. The realm of God is manifest in the ministry of Jesus. So, here we are at Advent, anticipating the first coming of the Christ child, but we also envision the day yet to come, when the realm will be established in its fullness. We wait for the little moments of perfection to explode into cosmic flawlessness. Waiting for the Messiah to complete the realm may feel a little like waiting in the cold, but we have the promissory note. The day, which has already dawned, will come in its full light. Already the Christ is at hand.

So choose to follow Christ. Take up the ministry of Jesus, for even now when Jesus' ministry continues, God's realm is made manifest. What the ministry means today varies from congregation to congregation, but whenever a church claims the ministry of Jesus Christ as its own, God's rule breaks in. For a Missionary Baptist Church in New Orleans, the ministry of Jesus Christ included spending their 20 year savings not on a new church building as they had planned, but on two abandoned buildings across the street. Drug dealers had turned the buildings into crack houses. The church decided the only way to redeem the houses was to own them. Instead of running away, the people claimed what they could for the realm of God. Rather than denounce drugs and build a new church building, the congregation sacrificed to take over the drug houses, and the realm was made manifest. Today there are 10 apartments on the property, and drugs dealers are not welcome. You can hear the call to carry on the ministry of Jesus Christ in this place. When you follow Jesus, the realm will blossom. Choose to follow Jesus.

So here we are, standing on the porch, waiting for the Messiah to open the door. To fight off the cold, we can huddle tight together, or we can get active in the ministry of Jesus. When we feed and heal and speak in the name of Jesus, the realm comes. The choice is ours.

Mary Alice Mulligan in 1995 was a student at Vanderbilt University and co-pastored the Love Lady Christian Church in Byrdstown, Tennessee.

Christmas Eve/ Christmas

LUKE 2:1-20

CHRISTMAS EVE
DECEMBER 24, 1976

In the Tate Gallery in London there is an arresting painting by Turner, usually noted for his glowing sunsets. This work, however, is quite different. It is entitled "Steamship Caught in a Snowstorm Off the Harbor's Mouth." The painting is a dark, twisting vortex of water, wind and snow, with a dim image of the steamship locked in its center. Dark smoke streams from the boat, and distress flares rocket into the night.

When the critics, accustomed to the peaceful landscapes of Turner, first laid eyes on this tortured painting they wrote, "Let us return when the storm has subsided. Hopefully, the sooner the better."

Turner was crushed. For what the critics little knew nor cared was that Turner himself had been on that boat. In eminent danger of his life, the renowned painter had ordered himself lashed to the mast where, at the age of 67, he remained for four hours in order to catch a vision of such a storm. He later wrote of his critics, "I don't know what they think the sea is like. I only wish that they had been there."

Into our world the Christ came. In the most unlikely story imaginable he entered the human scene, lashed to its fortunes, immersed in the vision of its need, committed to the life of its realities. For us today, the story is not yet comfortable. We are troubled, now by his humanity, now by his divinity. The story never fits. It is either too much of man or too much of God, not impressive enough or too impressive, too predictable or too improbable. We could understand it better, we think, if it were either plainly about gods or plainly about people.

Why is this story so unlikely? At first glance, it certainly doesn't seem to be. It begins as a story of business as usual. The Christmas story unfolds amidst our busy-ness. The scene opens in crowded streets, hurrying throngs, and packed inns. "No room, no room!" But who could be blamed? Business must go on, as we are often told, and so it did.

But so did God's! Right through the hubbub of taxation and the preoccupation of census. God's business also went on. Too long have we focused on the piteous nature of the surroundings of the birth and the negligence of that age. We should far rather notice how God, with the usual businesslike dispatch, continues with business as usual! God does not pause to ask permission nor wait to gain our sympathy. When the fullness of time was come, it was done.

And so God always does, not timidly asking our permission to exist, or wondering if Christ's coming will be an intrusion into our busy-ness, but firmly and without apology—he comes. Business as usual!—no more unusual for him than for us.

The story is unlikely too because of its missing persons. That is, this story is as notable for who was not there as for who was there. Really, no one who expected to be there was there. The king was not there, the high priest was not there, the myriad of other priests were not there, the Great Sanhedrin was not there, the political figures and soldiers were not there. No one who wanted to turn the story to their advantage was there. If the story later seemed hard to document, that is largely because God did not allow it to be exploited for anyone's use. Those who would turn it to their own advantage were simply not invited.

And they never are. Those kinds of people are never there. Again, we have wept for the King Child, ignored by the mighty. The fact is, they were not there because they were not invited! True, they had been invited many times before, but they had declined—and not respectfully. So those who would exploit it were simply not invited.

If we or anyone would come to this birth, we will come by faith or not at all. Exploiters, whether secular or religious, will always stand on the outside of this story.

But perhaps the most unlikely feature of the entire story is neither the indifference of those who passed by nor the ignorance of those who refused to come, but the unlikely choice of those who did come. For this is the story of a family gathering, as unlikely as that family might seem—an obscure Jewish girl of faith and her equally faithful husband, and the unlikeliest worshipers of all, shepherds from the hills. Our romanticism has likewise transformed the first century shepherds into wise, gentle folk of noble, if humble, bearing.

Nothing could be further from the truth. By the first century, shepherds were notoriously course, untrustworthy sorts who had great difficulty in discerning "mine from thine." Why then, you ask, did the splendor of the Christmas skies spill upon them and the glories of the angelic choirs ring over them? The answer is the same as for everything in this unlikely story. It was all of grace. The birth of God's son to a peasant girl—indeed, God's coming in the flesh to know us at all—God's revelation of salvation from on high to common sinners like shepherds: it was all of grace; thank God, it was of grace.

Clyde Fant in 1976 was pastor of First Baptist Church of Richardson, Texas, and author of Preaching For Today.

LUKE 2:1-20

CHRISTMAS EVE
DECEMBER 24-25, 1985

It's late. It's dark. You're tired. Bone tired. The sheep are finally settling down. They have been as restless as you these last few days. All the roads that lead through your grazing territory have been filled with travelers, going home to sign up for Caesar's new tax program. Some call it reform; some claim it is just tinkering with the system. What you know is what you see: Rome has soldiers everywhere and someone has got to pay to keep the chariots repaired and the swords sharp and the battalions on alert and the palaces of Quirinius and Herod invulnerable from the attack of zealots and revolutionaries.

You and your buddies have got to get home at some point or the IRS will be breathing down your back for failure to file. But when and how? Who is going to take care of the sheep? That's the problem with those government bureaucrats: setting up policy in their comfortable offices with no idea of what things are really like for us working folk, who can barely make ends meet now and who will have even less when we pay more taxes and people buy less lamb and wool because Rome is taking more out of their paycheck. You would be bitter, but bitterness would keep you awake and you want to sleep....

Light! Dazzling light! Sound! The sheep stand stunned. You are as frightened as they are—it must be Roman soldiers, a whole battalion with blazing torches come to round up those who have not signed up for the new taxation. All of your nightmares come true in a flash.

But wait. Your eyes adjust. A voice: "Be not afraid; for behold, I bring you good news of a great joy...." The stars turn into a sea of angels, wing on wing, circling and singing till the rocks and the trees seem to join them: "Glory to God in the highest and on earth peace among people with whom he is pleased!" Then silence and darkness again, and in the dimness of the starlight, words are shared with the others: "Did you see?" "Yes, yes I did. And I heard what was said." "And also the song, the glorious song?" "Yes, I heard it all. I was afraid at first, but now we must go, with haste, at once!"

You, who moments ago were bone tired and cursing Rome, stumble gladly through the night to find among animals who smell like the animals you keep, a young couple and their baby. When you return to your sheep nothing has changed: the tax decree is still in force, you are still anxious about signing up and about making ends meet, the soldiers are still on every corner. Yet everything has changed, for your heart is charged with the visionary gladness of knowing God is here with you in grace and in power to transform this world.

Thomas H. Troeger is a Presbyterian minister and in 1985 was professor of preaching at Colgate Rochester Divinity School/Bexley Hall/Crozer Theological Seminary.

LUKE 2:1-20

CHRISTMAS EVE
DECEMBER 25, 1986

Tonight in our hearts we travel to Bethlehem with all the countless millions who have gone there before, responding like the shepherds to the proclamation "For unto you is born a savior who is Christ the Lord."

A few years ago I journeyed to the geographical Bethlehem. In an effort to recapture some of the flavor of the place I walked the eight miles from Jerusalem to Bethlehem soaking up the Judean hills, the fields where shepherds still guard their sheep and the sun baked landscape Mary and Joseph crossed.

But it was Bethlehem itself which moved me most and especially the church of the nativity. Since 325 A.D. the Constantinian basilica has stood over the cave where ancient tradition has it that Jesus was born. It is one of the oldest churches in Christendom. To the right of the altar is a tiny narrow stair that takes you to the crypt beneath the chancel. The little niche where Jesus is said to have been born is marked by a silver star and encrusted with precious stones. Candles flicker all around and across the tiny room the manger site is marked by other costly adornments. There is a grandness in all the gaudy embellishments, a beauty which is not so much in the ornamentation itself but in the faith which prompted Christians to place them there.

I looked around the small room. The floor is covered with cool marble. The walls hang with ancient opulent tapestries. It is a pleasant place—a quiet and holy place. The pilgrims who gather speak in hushed tones as if there is a baby sleeping. I lingered in the warm candleglow. It felt good to be there.

When it came time to leave I suddenly felt overtaken by Yankee curiosity. I was unable to resist the temptation to lift the corner of one of the tapestries hanging on the walls and look behind it. What I saw gave me a jolt.

I really don't know what I expected but what I beheld was a rough stone wall, blackened by centuries of candles and censors, rubbed with the oils and sweat of millions of hands and bodies, colored by the dung of beasts and humans. It was the ugliness of that wall which arrested me. The contrast with the warm lighted space was so severe.

Of course I knew the story of Jesus birth, how he had been born in a humble stable and laid in a manger. I knew the stable was most likely a cave in the hillside where shepherds took shelter and animals were penned. Yet at that moment I suddenly perceived in a deeper way the significance of it all.

The dark walls under those tapestries spoke to me of the hard reality of the dark world into which Jesus was born and is still born. The words of Cyprian came to mine, "it is a bad world." It is a world full of sweat and smoke, full of suffering, war, depression, loneliness, fear, imprisonment, separation, sickness, in short, a world hungry for peace. The world that Jesus entered was a world of darkness and death. Jesus, born in an insignificant place, among a subjugated people in the darkest and loneliest time of night.

It struck me that this place of his birth was little more than a tomb. (In someways the place of the nativity is considerably more tomb-like than that which is revered as the place of the Holy Sepulchre.) It is as Tillich said, "The darkness into which the light of Christmas shines is above all the darkness of death" (Paul Tillich, *The Shaking of the Foundations*, Scribners, p. 169).

I put the tapestry down, smoothing it back to its original position. Then standing in the warm glow of the room again the words of the scripture came to me. "For unto you is born this day, a savior who is Christ the Lord."

The birth of Jesus Christ makes it possible for you and for me to hope that new life can come to our lives even when we seem entombed by all the darkness of our world. The birth of Jesus assures us that even in death we can live because unto us is born a savior, Christ the Lord. That has been the hope of Christians for all ages. It is the traditional message of Christmas. I suppose that is why the cave of the nativity is hung with exquisite tapestries. It is not to cover up the darkness and ugliness of the crypt but to proclaim to all that light has come.

I don't suppose I have ever been the same since Bethlehem. Nor has the world ever been the same since that night when angels sang a message of great joy and shepherds responded, all because Christ our Lord was born!

Karen Engle Layman, a minister of the United Methodist Church, in 1986 was pastor of the Mt. Rock United Methodist Church, Carlisle, Pennsylvania.

LUKE 2:8-20

CHRISTMAS EVE
DECEMBER 24, 1987

It is too late to do any more shopping. The stores are all closed. The little Peruvian shop with its stock of beautiful peasant art—the hand carved clay figurines of Mary and Joseph and the haloed baby; the miniature creche scenes, made to hang on trees, and painted bright blue, red, yellow, green, white, and purple—these things lie in the shop with only the light from the streetlamp. Occasional shadows pass of late night solitary walkers, shoulders hunched against the knowledge that on this night no one should be alone for long. And church steps scrunch with snow underfoot across the land as believers and would-like-to-be-believers together try to relive the hope of the world. Strains of "Silent Night" resonate throughout the lands. The whole earth pauses briefly to reflect on the mystery of this time.

This much we may all say. We live in ambiguity. It is inescapable. In this time of family gatherings, we may be with people who are not the easiest to be with, no matter how much we love them. Perhaps loved ones we want to be with are no longer here. There is a shadow side to Christmas.

We are no shepherds. But on the night of Christ's birth, when the earth paused for history to begin again, in a new age of hope, the shepherds were filled with fear. They were despised by their society, cast out like prostitutes and thieves, the lowest of the low, the least worthy by our standards. They thought destruction was upon them. They thought it was the end. And the first thing that the angel said to them was "Fear not." Almost before the shepherds could have named their own choking terror, "Fear not" came to them.

What would it mean if "fear not" came to us?

What would have to happen for all of the fear we have to be stilled? Would the banning of all nuclear weapons still the fear?—It would help, but the fear would not be gone. Would narrowing the gap between rich and poor so there would be war no more still the fear?—It would help, but the fear would not be gone. Would narrowing the gap between mother and father or sister and brother still the fear? Would increasing our life spans, curing our diseases, still the fear? They would help, but the fear would not be gone.

If we want the fear to be gone, we may look in a most unlikely place. Look to the lowliest place in our life. There you will find a newborn child who will end all your fears. And his name shall be love, peace, hope, reconciliation, comfort, freedom, justice, promise, healing, joy, fulfillment, creator, Lord, Savior, God. But you may call him Jesus. And you may put all your faith in him. And you need never fear again, for there is no meaning in life if this one is not that meaning.

"Fear not" comes to us. This is the real ambiguity of life, that God should come to us in this way, not imposing peace but offering it.

A woman was recently called to serve as the minister in a large church. At the first large gathering of parents and teenagers she felt very out of place. Her son was there, looking very much the rebel in Mohawk hair and torn denims. All of the other boys were in suits or sportscoats. They stood apart, she looking very much like the proper minister, blue suit, tight forced smile. And then someone reached out and touched her son and drew him into their group. In times of fear or joy, in places which are low or high, "Fear not" comes to us. The pause of the world for this birth will not be for long. Soon it moves on. But it moves on with hope.

Paul Scott Wilson is ordained in the United Church of Canada and in 1987 was associate professor of homiletics at Emmanuel College, the Toronto School of Theology

---

JOHN 1:1-14

CHRISTMAS DAY
DECEMBER 25, 1992

On a rainy afternoon in Florence, Firenze, my traveling companions and I sought refuge in Santa Croce, a Franciscan monastery where Donatello and Brunelleschi, (before they became Ninja Turtles), designed and built the Pazzi Chapel. The Chapel is perfectly proportioned, simple, serene, with Della Robbia porcelains around the circumference, porcelains of the twelve disciples and four apostles. But, as is so often the case in travel, what caught my attention that afternoon was not the Chapel as planned, but a fresco in the monastery itself. I came around the corner from the large refectory into a smaller chamber, and came upon "Madonna che allati Bambino", Quatrocento, a fourteenth century fresco of Mary nursing Jesus, and I was stopped in my traveler's tracks.

What was it that attracted me to the fresco, held me captive in its spell? In part, it was the rich tones, the Renaissance blues and reds and golds. In part, it was its Renaissance fleshiness, so lifelike that I imagined if I looked at it aslant, I might sense movement, Jesus' hand tugging at Mary, or might even hear the noises of a hungry baby sucking. In part, I was attracted because of the fact that that sweet stage of infant mother love is past for me now. We're into back talk when the dinner menu meets with disapproval.

But I believe what captivated me more fully is the fresco of Mary nursing Jesus, dove and saint's overhead, Jesus' leg kicking, jerking, was proclaiming to me Incarnation, God made flesh. God is found in that which is hungry and vulnerable and small. God is found in that which is in need and depends on us most of all. That's what attracted me, that truth in rich tones on a monastery wall. And the Word became flesh and dwelt among us full of grace and truth.

To hear the Christmas story and believe, to come to the stable, to accept Jesus and live as a disciple, a Christian, is to see God now in all that is human, to cherish all God's children, to love and to protect, to feed and to shelter, to support and to strengthen, especially those for whom there is no room, especially those who are hungry, especially the most vulnerable.

Marlene and Jose Padilla live in the South Bronx, Jose is a maintenance worker, Marlene is a homemaker. They grew up as neighbors in the South Bronx together, went to school, fell in love, married, started a family. A common story? Not at all. For the Padillas have two children of their own, and two foster children who are HIV positive, all four under four! So amidst the hectic routine of that young household, there are trips to the emergency room, special food and formula. There is the explaining the severe developmental problems of one of the children to the others, and explaining to all of them when they are spurned as a family because of misunderstanding, fear in the neighborhood. "These are children that nobody wants," Marlene Padilla says up in the South Bronx. "l want to be one of the ones to help out" (*NY Times,* December 7, 1991). And the Word became flesh and dwelt among us full of grace and truth.

Jesus said, "I was hungry and you gave me food, I was thirsty and you gave me drink, I was a stranger and you welcomed me, in prison and you came to me." The righteous scratch their heads and ask quizzically, "When did we do that for you"? Jesus smiles, shrugs his shoulders, and points to the mysterious truth, "Whenever you did it to the least of these, you did it for me...."

Sue Anne Steffey Morrow in 1992 was the Associate Dean of the Chapel at Princeton University and is a United Methodist Minister.

LUKE 2:1-14 (15-20)

CHRISTMAS EVE
DECEMBER 24, 1993

Ralph Milton points out that this beloved Christmas story is full of contrasts. It's stronger than that; the story is full of contradictions! "The child is special," writes Milton, "but very ordinary. Jesus is born in a barn, but there's a special star over the stable. The stink of manure is mingled with the fragrance of frankincense brought by wealthy astrologers who kneel in the dirt before a simple child. The baby is honored with extravagant titles, but his parents have to pick up and run because a dictator wants to slaughter their child. The Child of God is a refugee" (*Commonsense Christianity*, Winfield, BC: Wood Lake Books, 1988, 40).

We can add any number of additional contradictions. There is no room for this Child, but the whole of heaven opens to him. He is born of Mary and Joseph but the throne of David is his. He is born in a village because Caesar Augustus makes a decree but he will one day encompass the whole of Augustus' empire and more.

We may be intrigued by such contrasts and contradictions, but they make us uneasy. Either something is or it isn't. This yes-and-no, this-on-the-one-hand-but-on-the-other-hand, is confusing and finally irritating. Let's have it straight. If we don't know or aren't sure, let's find out for sure. If we're maybe losing tax revenue because we don't know how many taxpayers there are, then for heaven's sake let's find out: take a census.

The whole thing becomes more clamorous when we're talking about God. One ought to be sure about God, right? If this story about Jesus' birth is about God entering our world, then that ought to be perfectly clear, right?

Because we really ought to know about God. For sure. Shouldn't we? We really ought to know *for sure* about God.

Because life is tough. There's that little teenage girl. Only yesterday, it seems, she was delivering the paper to the house; there she is, on the street with her swollen belly.... Some say something about abuse. Maybe.

See that young man? He did everything right. He stayed in school and learned a good trade. Carpentry. Very good at it. Started his own little company. He's barely hanging on. He's started going to the Food Bank. He doesn't talk to anybody, though.

See that old woman over there? The one with a shawl? Never had any family. Or else they're dead or gone. She likes to go to the hospital and rock the babies.

And that couple. Black hair. Dark clothes. Watch. See how careful they are? They sort of hug the sides of buildings as they go down the street? Iraqis. I don't know how they got here—and together at that. I don't even know how they survived the war. I don't know if they will survive here. Refugees. And they're only two of how many in the world? Twelve million? Fifteen million?

A bishop from Dresden in eastern Germany told me a little couplet: "Unter jedes Dach, ein Ach!" "Under every roof, an ouch!" It's true. And he knew exactly how painfully true. But twelve million don't even have a roof.

So if we're to know anything about God at all, it had better he sure. There's too much to be set right in the world for fancy contrasts and puzzling contradictions. The Christmas story is nice for children on Christmas Eve, but the day after we want —and need—the straight goods. There's a lot that needs to be set right.

The shepherds knew that. There is a lot that needs to be set right. Maybe the shepherds knew that better than anybody. When you live on the edge of things you see things more clearly than do the people who are caught up in the middle of them. The people in the middle of things get whirled up and carried along, and can't any more sort things out. It's as though they get all mixed up about what is happening and what needs to be done and what's right and what's wrong. Maybe they forget to think like a human being! Take a politician. Starts out all right. Has a few things she wants to set right because people are hurting. But soon she's part of a ruling body; she's only one among many; she hasn't much clout. Pretty soon she's thinking like the others. She's not thinking like a human being anymore, she's thinking like the governing machine. Usually that means that people on the edge get pushed farther out. The things that need setting right don't get set right.

Now, take a shepherd. A good shepherd—a really good shepherd—has to learn to think like a sheep. Sounds silly, but it isn't. What do sheep do when they're hungry? Tired? Scared? Sick? When a storm comes? When it's breeding or lambing season? When they smell a stranger? When they get lost? When they're injured? A *good* shepherd knows because he can think like a sheep. And so he can set right what needs to be set right. Talk to a fisherman and he'll tell you it's the same for fishing: a good fisherman thinks like the fish he's after. Talk to a mother, for that matter. A good mother thinks like her child; she knows her child from the inside. And so they can set right whatever needs setting right.

Because they *know.* From the *inside.*

So, strangely, the Christmas story makes deep sense, after all. To set things right— *really* right—you've got to start from the inside. So that you know from the inside.

That is what God has done!

The shepherds knew it better than anyone.

Except God!

Eduard R. Riegert in 1993 was Professor of Homiletics at Waterloo Lutheran Seminary, Waterloo, Ontario, and an ordained pastor of the Evangelical Lutheran Church in Canada.

LUKE 2:1-14 (15-20)

CHRISTMAS EVE
DECEMBER 24, 1994

vee 1996

On this spectacular evening, the long hours of night are made brighter and shorter by our path to the starlit place of Jesus' birth. The path that we follow is a wide, well-trodden path over treed hills, between rocks and through fresh fallen snow, the same path that we may have traveled last year to Bethlehem, that many of our parents followed, and grandparents and forebears before them. And now at last in the starlit narrow streets of the town, we make our way once more to a stable behind an inn, to witness an event of such importance, that no matter what we think of it, our lives can never be the same again.

It is helpful to note who is making this journey with us. There are some college students, back after a long term away from the place that still feels like home. There are families reunited, even as there are some people journeying who are missing families and friends. Some are finding it hard to deal with all of the emotions that come from renewed relationships. There is a woman who once said, "You know, there has to be a better way. I spent so much time last year getting ready and preparing food, that when it was over I had hardly had time to visit." Some people may not want to be here. Yet most of us are excited.

We are right to be excited. Ready or not, whether we feel sufficiently prepared or not, the end of the journey is here now, as we kneel before Jesus, born of Mary, heralded by angels, and worshiped by shepherds and royalty. Here is a place to set down your load. Let go of all those things you have been carrying. This is the end of the journey for all of us who have been looking for meaning in all the wrong places. Sometimes the best gift that can be laid before the Christ child is the giving up of the wrong kinds of relationship, or drugs, or alcohol, or greed—whatever keeps us from praising the God who offers all purpose and true meaning in life. Whatever you have brought with you this night that prevents you from loving or being loved, you may leave it in the stable where it belongs, before God, who knows how to tend to such things and is the author of all love, and who holds you even now.

This is the end of the journey also, for all of those who have walked alone through the land of long night. The birth of Jesus is God saying, "Enough of sorrow and pain. I will lengthen the days that you may see that you walk with others." The birth of Christ, Emmanuel, God-with-us, is the birth of a new family in Christ, a family dedicated to love, to lives of service helping others, to praising God in the midst of both joy and hardship, knowing that this is the God who can work all things for good, no matter how bad or threatening they may be. If you have been walking alone to this night, know that the God who chooses to be known in Jesus as a tiny baby, is the same God who chooses to be known not just each Sunday, but each minute of your life on this earth, and in the life to come.

Eleanor is a woman in her thirties. She had been estranged from her family. Her parents had been alcoholics. She wrote to tell her father that she and her husband were expecting a child, but there was no word. There were complications that kept her in the hospital after the birth. One day when the chaplain came to see her in her hospital room, she seemed at peace. She explained, "I kept praying that my dad would come. And maybe he will. I don't even know what I would say to him. He might still not be able to love me. But I suddenly looked around and saw all my friends and family who love me, and now my baby, and I suddenly realized that while I want his love, I have so much love already." What she discovered in that moment was something of what we mean by the birth of Christ in our hearts.

We have arrived at our destination. Or we would be more accurate in saying, God's Son has arrived. There is no love that we seek, no healing that we yearn for, no purpose to be found, that cannot be found here, where Jesus is born in utter poverty, yet with all the wealth of the heavens. You have made it this far: do not give up, for the gift of this Son, is God's gift to you. God holds you near and dear. What you need the most God offers you freely. This is the true gift of Christmas. It is not something that we give. It is not some present we have bought. It is something priceless that God gives to us. And there is no power on this earth or in all creation that need prevent us from receiving what is offered to us for our loving care.

In this wondrous night of love, kneeling before Jesus at the end of this journey, we are also at the beginning of another. It is the beginning of a journey with Christ. On this journey, the straps of our knapsacks are comfortable and the burden we carry is light. There is no more looking back with guilt at all the wrong that was done, but only looking ahead with joy for all that God will accomplish through us and others. Rejoice in what God has done. Rejoice in the promise that has been given. This child Jesus is the One we have been seeking, perhaps without even knowing. This is the One who by his resurrection has shown us that God's love is stronger than the power of death itself. This is the beginning of the hope that ends all suffering, the healing that mends all wounds, the comfort that soothes all mourning, the justice that ends all poverty, the peace that silences all war, the righteousness that makes all the heavens ring with the sound of angels singing, "Glory to God in the highest, and on earth peace to all peoples. For your Savior has come, even Jesus Christ, the Lord."

Paul Scott Wilson in 1994 was Professor of Homiletics at Emmanuel College in the Toronto School of Theology.

JOHN 1:1-14

CHRISTMAS DAY
DECEMBER 25, 1995

You don't usually think about tents on Christmas. You think about tents in the summer when you are camping. Is the tent big enough? Is it still waterproof? Is the mosquito netting intact? How far away from the children's tent can you set up your own tent to be near if they need you in the night but, far enough away that their boom-boxes will not keep you up all night? We use tents for special occasions.

In the ancient world a tent was often a year-round dwelling. Can you imagine what it might have been like to live in a tent on a cold day such as today? The tent is made of animal skin or goat's hair, and you can still smell a trace of animal odor. Heat comes from a small fire near the entrance. The only furniture: rough straw mats for beds, a piece of leather for a table, a jar for water, a few small pottery dishes and bags made of spun animal hair. Can you hear the wind pulling at the tent poles? Can you feel it? Life in a tent was a tenuous existence.

After the Exodus from Egypt, the people of Israel lived in tents in the wilderness for forty years. They were freed from slavery, but their wilderness sojourn was still a very difficult time. The Israelites had been in Egypt for 400 years. They had settled into houselife. Now, they find themselves pulling up stakes every morning, and making a new camp every night.

The wilderness is desert. Hot and parching in the summer. Penetrating cold in the winter. Manna and quail day after day after day. But would there be wood to build a fire? And water? A tenuous existence. No wonder they murmured.

What do we need when we are living on the edge? In addition to food, water, clothing, and shelter, we need signs that the world is going to go on. We need assurance that we can make it. And we need reminders of who we are and what we need to do.

I believe that is why God had Moses build the tabernacle. The tabernacle was a portable sanctuary. The tabernacle was essentially a big tent, (I would now describe the tabernacle:)

The tabernacle is a physical reminder that the unseen God is always present and always working for the people's good.

The tabernacle was constructed of animal skins, and wooden poles, and other things from Israel's everyday world. The materials of the tabernacle represented their very life. In the very elements of the tabernacle, the people could see God present in their everyday life.

The tabernacle was laid out in a very orderly way. The design of the tabernacle itself was a symbol of God's order and reliability in the midst of the unpredictable, chaotic, and dangerous wilderness.

Three millennia later, we live in a tenuous world. Few of you are actually on the edge of physical survival. But it often feels to me like our world is living in a tent. So many things changing so quickly. So much uncertainty. So much wind pulling at so many stakes.

My denomination gets smaller every year. When I was born (1949) our denomination had 1.7 million resident members. This year (1995) we list just above 600,000 participating members. But next year (1996), we'll be below 600,000 for the first time. Which of my friends at our General (i.e. national and international) Offices in downtown Indianapolis will be riffed next? Good people doing good work, but no money to pay them. And will our evolving forms of church life help us make a significant witness?

In these middle adult years, I am preoccupied with five children at home. So much chaos in our house. Can the children navigate through the booze, the drugs, the violence, the false values? What kinds of jobs will they be able to get? Will their adulthoods be a series of race wars? Wars among different ethnic groups or social classes? In my heart of hearts, I do not want to release them into the future.

And in the broader world, so much unsettledness, so much violence. Last summer, in the Balkans, even the "safe" places were no longer safe. And who knows how long the eco-sphere can survive human exploitation. The wind is pulling at the stakes of this tent of a world.

But the Word becomes flesh and pitches its tent among us. Yes, in the Greek language the term means "to pitch one's tent." The term recalls God dwelling with Israel in the wilderness. John uses it to say that Christ is God's tabernacle with us in the church, even as God tabernacles with the Jewish people.

Christ is a visible sign of God's presence. Christ is one of us, a representative of our own life. Christ demonstrates that God is with us in our humanness. Christ reminds us of God's constant presence. When we feel the pull of the wind against the tent of our world, we feel the strength of Christ. And Christ promises to go with us through the chaos of life. Christ is a tent of meeting, a relationship through whom we meet the Living God.

The Word became flesh in Christ. And when Christ's living presence animates people, it continues to meet us in the flesh.

Today, December 25, is my mother's birthday. I think about her a lot this Christmas because she died (at the ripe age of 83) this past year. I remember ways in which she became a sign of the presence of Christ for me. In self-giving love, she almost lost her life giving me birth. One night, when I was in high school, I got a ticket for speeding "and trying to outrun the law." In a small town, such a report was headline news. I thought my life was over. But she went to municipal court with me and stood beside me and vouched to the judge that she would watch out for me in the future. When my Dad's health collapsed, and he was no longer able to work, she supported our family. And when my Dad died, she wrapped me in her arms. Beneath the aching and the weeping, I felt a fresh sense of security. And when she died, the people she had touched came forward and embraced me.

So, on this Christmas morning, we tent dwellers can take heart. The Word becomes flesh and pitches a tent among us. From this fullness we can all receive, grace upon grace.

Ronald J. Allen, ordained in the Christian Church (Disciples of Christ), in 1995 was Associate Professor of Preaching and New Testament at Christian Theological Seminary, Indianapolis, Indiana, U.S.A.

Season of Christmas

JOHN 1:1-18

THE SECOND SUNDAY AFTER CHRISTMAS
JANUARY 3, 1982

The prisoners could hear the guards casually talking about the coming of spring. But they could not know for themselves. Neither from their confining cells nor from the walled exercise yards could they see the hills becoming green or the flowers blooming. Imprisoned, they were totally cut off and isolated from new life and new beginnings, locked in a gray, hopeless, impersonal world. In his poem "Estrangement," Sir William Watson describes this kind of world where imprisoned people can only hear of spring. Spring is, "A legend emptied of concern; And idle is the rumor of the rose."

Most of us know this kind of imprisonment. We shuffle in lockstep from day to day along the gray, shabby corridors of our lives, isolated by pride or fear or greed or guilt, unable to believe the rumors that speak of a realm of the spirit that exists beyond the walls of our narrow, limited lives. Yet we have heard the rumor of the rose and, on rare occasions, have stood silent, stilled by a drift of fragrance.

In his *Paradiso,* Dante came to the end of his journey and saw the eternal rose of harmony, fulfillment, and spiritual perfection. Unable to see Divine Love directly with his mortal eyes, he was told to bend down and drink of the river of light that flowed through Paradise. In a moment of vision his eyes became mirrors reflecting the tiers of angels and the blessed who as a mystic rose opened to the sun of God. In this symbolic rose, God's heavenly kingdom blooming eternally, human love entered into union with Divine Love.

Dante's tale is but one voice in all the rumors of a rose that speak of a divine love able to bring about salvation in human hearts. But do we listen to these rumors? Or do we move through Christmas with unhearing ears, choosing to discount reports of a God who took on human flesh to walk among us so that human creatures, like the earth, could be born anew. At times during the Christmas season a few words catch our attention and our hearts leap with hope, but then as Christmas passes, we walk dully back to our narrow cells of existence. Convincing ourselves that the rumors of the rose were mere fantasies wrought by sentiment, we passively allow ourselves to be locked again into a world walled by our limited mortal perceptions.

Even so, we preserve some dim awareness of the promise that Christ's coming may bring spiritual transformation, for we associate him in painting and legend with the symbol of a rose. If we could accept this rose as a symbolic representation of a reality of which all else is an imperfect shadow, we could walk free of our prisons, discover new beginnings, and begin the pilgrimage toward fulfillment.

John's Gospel tells us this. He writes of the Word that came among us in Jesus Christ bringing "beginnings" and "light" and "Truth" and "life" because of God's love. For ages men and women had heard through law and legend of God's faithfulness in mercy and gracious favor toward his children. But in one liberating moment, the prison doors that shut off human from divine reality were set ajar. In the person of Jesus Christ, who came to set the prisoners free, rumors of God's love became validated. "And the Word became flesh and dwelt among us, full of grace and truth; we have beheld his glory, glory as of the only Son from the Father.... And from his fullness we have all received, grace upon grace...."

But has the rumor become reality for us? John suggests that the key to liberation from all that binds us is our response. The rumor will never become a validated reality in our minds and hearts if we insist that it must be a reality that we can see and touch. Spring came in the greening hills and blooming flowers even though the prisoners could not see it. John says, "No one has ever seen God." Even in Dante's imaginative vision, mortal man could only see God in the reflecting waters of the "sweet stream that flows its grace to us." Only the eyes of faith, washed by the waters of grace, can perceive the rose of the eternal.

Recently I sat with a friend who has only a few months to live. Her illness has drained her body of strength, but her spirit and vigorous mind keep sending signals of life. I said to her: "You are a very courageous person. We all admire your courage." Always direct, she answered: "It isn't my courage that keeps me going. It is faith—faith that helps me go on believing when everything I see about me is fading away."

Of course, she is quite right. She is living by trust in Christ. She already possesses eternal life. "He that believeth on me hath eternal life" (John 3:15). No rumor of the rose here! My friend is in touch with reality, and clasps the beauty of the Lord's Presence at the center of her being. No more a prisoner of this world, she is walking free!

Christmas *is* over, but you and I need not go on locking ourselves away from life. We may walk free, for the rumor is reality. The Lord is with us!

Robert Drew Simpson in 1982 was Senior Pastor, Chatham United Methodist Church, Chatam, New Jersey

---

JOHN 1:1-18

THE SECOND SUNDAY AFTER CHRISTMAS
JANUARY 4, 1987

The kitchen storm door slams shut and the child stands bawling in the middle of the floor. Hot tears melt the snow caked on her boots. "That big kid pushed me off the sled and called me a nerd." The father lays down the knife from slicing the potatoes for the soup, and kneels down and takes the child in his arms. "And the word became flesh and dwelt among us."

The student closed the door to the professor's office. An F. Couldn't believe it. The teacher had noticed the lines in the paper which were taken directly from an unacknowledged source. As he stepped slowly down the hall, he heard the professor's door open and her throat clear. "Could you come back for a moment. I was so disappointed by the plagiarism that I forgot to mention something else. The general idea of the paper is very good, like the rest of your work this semester. If you do the paper again, in your own way, you can pass the course. And I will write you a strong letter of recommendation for graduate school." And the word became flesh and dwelt among us.

The man sat down on the edge of the bed, his head in his hands. When he had left for work that morning, everything had seemed so ordinary. She said she was going to take down the Christmas tree and run to the store to buy some ornaments that were on a clearance sale. The police did not know exactly what had happened on the ice. But when the car hit the tree she was killed instantly. The thirteen year old stood in the doorway, eyes red, and came over and put her arm around her father. "We'll make it, Dad, we'll make it. It'll be tough sometimes. But we'll make it." And the word became flesh and dwelt among us.

The board meeting was over. The pastor turned the key in the lock and stepped out of the alcove and into the bitter wind. The first woman in the judicatory. A church with a tiny membership in a vast changing area. A sanctuary that seats over 600 and leaks around the old dome so that when the wind blows the women in skirts cover their legs. Only four at the meeting tonight and their average age was over seventy. But tomorrow should/would begin the survey to see what was needed in the neighborhood. And two of the Board members would go with her. And the word became flesh, and dwelt among us.

The property line of the military base was only a step away. But if any of the peace marchers crossed it, they would be arrested. Their attorneys explained that they would be fingerprinted, have a police record and could be prosecuted. They looked each other in the eye, gripped each by the hand, and stepped across the line. And the word became flesh and dwelt among us.

He came down the aisle on the invitation hymn. His life was not a mess. He had never cheated, robbed, stepped out or even gotten drunk. A good job. A good house. A good family. But today, during the sermon, it had all come together as if for the first time. And a surge of gratitude lifted him up from his seat and sent him down the aisle. And the word became flesh and dwelt among us, full of grace and truth.

Ronald J. Allen in 1987 was Assistant Professor of Preaching and New Testament at Christian Theological Seminary, Indianapolis, Indiana.
Linda McKiernan-Allen in 1987 was ad interim Associate Pastor of First Christian Christian Church, Noblesville, Indiana. Both are ordained in the Christian Church (Disciples of Christ).

How does the Word become flesh in your life

LUKE 2:22-40

FIRST SUNDAY AFTER CHRISTMAS DAY
DECEMBER 26, 1993

There's a painting by the Italian artist Ambrogio Lorenzetti called *Presentation in the Temple*. The major characters are gathered at the altar. Mary and Joseph look on in amazed silence. The prophetess Anna fixes her eyes on the child. The bearded priest Simeon, with a look of great solemnity, stares at the baby in his arms. Yet the Christ child in the center of the picture is surprising! Simeon, Anna, Mary and Joseph are gazing awestruck at a baby Jesus *sucking his thumb!* Well what child is this? The family may marvel, the aged Simeon and Anna may prophecy and witness, but the little child—this thumb-sucking baby Jesus—*he's* not what was expected at all!

Of course, we can surely understand Jesus' parents! They only expect their son to fulfill the law. Mary and Joseph, after all, do things by the book. Out of devotion to the law Jesus' parents do ritual purification and go up to the temple to present baby Jesus along with the stipulated sacrifice for poor folks —two small birds. Surely law-abiding parents like these simply want their son to learn the value of righteousness. They hope that a little piety will rub off on the boy. Call it: family values. Jesus' parents expect him to do what a child of the covenant ought —fulfill the law.

But the priest Simeon reveals that this baby will also fulfill prophets' dreams! Old man Simeon somehow sees Jesus as salvation incarnate! Who'da thunk it? In the movie *Babette's Feast* two elderly Danish sisters devote their energies to preserving the teachings of their late, pietistic minister father. They reluctantly take in Babette, a French woman, who has had to flee Paris, as their maid. After winning the lottery, Babette expresses her gratitude by spending all the money on a sumptuous feast given at a gathering to which the sisters had invited disciples of their pietist father. As delectable course after course is brought out the table conversation revolves solely around late minister's teachings concerning disdain for the world and its pleasures even as they obviously enjoy the feast. Yet one guest—an old, decorated military man—more explicitly revels in every delicious gourmet dish brought out. While the others are less aware of the precious gift on the table, the old officer blurts out what they all are beginning to realize *that a costly feast has been set before them all!* Just like old Simeon—he has eyes to see the salvation before his very face. Simeon recognizes Jesus as the fulfillment of every prophet's dream!

Well naturally Jesus' parents marvel at the news. No doubt they must already be imagining the headlines back home. "LOCAL BOY MAKES GOOD" splashed right below the Galilee Gazette's masthead. And how about a banner headline across the Jerusalem Journal: "SOMETHING GOOD COMES OUT OF NAZARETH". Then there are the photos. Naturally a young boy with such prophetic promise will need to be shot with all the bigwigs—high priests, teachers, local government officials. And then, of course, there are official parties. Such a long-awaited person deserves the red carpet treatment. Oh, Joseph and Mary must be proud of their son— destined to fulfill all of Israel's hopes! After all, Simeon's news about this little boy is marvelous!

But stop the presses: Simeon's revelation promises not just good news. The fulfillment of Israel's hopes will bring opposition to Jesus. Of course, Joseph and Mary should have seen it coming. Even the law can't guarantee parents their children will grow up in ways they expect. After all, Dear Abby's columns are full of parents' letters about kids not turning out as hoped—even when they did follow Dr. Spock's baby book to the letter! But what law-abiding father wishes to have his son described as a "sign that will be opposed?" What kind of mother could be happy with a son whose life pierces her own soul like a sword? Apparently, there's a dark underside to this good news: the reality that Mary and Joseph's son will not be some rags to riches story! Mary and Joseph may "do things by the book," but in the Temple Simeon already sees the outlines of a cruciform shadow—cast across baby Jesus' face.

But to folks awaiting salvation Jesus is good news nonetheless. For people expecting God's redemption the promise and the cross go together. The prophetess Anna catches sight of this baby Jesus, this "sign of contradiction," and runs out into the street—even with Simeon's second prophecy still ringing in the air! Immediately old Anna is set in motion, praising God and telling others about the child. Perhaps Anna has awaited redemption long enough to know that the promise and the cross are of a piece. A church in South Dakota decorates its sanctuary in an odd way every Lent. Like other churches, they set up in the sanctuary a wooden cross—cumbersome and rough-hewn, like the season of Lent itself. But in order to get it to stand, they do more than simply lean it against the wall, or suspend it from the ceiling. This congregation sets the rugged cross in a *Christmas tree stand*! After all, they think the reality of the cross and the promise of Christmas belong together. Besides, nothing but the hopes of Christmas can bear the weight of the cross. And that is good news indeed!

David Schnasa Jacobsen in 1993 was a Ph.D. student in homiletics and the Christian scriptures at Vanderbilt University in Nashville, Tennessee and is an ordained elder in the South Dakota Annual Conference of The United Methodist Church.

Epiphany

MATTHEW 2:1-12

EPIPHANY
JANUARY 6, 1977

4/5/97

Those of us who come to worship the Christ child sometimes have the problem the Wise Men had— namely, finding the place where his parents laid him.

So where would we look today in an effort to find him? Some people might look for a place that gives them a sense of calm, peace and tranquility. After all, that's the feeling depicted in many creche scenes displayed at Christmas time. Remember the glass balls which were filled with liquid and contained a creche scene? Turn the ball upside down and plastic snow gently descends on the manger scene. There is Mary, poised and composed, holding a cute baby Jesus. Alongside her are antiseptic animals. Maybe we would look for a place like that, where everything is sweet and calm and pure.

But that isn't the kind of place in which he was laid. Thank God for that! Otherwise we would probably have to jump out of our skins in order to find him. Let's face it, not much of our life is sweet and calm and pure. And the amazing proclamation is that God chooses to take his place right among us, live the life you and I live day in and day out, face the threats and needs you and I face day in and day out.

So where would we look in an effort to find the place where they laid him? Possibly at the place of tension and conflict in our lives. For the place in which they originally laid him was riddled with tension and conflict. Israel was under foreign domination. Soldiers were in the streets. Refugees lined the roads. King Herod felt somewhat insecure about his authority and position, especially after he heard the news of a new-born king. Immediately he began to formulate plans to destroy any threat to his position. Tension and conflict were widespread.

But what about today? Would we likely find the Christ child in Marquette Park where racial tensions are boiling? Or in Calvert House where elderly people are eking out an existence and fighting for more humane treatment? Or in an office at State and Washington where people argue over the values that should prevail in corporate decisions? Or in your very own heart where you sometimes gasp at what you have become in light of what you might have been? We will probably find the Christ child at the place of tension and conflict. That's a start.

What's more, we shouldn't be surprised to find him among God's folk. The Wise Men were led by a star. Nevertheless, they went to Jerusalem, symbol of the people of God's promise, to inquire of the whereabouts of the new-born king. Although they didn't find him in the Temple at Jerusalem, they were informed by the leaders of the Temple where he might be found—among God's fold at Bethlehem, the place of which an ancient prophet had said, "from you, (O Bethlehem), shall come a ruler who shall govern my people Israel."

God's working among God's people has a continuity. And to deny ourselves access to this living tradition among the brothers and sisters who praise and serve and care means that we will wander more aimlessly in our search than is really necessary.

A place of tension and conflict, a place among God's folk and finally, a place where we stand in awe and wonder, surprised by the presence of love and new possibility. It's a place where worship is natural and real. That place might be right here—right now. It may also be elsewhere. But wherever it is, it is a holy place for you. For one man it is a workshop attached to a barn. "There is a wood burning stove in it made of an oil drum. There is a workbench dark and dented, with shallow, crammed drawers behind ore of which a cat lives. There is a…calendar on the wall, plus various lengths of chain and rope, shovels and rakes of different sizes and shapes, some worn-out jackets and caps on pegs, an electric clock that doesn't keep time...." The man has no idea why this place is holy for him. But he does know, "For reasons known only to God, it is one of the places he uses for sending his love to the world through" (F. Buechner, *Wishful Thinking,* p. 39).

That's the final clue we need to find the place where they laid him. It will always be the place where God sends God's love to you.

Morris J. Niedenthal in 1977 was Professor of Preaching at the Lutheran School of Theology at Chicago, Chicago, Illinois.

MATTHEW 2:1-12

EPIPHANY
JANUARY 6, 1980

The old church downtown was a big barnlike place on the Akron plan. It smelled of varnish, oiled floors, plaster that was damp from a roof leak and ladies' toilet waters. A pipe organ presided over the room and its fake, ornamental, gold pipes caught the brightness of the stained glass windows—Jesus the good shepherd, a resurrection angel and one I have forgotten. Everybody was proud of the rheostat, a big black affair controlled by dangling ropes that hung in the vestibule.

The good thing about the rheostat was that on Christmas Eve all the lights could be dimmed for the Children's Program. Even though you may have lived in Maine or Arizona, you've been there: little children in white smock-like robes with big red bows opened the program. Then came the pageant put on by the fifth and sixth grades. Every boy's mother got the idea of making her son's costume out of a bathrobe with a striped towel for a headpiece. The girl's mothers appeared to use white bedsheets with blue bathtowels, though I can't be too sure about that since I didn't have any sisters. We all smelled like Fab detergent with a touch of Purex to impress the other mothers.

The old sanctuary was enough like a barn not to require much scenery—a crude crib with straw poking out of the cracks and the gleaming heads of tenpenny nails, haloes made of coathangers painted silver, *papier maché* angels' wings that were usually lopsided and a cardboard star (covered with aluminum foil). The star was taped to the top of the tallest fake organ pipe and illuminated by a flashlight hidden in the baptistry. I always watched the star because as the program got longer the batteries got weaker until at the finale (when the choir director sang "O Holy Night") the star was the color of putrid yellow—if you could see it at all. Just the reverse of the way the Bible has it.

When I was in the sixth grade I was Joseph. I tried to act holy but I had an itch in an embarrassing place. My friend Johnny was a wise man. After they had tramped down the aisle with their cigar-box gifts, he positioned himself in such a way as to catch my eye. Then he flashed me an obscene sign with his hand which he had just learned from the seventh graders. That didn't do much for my attempt to act holy.

Johnny was always doing stuff like that. His favorite Sunday School sport was shredding the plastic rim on the table. During worship he liked to sit in the balcony and bring out the hitherto unnoticed sexual overtones of the hymns. He liked to ride his bike up and down the white tiled halls and jam on the brakes, thus leaving a long black mark. If he knew somebody was in the windowless men's restroom, his hand would slip inside the door and flip off the lights. There were a lot of Elders who wanted to flip off his lights.

But something must have been going on inside of Johnny. It was at least as inconspicuous as astrologers riding their camels across the desert in the dead of night with one eye fixed on the stars. Johnny went into the ministry. When I visited him last week, just for a night on the way back from vacation, he seemed to have offered up all that imagination to the church. As he might have said, if he hadn't been trying so hard to act holy, he's a hell of a preacher.

There must have been more juice in those flashlight batteries than anyone ever suspected. Of course, there was more in Bethlehem's star than met the eye.

Ronald Allen, a minister of the Christian Church (Disciples of Christ) in 1980 was co-minister with his spouse of First Christian Church, Grand Island, Ne.

MATTHEW 2:1-12

EPIPHANY
JANUARY 6, 1985

Christmas was God's doing and not our doing. Whether it is Isaiah, or Paul, or Matthew, they each say that it is God who has revealed the good news of which they speak. They all say that it is God who has acted in our world— "the glory of the Lord has risen upon you," "according to the gift of God's grace," "an angel of the Lord appeared to him." As we approach our Christmas celebration we become so involved in imagining and in planning, in going and coming, in doing and decorating, in gifting and getting, in carding and caroling that we come to feel that Christmas is in what *we do* and in the way *we act*.

But now that we have completed our human celebrations it is time to have our heavenly celebration and pause with the wise men to adore God's gift of the Christ-child. Now that the excitement of the birthing has subsided we can give ourselves to admiring the radiance of the new arrival. We can match the gift of Divine presence with the gift of our undivided and attentive presence.

We may find it more comfortable actively to enter the nativity drama at this juncture because it has ceased to be an all Jewish show. Especially would this be true if we have felt some empathy with the poet who wrote "How odd of God, to choose the Jews." Three gentiles of stature and means are being drawn center stage through God's leading to signal that God's gift is to be for all people—"they all gather together, they come to you," "the gentiles are fellow heirs, members of the same body, and partakers of the promise through Christ Jesus." Though the gift was delivered in a Jewish town to a Jewish family it is intended to be for gentiles as well. It would be wrong to attempt to keep God's gift for ourselves because it is intended for all people. This gift of divine light has the potential for illumining the lives of all people. The largess of the gift can only be known and experienced through manifesting the gift to all.

It is at this juncture that we become caught up in God's act of giving. Responding to God's gift in Jesus Christ means becoming caught up in God's giving to the world and the abandon with which God gives Christ and us to the world for its healing and salvation both astounds and awes us to the point of fear and incredulity and we are inclined to exclaim, "What have we gotten ourselves into?" The wise men in T. S. Eliot's "Journey of the Magi" lament that they are no longer at ease in the old dispensation. In Matthew's gospel we find them being warned not to return to Herod and departing to their own country by another way, while pondering the risks of deliberately defying the Jewish king. The apostle Paul has accepted the role of the "least of the disciples" and become a prisoner in his endeavor to preach the "unsearchable riches of Christ." The call to become part of God's Jesus Christ—gift to the world is clearly sounded in the words of the prophet Isaiah—"Arise, shine!" See! Be radiant! Rejoice! Let yourself be swept away with the wave of wondrous love which God is giving to the world. Such an attitude is reflected in the covenant for binding ourselves to God which John Wesley proposed to his followers.

"I am no longer my own, but thine. Put me to what thou wilt, rank me with whom thou wilt; put me to doing, put me to suffering; let me be employed for thee or laid aside for thee, exalted for thee or brought low for thee, let me be full, let me be empty; let me have all things, let me have nothing; I freely and heartily yield all things to thy pleasure and disposal" (p. 387, *The Book of Worship*, The Methodist Church. Nashville: The Methodist Publishing House, 1965).

It is time for us to move to an understanding of Epiphany as a season when God includes and uses us as a part of the gift of Jesus Christ for the healing and salvation of the world.

Harold A. Brack, a minister of the United Methodist Church, in 1985 was professor of Speech and Homiletics in the Theological School of Drew University, Madison, N.J.

MATTHEW 2:1-12

EPIPHANY
JANUARY 6, 1986

One sure sign of the passing of Christmas is the tinseled trees which lie by the sides of the roads, at the ends of driveways, along the curbs. One such tree caught my eye on the day following New Year's Day. It was the first one of the season. It lay, bottom up, with twists of tinsel blowing sorrowfully in the wind. It became for me a symbol of two things: An efficient householder who was anxious to get the house back to "normal," and the passing of Christmas. In one sense, I wasn't quite ready for "Christmas" to go back into the attic, or be sent off to the local Christmas tree recycling center! But there it was—a single, tinseled tree by the side of the road. It became a parable. It raised a question: Christmas has gone, and with what are we left? Ah, that's the real measure of Christmas! And it occurred to me that at Christmas we remember that Christ came—but then life goes on, sometimes just the same.

The seasons of our lives move on relentlessly. Several days after Christmas I walked through a department store and was surprised to find spring hats for sale! And that, too, became a parable: While we religious types still muse around the manger, the merchants haven't dropped a step in the march of the seasons! But that's the way life really is. "One season following another," as The Fiddler on the Roof said. And when you think about it, that's nothing to be mourned, really. Even the Bible picks up the pace just as rapidly as the merchants. In Matthew 2, we read the story of the birth of Jesus, the visit of the Wise Men, the flight into Egypt. In Matthew 3, we are launched into the orbit of the public ministry of our Lord Jesus beginning with John the Baptist, the baptism of Jesus, and the affirmation by the Voice from heaven: "This is my beloved Son, with whom I am well pleased."

As I have confronted the Scriptures and have seen more and more tinseled trees by the side of the road, I have come to conclude that Christmas tells the SEASON of His Coming, and Epiphany spells out the REASON of His Coming! It's as though God is reminding us that both Scripture and Season answer the human question, He came! So what? The tinseled tree is not really a tragic, lonely reminder that Christmas is gone. Rather, it is a powerful statement about the nature of reality and the character of God. It's really a reminder that we are called to go on with the necessary work to get Christ out of the cultural and economic event which has been called Christmas, and into our daily lives and the life of the world. Indeed, when it comes right down to it—one of the great problems which God faces in our time MAY BE the well-intentioned slogan: KEEP CHRIST *IN* CHRISTMAS!

Epiphany is the outward movement of the inclusive spirit of God's love. The tinseled tree at the side of the road, and the long journey home for Three Wise Men to take his name to the gentiles are part of the rhythm of God's plan. God won't be kept in pastoral settings of plaster and plastic creches; he will get out somehow into our homes, and into the marketplace, and into our personal struggles, and into the great movements for the liberation of the human spirit. The Herods of this world will not finally prevail!

So when you see those tinseled trees at the side of the road, try to feel the awesome power of the movement of life where one season follows another, and remember a statement by Churchill who, when he was asked to sum up his reflections on the significance of history, said simply: IT GOES ON!

I like that! And I commend it to those of you who are feeling the pain of the passing of the seasons: some who wrestle with important decisions in marriage; others who know firsthand the threat and power of disease; those who have had to deal recently with the loss of a relationship, of a job, of self-esteem; those who wonder if they can make it without the presence of one around whom their world has turned. The tinseled tree by the side of the road is a *sign of pain* and a *sign of hope*—for life goes on, and that's where God is to be found.

The Invitation to Communion reads: "Come and take this Holy Sacrament to your comfort!" It reminds us of another Tree which stands forever by the side of the Road. It, too, is a sign of pain and hope. Come, and embrace *your* life with all its ambiguities and certainties, as you embrace the Christ who once adorned a Tree that stands not only at the side of the Road but also at the center of history!

W. James White, a minister of The United Methodist Church, in 1986 was Senior Minister of The United Methodist Church in Morristown, New Jersey.

MATTHEW 2:1-12

EPIPHANY
JANUARY 6, 1994

I grew up in Racine, Wisconsin on the shores of Lake Michigan. As a little girl, I remember going to one of the beautiful beaches and jumping into the cold, cold water. I also remember going down to one of the piers with my dad to fish for perch. In the summer, we'd drive down and sit along the shoreline because it was always 10 degrees cooler. Mostly as I grew older I became indifferent to the lake. During the 60's the beaches were closed due to pollution. In the 70's there was an environmental thrust to clean up the lake. Yet, living by something that you see every day of your life can leave you disinterested. In the 80's, however, I worked very near the lake and would walk every day in summer along the top of the lake's embankment. There was a nice trail, with trees and benches and a group of us would often stop and sit to eat our lunch. One day as our group approached the lake we saw people standing on the embankment pointing. Cars were slowing along the drive that followed the shoreline. We thought that perhaps somebody had drowned, and people were watching the divers. As we got closer we saw what all the commotion was about. The lake, a pale blue, was as smooth as glass and perfectly transparent; we could see right to the bottom all the way out to the mile breaker and beyond. We could see every rock; we could see the huge schools of coho salmon and rainbow trout. We could even see the hulls of boats that had sunk. It was amazing. It was a miracle. It was an Epiphany for the lake was showing forth all its radiant beauty and the wonders that it held. We stood in awed silence with all the others who had stopped to look.

Finally, we had to leave—we had to go back to the world of work and ordinary life. But all of us were changed. I am sure that those who saw that miracle will never forget it. We all rushed back the next day, but the magical world was closed. The glass had turned dark again.

Epiphanies are rare and will likely show up in the most unexpected of places—God can "show forth" using the most common of elements like a lake or a manger. For the Wise Men, the Epiphany showed up in a dirty stable, among the common, ordinary of life, as a new baby in a tiny manger. No one captures what that must have been like better than T.S. Eliot in his poem "Journey of the Magi." In the poem, Eliot has the last living magus reporting to Matthew what the trip was really like. It is not the picture we get on the beautiful greeting cards that we send at Christmas. It is rather a picture of struggle, doubt, loss and despair. The journey was, we often forget, a risk. Eliot writes: " 'A cold coming we had of it, / Just the worst time of the year / For a journey, and such a long journey: / The ways deep and the weather sharp, / The very dead of winter.' " When the magi finally arrived, they weren't sure what they had seen... whether they had come all that way for a birth or a death. Eliot writes: "this Birth was / Hard and bitter agony for us, like Death, our death." And each of them knew that their worlds would never be the same. Each of them realized that all they enjoyed in the old life must pass away—had passed away. Birth and death are always one and the same.

Today Epiphanies are rare. Even so, today they still signal both a birth and a death. For me that lake Epiphany showed me once again God's glory, and caused me to reflect on how I took it all for granted. When Jesus Christ enters your lives, the old must pass away. Out the window go the comforts of ignorance, in come all the responsibilities that go along with being shown. Like the magi of Eliot's poem, we can be "no longer at ease here, in the old dispensation."

And yet, Epiphany reminds us once again of the glory of the Lord and the promise of the child who becomes the man of the cross. That last magus that was left, ready to die, giving his story to St. Matthew, perhaps says it best: "I should be glad of another death."

Cynthia Lee Ruud in 1994 was a Local Licensed Pastor in the South Dakota Conference of the United Methodist Church serving the Rockham, Cresbard and Miranda UMC's.

Sundays after Epiphany

JOB 7:1-7; MARK 1:29-39

THE FIFTH SUNDAY AFTER EPIPHANY
FEBRUARY 4, 1979

I once heard of a submarine which sank in the Atlantic during World War II. A team was sent down in a diving bell to attempt to rescue the trapped crew. When the bell settled against the sub, the crew was able to communicate with the world outside for the first time since they were sunk. Tapping in Morse code against the connecting steel the men asked their fateful question: Tap, tap, tap "Is...there...any...hope...?"

Is there any Hope? This is one of the crucial questions of life. In many ways each of us taps out the question from the various situations which sink and imprison us.

In the face of a serious illness, we ask the doctors, "Is there any hope?"

In a caring relationship with another which may extend over a long time or end tonight we ask, "Is there any hope?"

As twilight falls over our advancing years we ask, "Is there any hope?"

As persons struggle against the bonds of social oppression which tie them down because of race, ethnic origin, sex, or status, they cry out, "Is there any hope?"

The question is ancient as well as contemporary as the Old Testament lesson from Job reminds us. In the depth of his loss and despair it seemed that his days were passing faster than a weaver's shuttle and were spent without hope. But what distinguishes Job is his profundity, not just antiquity. Job wants to know if there is hope in an *ultimate* sense.

Job uses the Hebrew word for hope which means literally a cord attachment. Job has no hope, no cord that ties him to the future. Thus he drops to the depth of despair. Job believes that he could bear his losses and his pain if he could believe that one day he would be connected to a new possibility lifted up to a new life. One day he might know that his Redeemer lives and will at last stand upon the earth.

What Job longs for is not just the cessation of his particular complaints but Hope with a capital "H" by means of which he can be lifted above his hopelessness. If there is an ultimate hope beyond the grave then there is hope for us now in the midst of our suffering.

Jesus Christ is our answer to Job's lament. Jesus is the assurance that our Redeemer lives. There is hope!

The Gospel lesson from Mark shows us how Jesus brings hope in the healing of Simon's mother-in-law. Lindsay P. Pherogo writes: "The healing of Simon's mother-in-law is a 2nd example of Jesus' power. He does not rely on magical formulas that bring some outside supernatural force into the situation, but he himself is the power to heal" (*The Interpreter's One-Volume Commentary on the Bible* ed. Charles M. Laymon, Nashville and New York: Abingdon Press, 1971, p. 647).

Jesus had been teaching with authority in the synagogue at Capernaum. He left the synagogue and immediately went to the house of Simon and Andrew where he found Simon's mother-in-law sick with fever. Jesus acted in the home with the same authority which had marked his teaching in the synagogue. Jesus sized up what was going on, took her by the hand. He lifted her up clearly in more ways than one. She went on to get dinner for them.

Jesus brings Hope with a capital "H" to the otherwise hopeless situations of our lives. As a Modern Affirmation of Faith puts it, Jesus Christ is "the ground of our hope, and the promise of our deliverance from sin and death."

Jesus speaks with authority in the synagogue. Had he done no more he would have been known as a great speaker. But he brings his healing power into our fevered lives and lifts us up with hope. Therefore, he is more than a great speaker. He is a great Saviour. This theme can be developed in at least two major dimensions which are related.

I. Hope in Jesus Christ helps us handle problems which otherwise would destroy us. Illustrate from individual experience.
II. Hope in Jesus Christ helps us transform social situations which otherwise imprison people. We may confirm this from social settings, for instance, the role of the churches in Youngstown, Ohio, as shown in the ABC-TV film, "The Town That Refused To Die."

David Randolph in 1979 was minister of Christ Church, United Methodist, in New York City.

MATTHEW 5:1-12

THE FOURTH SUNDAY AFTER EPIPHANY
FEBRUARY 1, 1981

One of the most remarkable human beings it has ever been my privilege to know is a man named Albert. He lives in a small town in the deep South. I first knew him when I was his neighbor 16 years ago.

Albert had grown up in a place called Hermanville, which is about as big as it sounds. He reached adulthood during the Depression and ended up selling Fords in the town where he now lives.

Albert believed that it was wrong that 80% of the eligible voters in his town had never been allowed to register to vote and that the registrar had publicly stated that the first one who tried would end up dead on the sidewalk in front of the county office building. Albert believed that it was wrong that a highly disproportionate share of the county's school tax money went to the smaller of two separate and very unequal public schools. Albert believed that it was wrong that it was virtually impossible for a white person to be convicted of a crime against a black and just as impossible for a black to be acquitted of a crime against a white. Albert believed that it was wrong that the town government maintained two little league baseball fields, one beautifully manicured with chain like fences, field lights, a press box and a public address system and the other a literal weed patch with stumps, briars, and not even a backstop behind home plate. The list went on.

For 30 years Albert had quietly but forcefully voiced his beliefs: among business owners of which he was one, in the town council, in the governing board of his Methodist Church, in casual conversations. His message was singular: friends, if we don't make things right in our town, then one of these days the federal government is going to come in here and make them right for us, and we'll all be better off if we do it ourselves.

I remember a Kiwanis Club meeting held in the town restaurant. The speaker was an executive in an area utility company. He gave a fairly typical speech, exposing communist influence throughout the federal government and branding the civil rights movement a Kremlin plot to subvert traditional southern virtue. When the speech was finished there was enthusiastic applause. After a brief silence, Albert rose to his feet. "Sir," he said humbly, "with no disrespect for you or your office, and with malice toward no one in this room because they are all my friends, I have to disagree with many of the things you have just said." He went on briefly to state his own case in behalf of justice and fairness for all people.

One morning as I walked downtown to get the mail—downtown was 2 blocks from our house—I heard news that there had been trouble at Albert's Ford place during the night. The Ku Klux Klan had had a rally, had heard some rousing speeches, had put a few beers under their belts, and then had decided they were ready to persecute their favorite villain. They had thrown rocks through Albert's plate glass windows, and poured gasoline over several of his used cars and set fire to them. His place was a charred mess when I got there. "What does this do to you, Albert?" I asked him.

"I've gotten so used to it it doesn't do much of anything," he replied. "The only thing that worries me is that the insurance company has threatened for some time to cut me off. I don't even report little incidents like this anymore because I need to keep my insurance in case something really big happens."

"What happens if they do cut you off?" I asked. I expected his answer to be: I'll have to move to another town and start over; or, I'll have to learn to be quieter about what I believe. Instead, he quietly spoke words that told me what his life was made of.

"I'll have to operate my business without insurance." Albert had no *intention* of giving up any thing.

Albert will never be blessed with the biggest Ford dealership south of Nashville. He will never be governor of his state nor outstanding layman in his Methodist district. And there's not much I can say about rewards he will receive after he dies, except that I know the Lord will be with him. But this much I can say: Albert is a clear sign of what is to come. His life is poetry that implicitly summons all who can hear to integrity and truth. His story will live, because it is the kind of story that empowers other people to live, and to be the human beings they too can be. No greater gift can one person give to another.

James O. Chatham, a minister in the Presbyterian Church U.S., in 1981 was associate pastor of Highland Presbyterian Church, Louisville, Kentucky, and Adjunct Professor of Homiletics at Louisville Presbyterian Seminary.

ISAIAH 58:5-12

THE FIFTH SUNDAY AFTER EPIPHANY
FEBRUARY 8, 1981

When I was a child I used to give up peanut butter and ginger ale for Lent. It was my way of showing my best buddy, Roy Barnhardt, that I was as good as he was. It was also my insurance that God would not push me through the trap door to hell. Roy was the one who had taught me about the trap door: "When you die, unless you're a saint, they put you into this middle room. Then if your friends pray a lot for you, an angel lowers a rope ladder like a police helicopter making a rescue and they fly you away to heaven. But if you stay too long in that room and they got to make room for fresh dead people, they shove you through a big trap door to hell. But if you give something up for Lent, God writes it down and sends the helicopter and you make it into heaven." Well! as a second grader that was all I needed to hear. I decided then and there to give up my two most favorite foods for Lent, peanut butter and ginger ale.

It is easy now to look back at this story and laugh with all the wisdom of our adult sophistication. And yet there is something in this story that is more than the entertainment of a youngster's stumbling efforts to please God. For when it comes to religion it is true that "The Child is father of the Man" and mother of the woman. Our childhood responses of faith and fear rumble in the heart long after we have grown up and erupt in patterns of belief and behavior. When life seems against us we fall back into simplistic efforts to win God's favor, even as children regress to earlier patterns of dependence when confronted with fearful situations This is exactly what happened to the Israelites when they returned to Jerusalem from the exile. The holy city—which they had grieved and yearned and prayed for while they were in Babylon—turned out to be a dump when they arrived home. Streets, homes and the protective wall were in rubble. Violence reigned. The stamp of urban blight was everywhere. And how did the Israelites react to the scary social situation that engulfed them? They became religious, very religious, too religious. In effect, they went back to giving up peanut butter and ginger ale when they should have been taking adult responsibility for the world in which they lived. They fasted. They called on God. But God was not interested. God did not want them to be religious. God wanted them to be faithful, to be loyal to the divine demands for building a just and decent city.

Like those Israelites and like Roy Barnhardt and myself as children, we are tempted to revert to the simplest religious activities to win back God's favor. Most of us are familiar with Roy's trap door. It is located inside our minds, at that spot where our fears overtake us and the bottom of our world seems to fall out from under us. It happens to us individually and as a society. The trap door has been opened by urban unrest, the scars of Viet Nam, Watergate, and an economy that no longer functions by the old theories—conservative or liberal—and we have felt ourselves falling, falling, falling toward hell, toward the chaos of a world that threatens to overwhelm us with its violence and brutality. So we have become religious. The electric church on television, the upsurge of piety and personalistic experiences are like my childhood peanut butter and ginger ale—ways to please God, ways to win God's favor. But today as God looks at our cities swelling with refugees and still boiling with the legacy of prejudice and poverty, God asks us the same question that God asked those Israelites returned from Babylon: "Is not this the fast that I require: to loose the bonds of wickedness, to undo the thongs of the yoke, to let the oppressed go free, and to break every yoke?"

Prayer and praise are the wick and candle of a Christian's inner light. But who lights a lamp and then puts it under a bushel basket? "Let your Light so shine," says Jesus. Let it shine in your politics, let it shine in this neighborhood, let it shine in your acceptance and care of all people. Then God will send Roy's helicopter, not only in death but in life. Or as Isaiah puts it, "Then you shall take delight in the Lord, and I will make you ride upon the heights of the earth."

Thomas H. Troeger, a minister in the United Presbyterian Church in the U.S.A. in 1981 was assistant professor of preaching and parish, Colgate Rochester/Bexley Hall/Crozer Divinity School, Rochester, N. Y.

MARK 1:4-11

FIRST SUNDAY AFTER THE EPIPHANY
JANUARY 10, 1982

The wilderness in which the voice of John cried out was basically a physical wilderness, a desert. But he cried out, "Prepare the way of the Lord." And when Jesus appeared he pointed to him and cried out, "Behold the Lamb of God." Today we live in a wilderness nonetheless real for being urban. It is our calling as Christians in our time to prepare the way of the Lord and to point the way to the Christ.

Now the wilderness is not only a deserted place, it can be a spiritual wasteland. And most of us know what that can be like. We know what it is like to have a sense of enormous loneliness, even though other people may be around us. We have a sense of grief and loss when someone whom we have loved is taken from us. We've sensed the wilderness of a world which prepares for war while it talks about peace. And we sense the grimness of life in what is often a cliché but nonetheless true: an urban jungle. So at least we know that in our time we live in a wilderness nonetheless real for being different from the wilderness in which John the Baptist first appeared. Indeed, there are surely few of us who have not felt the impact of the rising violence and crime which we not only see around us but come to experience and the reports of a number of you have indicated to me that you, too, have been victimized by the signs of this urban jungle. That's the trend, the sign of the times, the way in which there's a kind of violence that breaks in upon us, a violence which makes all the more vivid the need for you and for me and for all of us as Christians to prepare the way of the Lord. To be a voice in the wilderness.

Now to prepare the way of the Lord is to do those things which lead to the coming of the kingdom. It is not our calling to be kings. It is our calling to be servants of the king. And by deeds of loving mercy to prepare the way so that the king may come. I believe that as we give generously to the church and its mission we are preparing the way of the Lord. When we act responsibly to root out the causes of violence and crime we are preparing the way of the Lord. I believe that when we provide music, as we hear consistently in church, we're preparing the way of the Lord. And the ministry which cries out in song which is often beautiful is nonetheless a cry in the wilderness; there's so much ugliness around us. And when we hear a beautiful voice and a beautiful organ being beautifully played, that comes as a voice in the wilderness. When we preach the word of God, truly we may be a voice in a moral and spiritual

All these activities are not just activities; they are not just things to do to keep us occupied. I believe that they are ways in which you and I can prepare the way of the Lord and be a voice crying out for love, for justice, for truth, and for beauty in the wilderness of our modern world.

Yes, at times we could wish that we were kings. How happy we would be, we think, if we could bring in our kingdom and have things our way. But it is not our calling to be kings. It is our calling to prepare the way so that when the Lord comes He will have a way to travel before Him. How much many of us would like to have some kind of a personal promoter who would point to us and keep us in the spotlight. That is not our calling. Rather, we are to be like John the Baptist whose very life, as indeed his word, is like a finger pointing to the Christ in all that we are and all that we do, crying out, "Behold the Lamb of God."

David James Randolph, a minister of the United Methodist Church, in 1982 was Senior Minister of Christ Church—United Methodist, New York City, New York.

MARK 1:40-45

THE SIXTH SUNDAY AFTER EPIPHANY
FEBRUARY 14, 1982

How appropriate—to be talking about healing lepers on Valentine's Day! The gift of love, the epiphany that occurred when Jesus reached out to touch the leper.

The phone company, "Ma Bell," has been running an advertising campaign to encourage people to call long distance. It's based on the human longing to be loved and it's called, "reach out and touch someone." A gangly teenager holds her roller skates in one hand, the phone in the other while she teeters in her first pair of high heels while telling her faraway aunt about the coming prom. A father holds baby's hands while mother dials the grandparents to tell them their grandchild has just taken a step. All part of reaching out and touching. All part of keeping people within the community, the circle of love. (And, for Ma Bell, it's all part of making money.)

Recently, I read about a psychologist who claims that all humans need at least one good warm hug a day to stay mentally healthy. If that's true, it is both reassuring and frightening. It's reassuring because a hug is so easy and inexpensive to give. Imagine, instead of paying a therapist sixty to a hundred dollars an hour, you could go to a dear friend and say: "Life is too much for me right now; please put your arms around me and hug me for two minutes." But the frightening part about this theory is that there are so many people who have no one to hug them or who are afraid to ask for a hug.

Think of the prisoners in our over-crowded jails. Who could they possibly ask for a hug? Who would want to hug them? Yet, who needs a gentle, caring touch more than a criminal? Think also of other prisoners of our society, not behind iron bars, but trapped in loneliness or ignorance. There is a short movie entitled, *Minnie Remembers*. Minnie, an elderly woman, sits in her rocking chair; and, in a series of flashbacks, we see her life. She is holding children, being touched by her husband, reaching out to take flowers picked for her on a picnic. At the end of the film she is still alone in her rocking chair, saying to herself: "No one ever touches me anymore. They come to pay a visit and then they leave; but they never touch me." Minnie had a family who visited. We can only wonder at how many older people live alone, and like the prisoners in jail, have no one to ask for a hug even if they had the courage.

I wonder how much courage it took for the leper to ask Jesus for help? I think of my teenage stepson who went through a period of being a "prickly pear." When I would reach out to hug him he would pull away—not just from me, from anyone who tried to help. He was lonely, miserable, unsure of himself (just like many teenagers)! In his fear of being rejected, he rejected anyone who tried to help. It was several years before he learned how to ask for help and to be willing to receive it. Anyone who has tried to get volunteers for a church youth group knows many people fear reaching out to teenagers. It's no wonder they, in turn, fear reaching out and asking the adult world for help!

If we, as the Church, are going to take Paul's words seriously about imitating Christ, then we need to be looking at the lepers of our society and how we can touch them. Unlike

Ma Bell, we're not just reaching out to those who love us —even sinners and publicans do that. We need to be touching the untouchables so that they enter into the community—the mainstream. An occasional visit to a lonely old person who cannot drive a car and get to town is not sufficient. We need to think of changing the system so there is cheap and safe transportation. Then the elderly person can really be in the mainstream. Visits to people in prison are fine; but what about the whole philosophy of putting people away from loved ones and never providing them with adequate rehabilitation. Where is the system that allows them meaningful work after they are let out?

When you care enough to send the best... you send yourself. That's what God has done. What a valentine—Jesus has dwelt among us. We are called to follow that example. We are to be the valentine lovers of this world.

Barbara Martin, a minister of The United Church of Christ, in 1982 lived and worked in Pasadena, California.

MATTHEW 5:1-12

THE FOURTH SUNDAY AFTER EPIPHANY
FEBRUARY 1, 1987

"Blessed are the poor in spirit, for theirs is the kingdom of heaven.

"Blessed are those who mourn, for they shall be comforted.
"Blessed are you when men revile you and persecute you and utter all kinds of evil against you falsely on my account."

Wait a minute. What kind of blessings are these? When we say count your blessings we usually think of health or a good family or an excellent position in a sound company. Blessed are the rich. Blessed are the happy. Blessed are the popular. These are the beatitudes of our society, the blessings of our culture that are celebrated in the media. How can we ever understand that the poor, the grieving, and the persecuted are blessed?

One place to begin would be with the word "blessing." Many modern translations find the term so antiquated that they render the biblical word as "happy" instead of "blessed"—"Happy are the poor in spirit, happy are those who mourn, happy are the meek." This translation is filled with problems. In our everyday speech "happiness" is primarily a term of feeling, a psychological state of inward satisfaction. But for the biblical writers it was clear that being blessed had its roots in "God from whom all blessings flow." Certainly to know God's blessing is a happy thing! But happiness alone is too constricted a meaning for blessing, and it is too constricted a purpose for anything so complex and wondrous as human life.

Understanding the word "blessed" gives us a glimmer of the meaning of the beatitudes, but in the last analysis we have to move beyond speech to the reality of the difference between happiness and blessedness. I can think of many times when I have been happy in the conventional sense of the term: I bought a new car and I liked the color and the way it shone and the way it ran before the first rattle. But in a few weeks as it got as muddy as every other car and lost that new car smell, it became just a way to get around. That car had made me happy but it had not blessed me.

I think of another time in my life, when my happiness had shattered and I was in deep grief. But there was someone I loved who was with me, who listened and held me when I wept. Then I knew "Blessed are those who mourn, for they shall be comforted." And it was a blessing, not a happiness. I did not feel it as some inward state arrived at by my own thought, but I felt the blessing as something coming from beyond me, coming even from beyond my friend, as though she were drawing on some gracious source that steadied us both, a reality worthy to be called "the kingdom of heaven."

And that is a single personal story. Think of that story amplified a million times over by the poor and the persecuted and the peacemakers, "for theirs is the kingdom of heaven."

Thomas H. Troeger, a Presbyterian minister, in 1987 was professor of preaching at Colgate Rochester Divinity School.

MATTHEW 5:17-26

SIXTH SUNDAY AFTER EPIPHANY
FEBRUARY 15, 1987

Invitation to the Dance—
"I danced for the scribe and the pharisee,
but they would not dance and they wouldn't follow me…."
(from "Lord of the Dance," by Sydney Carter)

Scribes and Pharisees don't dance much. If they do, they dance alone, picking their feet up and placing them carefully, just so—one, two, three; one, two, three. They dance alone because for them the essence of the dance is to get it right, not to put the left foot here when it should be there, the angle of the right foot not a degree too much to left or right. To dance with partners, or to dance in a circle would be to court disaster, to be pulled hopelessly out of position, or to be distracted by another's clumsiness. After all, if one must dance (and I suppose occasionally one must) then it must be done correctly, paying as little attention as possible to the music (another source of distraction) and no attention to others on the floor. Eyes on the feet, concentrating on the steps, they cautiously but flawlessly perform the intricate maneuvers, and congratulate themselves as they exit. They got it right, again. But then, it would be unthinkable to dance and get it wrong.

Such is the righteousness of scribes and Pharisees, a solitary virtuoso performance which others may watch, and perhaps applaud, but never share in. For after all, salvation is at stake and it would be a shame to mess it up by trying to do it with someone who doesn't know how. "Watch me; do it this way," they cry, "but keep your distance until you can do it perfectly!" That may be righteousness of a sort, but it resembles the righteousness of Jesus about as much as my dancing resembles Tina

Turner. "Unless your righteousness exceeds that of the scribes and Pharisees, you will never enter the kingdom of heaven," said Jesus. What could that possibly mean? Is there more to righteousness than "getting it right" every time? Is there more to dancing than not making any mistakes?

I was among the scribes and Pharisees at the school dance. We were, most of us, grade seven boys, back against the wall, hands in pockets, staying well clear of the dance floor, but making wisecracks at the expense of those who were out there. "Look at old George trying to dance!" "Yeah; I hope his girl is wearing safety boots!" In vain the teacher in charge tried to get us to mix in with the others. But not a chance. There was no way we were going to make fools of ourselves on the dance floor.

I really don't know why I was there. I couldn't dance, and I was frightened of girls. But everyone else was going, and it would be fun to make jokes about those who were actually dancing.

The teacher had one more trick up her sleeve. She announced a Sadie Hawkins, and I was too slow to figure out what that meant. I might have noticed that the other scribes and Pharisees had suddenly headed to the washroom had it not been that I could see a girl coming in my direction. It was too late to run. She knew I had seen her. I was trapped. All I could do was stand my ground.

"Will you dance with me?"she asked.

"But, but I don't know how to dance," I stammered, knowing all that while that such an excuse would never save me.

"Well, come and dance anyhow," she said, and taking my hand she led me onto the dance floor. The circle I had drawn to exclude myself from the possibility of making mistakes (committing sin) was suddenly redrawn to include me. I was going to make mistakes in spite of my intentions to avoid any such possibility.

When Jesus talks about the righteousness of the scribes and Pharisees he reveals our foolishness. We suppose that we can draw the circles in our lives so as to keep ourselves free of sin. We draw the line between sin and righteousness so that murderers are clearly sinners, but the rest of us are not. Jesus draws the line so that the rest of us with our angry thoughts about other people find ourselves in the same circle with murderers.

And having drawn us into a circle we thought we could avoid, and shown us the futility of the righteousness of scribes and Pharisees, he turns the tables by revealing a different righteousness, a righteousness that is rooted in the cross and made valid by God's love. It is marked by forgiveness, affirmation, and the joy of community found among those who have given up the pretense of being righteous by their own virtue.

I began to discover a different righteousness that warm fall evening. A girl, whose name I have forgotten, drew me in and made me part of a different company where righteousness was an infectious smile, an invitation that wouldn't take NO for an answer, that forgave my clumsiness with an encouraging word, that made it possible for me to believe that I belonged to a better fellowship than ever scribes or Pharisees may know. And as I danced it was then, I think, that I began to live.

'Dance then wherever you may be;
I am the Lord of the dance,' said he.
'I'll lead you all wherever you may be,
I will lead you all in the dance,' said he.

Frank Meadows in 1987 was the minister of Fairlawn United Church, Toronto.

MATTHEW 5:27-37

THE SEVENTH SUNDAY AFTER EPIPHANY
FEBRUARY 22, 1987

She was sixteen years old and a bridesmaid at her father's wedding. It was his second marriage and, for many of us at least, an occasion which signaled a triumph of joy over pain, of hope over despair. We shared a giddy exuberance and confidence that comes from long, fierce struggles, but she was not a part of that. I was already wrapped in my dark robe and white stole when she came softly rapping on my office door. Her eyes were uncertain and moist with tears. She had started attending a Bible study after school, she explained, and just a week or so ago... her voice gave way and a dark, mascara-soaked tear dropped onto the lap of the pale peach bridesmaid's dress she looked so pretty in. She opened a Bible and silently pointed to these words (read Mt. 5:31-32).

The words were Jesus' words, and I wished he had never said them. They have given so much pain to so many women and men who have broken themselves against him, but here was only this child—no, this young woman— who had done nothing but love two parents whose love for each other had not been strong enough or wise enough to sustain their marriage. It hurts to read such words.

We don't expect words like these from Jesus. The words strike us as insensitive, uncaring, judgmental, legalistic, wholly lacking in compassion and understanding, precisely everything Jesus was not and is not.

Jesus was not simply against divorce or against people who are divorced or do divorce. As long as we approach these words feeling guilty we will read them only as a law we cannot keep. Jesus said that because he trusted in God's goodness and believed marriage to be a good gift of God. When Pharisees (like us) came asking about the law for divorce Jesus reminded them that before the law there was the good hope of God for marriage: God who made them *from the beginning* made them male and female (Mt. 19:4). Made them sexual. Made us for each other. Jesus recognized, and the church has affirmed marriage is a good gift of God. We say so at weddings. (Here might be quoted portions of your tradition's wedding rite.)

Marriage is God's good gift but I cannot read the "Statement on the Gift of Ma... our Presbyterian service without wondering what protests are stifled in the back p... wait for the day someone stands to announce, "It's not that simple!" And it isn't.

Marriage services seem designed for the very young and very brave and very innocent, yet there is this prayer (in many traditions): "Give them the courage, when they hurt each other... to seek your forgiveness and to forgive each other." Not *if* they hurt each other, when they hurt each other: a blunt acknowledgement of what is involved in this gift. We know the struggles, married or not.

We confess we misuse God's good gifts: the gift of the creation, of land, wealth, knowledge, sexuality, the very gift of our life, and the gift of marriage, too. We call such misappropriation of God's gifts "sin," a "falling short" of God's happy, hopeful intention for us. But sin is not the church's or God's final word on divorce. Forgiveness is. New creation is. Hope is.

Deep in our lives, where the Spirit calls to us, we find judgment and brokenness overwhelmed by a greater power. We bind our wounds. We forgive others—and ourselves— and seek God's forgiveness for a new start. We find new beginnings within our marriages. We divorce and we try it again. Some would say this is evidence only of our deep loneliness and ability for self-deception. Certainly we are lonely creatures and self-deceived, but there is more. We move forward, we move toward each other with new promises because we have received from God a vast promise and a gracious gift: the gift of each other and the hope we may yet be a blessing, one to another.

Patrick J. Willson, a minister of the Presbyterian Church (U.S.A.) in 1987 was pastor of Grace Presbyterian Church in Midland, Texas.

MARK 1:14-20

THE THIRD SUNDAY AFTER EPIPHANY
JANUARY 27, 1991

"And immediately they left their nets and followed him." What do you think of when you hear the word "immediately?" I think of microwave popcorn, instant-on television, push-button readouts on gauges in my car, and high-speed photocopying. I think of *things* that produce an instant response, not people.

As a father of a six-year old boy and an eighteen month old girl, "immediately" is no longer part of my vocabulary. We don't do anything immediately at our house! Our son Ben's response to my call (Right now!) to brush his teeth or to put away his Teenage Mutant Ninja Turtle menagerie is almost always "In a minute!", "Just a second," or "I can't hear you!" Traveling with our daughter, Gretchen, also frustrates my desire for immediate mobility. "Is the diaper bag stocked? Is the stroller in the trunk? Did we get...? Did you remember to pack...?" Sometimes I think I could make it to the grocery store and back in the time it takes me to buckle the belts and secure the snaps on her car seat.

ـn is really no different. Change takes time. Very little if
ـdiately. "We'll bring that up at next month's committee
ـll have to wait until next year's budget." "Maybe we'd better
ـ until the new minister arrives...." The only place I regularly see
ـng immediately is at the hospital, when the words "Code Blue" or
ـver the public address system.

ـl, "Code Blue!" He simply said, "Follow me." But why the immediate
ـy didn't these four men express hesitation, as did Jonah, and Moses, and
ـ have been called? What was it about this man that made Simon and
Anـ ـeave their nets by the seashore? Can you imagine these two men, sweaty and
stinking of fish, their hands raw from years of handling nets, tossing their livelihoods
aside on the basis of some stranger's call to follow him and be made "fishers of men?"
James and John leave dad sitting in the boat with a partially mended net. The hired
servants watch the two men walk into the sunset with some passerby and wonder,
"What's gotten into them?" How do you think Zebedee reacts? Do you think he yells,
"You guys come back here and help me clean these fish!"? Or does he shrug his
shoulders and declare, "Well, they've always had a problem with peer pressure"?

How could this man generate such an immediate affirmative response? Could they
instantly perceive that this was a man unlike any other, about to proclaim a message
unlike any other? What was it about him? What was it about them? Were they not like
the rest of us—looking for a sense of meaning, a reason for getting up in the morning?
Gene Boring has suggested that the question of God is still really the only question in
town. Were James, John, Simon, and Andrew searching for meaning in their lives?
Were their souls "restless until they found their rest in God" (St. Augustine)? Is that
why they dropped what was in their hands and responded so quickly to Jesus?

This text leaves us with mixed feelings—perhaps a combination of intimacy and
distance. Intimacy because we have all been there. We all wanted something more in our
lives—wanted to turn in our resignations and find jobs and lifestyles that were life
enhancing. Most of us want to wrestle with the only question in town. It is not easy to
identify with the disciples' desire for a change in direction.

And yet, we experience distance from the scene at the seashore. We envy the
immediate, life-changing response of those men, but wonder if it's not more difficult
for us today. "Sure, they could leave their nets—they didn't have to worry about the
mortgage payment, the church pledge card, the VISA balance, child care, and gas
prices." Most of us have difficulty in seeing ourselves responding totally and quickly
to the call of Christ. We'd rather give excuses. How many pastors have heard: "Sunday
is the only day I have to sleep late." "We'll become involved in your church when we
have children to bring to Sunday School." "Teach Vacation Bible School? Are you
kidding? Me in a room full of eight-year olds? Try me again—in about five years!"

If you're searching for answers, if you are hungering for a deeper relationship with God, perk up your ears! Christ is calling! Aren't you getting tired of responding "I can't hear you," or, "Be there in a minute!" Why not respond today, this hour, this minute, right now? Why not immediately?

Neil Engle in 1991 was the Associate Pastor of Hillside Christian Church (Disciples of Christ) in Kansas City, Missouri.

MARK 1:29-39

THE FIFTH SUNDAY AFTER EPIPHANY
FEBRUARY 10, 1991

Like the crowd at Jesus' door, we all seek deliverance from calamity. We look for a savior who will undo life's suffering and loss. We look for a miracle.

The Ugliest Pilgrim by Doris Betts (*Stories of the Modern South*, edited by Benjamin Forkner and Patrick Samway, S.J., Bantam books, 1979) is a story about a woman who spends the better part of her life building a case for a miracle. Night after night she looks out at the sky from the side of the mountain which is her home in Spruce Pine, NC, and studies the scriptures. Day by day she builds the case which she will present to the miracle working preacher in Tulsa, Oklahoma. She wishes healing for her face which is hideously deformed by a senseless accident and she seeks relief from the barrier that it creates between her and others.

"Lord! I am so ugly!

"Maybe the Preacher will claim he can't heal my ugliness. And I'm going to spread my palms by my ears and show him this is a crippled face! An infirmity! Would he do for a kidney or liver what he withholds from a face? The Preacher once stuttered, I read someplace, and God bothered with that. Why not me?...

"I've seen the Preacher wrap his hot, blessed hands on a club foot and cry out "HEAL!" in his funny way that sounds like the word "Hell" broken into two pieces. Will he not cry out, too, when he sees this poor clubbed face? I will be to him as Goliath was to David, a need so giant it will drive God to action" (p. 39).

So powerful is her case and so great is her faith, that as the bus rolls toward Tulsa, we also cannot believe that God would ignore such a request.

When she tells her fellow travelers on the bus the purpose of her trip they, like Job's friends, look sad and try to help her to accept her fate.

"Maybe the preacher's a fake," one says with a worried look. But she's thought of that. "…it may be what I believe is stronger than him faking. That he'll be electrified by my trust, the way a magnet can get charged against its will. He might be a lunatic or dope fiend, and it still not matter" (p. 42).

We accompany her to the Preacher's church but he is out of town, his shows have been taped weeks in advance. Finally she enters the assistant's office and lays before him a case as impressive as any prepared by a jurist since Job. When he has read every page the assistant says, "My child, I understand how you feel. And we will most certainly pray for your spirit."
"Never mind my spirit."
"Our Heavenly Father has purpose in all things."
"Ask him to set it aside."
"We must trust in his will."
"Let us pray for inner beauty."
"No, I will not" (p. 55).

She leaves the assistant's office and storms down the hall to the auditorium and goes straight to the pulpit where the Preacher stands. "there is nobody else to plead." Then she tells Jesus "how it feels to be ugly, with nothing to look back at you but a deer or an owl. She reads Him her paper out loud…
"I have been praising you Lord, but it gets harder every year" (pp. 55-56).

Our author argues not one case but two. In her hand the woman clasps a Mappop flower brought all the way from Spruce Pine, NC. She brought it because the crown of thorns and the crucifixion nails grow in its center. And the miracle that she seeks is not recorded in the curved hardness of the mirror in her pocket but in the faces of her companions on the bus who have come to care for her in the course of their long journey together. Here, our author argues, has been worked a transfiguration as real and sturdy as any that could be captured by a photograph. And she, almost without our knowing it, reminds us of our calling to be the mirrors of God's restorative grace. The story ends with the woman trusting the miracle that has been given and leaving the mirror's image behind that she may believe in the reflection seen in the faces of those who love her.

Jill Edens, a minister of the United Church of Christ, in 1991 was Co-Pastor of United Church of Chapel Hill, Chapel Hill, NC

DEUTERONOMY 30:15-20; MATTHEW 5:21-37

EPIPHANY 6
FEBRUARY 14, 1993

I imagine that many of those who gathered to hear Jesus were completely shocked when he quoted a law from Deuteronomy—"You have heard that it was said to those of ancient times"—and then revised that law—"But I say to you...." After all these were God's words that had been passed down through the great leader Moses and Deuteronomy's injunction against altering any laws was always honored. No one rewrote legislation. Ever.

But Jesus is demanding something more than the best of the tradition. He advocates a higher righteousness. These demands must have sounded as impossible then as they do today.

Be reconciled to your neighbor. Do not look lustfully at another. Do not commit adultery in your heart. Do not swear oaths. Let your yes mean yes and your no mean no.

What is at stake here is the sacredness of person-to-person relationships. Jesus confronts us with who we are and how we relate to one another as God's people. As much as we might like to be obedient to this higher law we find ourselves constantly distracted by our own attitudes of mistrust and arrogance that keep us separated from one another. Often we feel more than justified in holding grudges against others or withdrawing our care and support from those who have hurt us or perhaps humiliated us in some way. We are so easily caught in the cycle of success and reward that we spend most of our time competing with each other for the highest marks that will get us into the most prestigious schools that will land us the best jobs.

It doesn't matter whether we are waiting in line at the checkout counter of the supermarket, working at the office, or standing around at the coffee hour after church, we catch fragments of the same conversations. We constantly hear the noisy chatter of our incessant striving to prove that we are capable, important, and trustworthy.

The demands of Matthew's text are impossible for people like us. And yet every now and again God manages to break through all of our perverseness and noisy chit chat whether we want it or not, and gives us a taste of this higher righteousness.

I don't know why I gave her the money. I had passed her by many times before, always pretending I didn't hear the whisper; "Have you got an extra dollar, ma'am?" But this day was different. She was standing outside Eaton's Department Store at the corner of Yonge and Eglinton in Toronto. She made the same request she always made and as usual I ignored it. When I had finished my shopping she was still there. I moved as far as I could to the far edge of the sidewalk hoping she would not notice me. "Do you have an extra dollar, ma'am?" she shouted. I don't know why I did what I did but I shouted back, "Yes." I walked over to her and stuffed a two dollar bill into her hand. "Gee, thanks!" she said. As I turned away I could hear her call out after me; "Now you have a good weekend." That was Saturday afternoon. On Monday evening I was having a late supper at a neighborhood restaurant and who should walk in but this same street beggar. The hostess of the restaurant greeted her like a long lost friend. "Hi Mary. It's nice to see you. How are you tonight?" "Just great," replied Mary. The hostess moved closer to Mary and I overheard her say, "I'll have your table ready for you in a few minutes." When I left the restaurant I peeked into the place where Mary was. She was seated at her very own table which was covered with a fresh blue and white checkered cloth. She was sitting tall, smiling a wide smile, smoking a cigarette and sipping a steaming cup of freshly brewed coffee that had been set before her. At that moment I was, well, I was filled with something quite close to ecstasy. A taste of this higher righteousness? Perhaps. But for certain, a broadened vision of what it means to be one of God's beloved.

On our own it is impossible to achieve or earn righteousness. But we can trust that God is always working to bring us to that place of integrity—where our actions match our intentions, where there is honor and dignity for our own person as well as others, that place of integrity where God's warm reconciling healing love embraces us and frees us to live an abundant life and to walk in the light of truth.

Susanne Vanderlugt is an ordained minister in the United Church of Canada, and in 1993 was serving North Minster United Church, Toronto.

---

1 CORINTHIANS 1:1-9

EPIPHANY 2
JANUARY 14, 1996

One Sunday a few years ago, the minister in the church that I was attending began his sermon with a question that called for a response. He asked everyone who would like God's judgment to begin "right now" to raise his or her hand. There were a few uncomfortable moments. He looked around for raised hands. Only one middle-aged man raised his hand. Everyone else voted for judgment delayed.

But Paul paints quite a different picture of the Corinthians in today's Bible reading. Paul says that the Corinthians were actually looking forward to Jesus' return. Paul pictures them bright-eyed, waiting on tip toe: "You don't lack any spiritual gifts as you eagerly wait for our Lord Jesus to be revealed."

Of course, when what Paul says about the Corinthians in the verses that we read sinks in, it isn't too tough to imagine why the Corinthians might be able to vote enthusiastically against any delay in the return of Jesus. Paul reports that Christ's grace had been poured out upon the Corinthians so richly that they were fairly brimming with sparkling spiritual gifts of speech and knowledge. You aren't lacking in any spiritual gifts, Paul says. Paul says that he sees faith so strong that he has no doubt whatsoever that it will hold up until Christ returns and that they will get straight A's on their final report cards. No wonder they were waiting on tip toe for Jesus to return.

Not like most of us. If it were up to us, most of us I suppose would probably not vote for Jesus to return this morning or even later this afternoon. And we all know why. Most references to the second coming of Jesus highlight Jesus' coming as judge, *the* judge. And if he were to appear as the judge of the whole universe, why, who in his or her right mind would ever look forward to that. None of us has spotless records, far from it.

But if you go on to study or even casually read the rest of Paul's letter to the Corinthians, you might wonder how Paul could have ever written about them as he did.

You would think that if anyone had reason to be less than eager for Jesus' quick return, it would be the Corinthians.

To start with, Paul mentions that the church in Corinth is chock full of divisions, quarreling, and infighting. And worship at Corinth could only be described as a discourteous, disorderly mess. And when the Corinthians celebrated the Lord's supper, disorder and discourtesy reigned supreme. Some people brought huge coolers chocked full of gourmet food, cracked open bottles of wine, made pigs of themselves, and got stinking drunk. Others had little to eat, felt excluded, and went home hurt and hungry.

Problems persisted during the week. A man in the congregation was shacked up with his step-mother and the church in Corinth pointed to him proudly as an example of how open and accepting they were. Other men in the congregation were patronizing prostitutes in the pagan temple. Still others were suing the pants off each other. So you might wonder what has come over Paul in I Corinthians 1:4-9. What in the world makes him think that these Corinthians' faith would hold up until Christ returned? And if they did manage to limp to the finish line, whatever made him suppose that they would be declared blameless on judgment day?

The key to understanding Paul's upbeat thanksgiving in the face of such major Corinthian problems can be found in the last two verses of our reading. Paul points directly to God's faithfulness in hanging on to them. God, who called you into the fellowship of his Son, is faithful.

God holds us fast as the chaos of life swirls around us. Our heavenly parent grips our hand holding us in relationship. If Paul were to look at all of us sitting here this morning, he could say the same thing to us that he said to those Corinthians. God who has called you into the fellowship of his Son is faithful.

God holds us fast as the chaos of life swirls around us. Our heavenly father grips our hand holding us in relationship to him. If Paul were to look at all of us sitting here this morning, he could say the same thing to us that he said to those Corinthians. God who has called you into the fellowship of his Son is faithful. He won't let you go.

And that is why we are so confident. Not that we're so good, so smart, or so spiritually keen, but confident that each moment of our lives we walk hand in hand with Jesus Christ. In intimate relationship with God who hears and answers our prayers. Hand in hand not with a God who drags us along, but a God who cares about each one of us like a Father or Mother. The one who has called us is faithful. God is holding on to us and won't let us go. And God will hold on until the end.

Paul refers to that end as the day of our Lord Jesus Christ. God will keep you strong, Paul tells the Corinthians, so that you will be blameless on the day of our Lord Jesus Christ. Now given the greatness and faithfulness of God, it's possible to see how the Corinthians might just barely squeak by. But how could Paul expect them of all people, with hormones surging, lawsuits raging, and chaos reigning to be found blameless by the heavenly judge? How could they be expected to do so well on judgment day?

You know the reason, and so do I. Paul expects the Corinthians to receive Jesus' report card on judgment day instead of their own. As those who belong to Jesus, God will judge their performance not in light of what they have actually done, but in light of what Christ has done on their behalf.

As those who belong to Jesus we know, don't we, that the judge will declare us blameless on judgment day, too. We'll get straight A's, not by mistake, but because of what Jesus did for us on the cross. And so not only do we have nothing to fear on judgment day, we look forward to it. We are eager for the day when God will put an end to sickness, injustice, and pain and generously give us what we don't deserve.

John Rottman is part-time pastor of the Grace Christian Reformed Church of Scarborough. He is married to Marilyn.

Transfiguration Sunday

DEUTERONOMY 34:1-12

TRANSFIGURATION
FEBRUARY 17, 1980

Imagine standing on a hill overlooking a calm and beautiful lake. Your heart is pounding inside as you anticipate getting to the shore, and then possibly diving into the water for a refreshing swim, or skipping pebbles across the water, or rowing a boat out on the lake and casting out a fishing line. But, for some reason, you can't get to the water. You can only see it from afar.

There's something disconcerting and frustrating about such an experience. Maybe that's why we try so desperately to deny that that is an accurate picture of our human life and experience. Note the penchant we have these days for instant success, community, sex, even education. Who wants to see anything only from afar?

But my impression is that all of us, at one time or another, have had to experience God's goodness from afar. This condition should not surprise us. For it points to what one writer has called the "inconsolable secret" in each one of us, namely our "sense of exile on earth as it is."

People of faith in all generations have sensed this truth of life. Near the end of his career as Israel's greatest prophet, leader, lawgiver and judge, Moses stood on Mount Nebo and the Lord showed him all the land which the Lord had promised to give to Moses' ancestors. It must have been a magnificent sight. At long last, there was the land which had been promised, and, now, Moses could finally settle down and be at home in the land.

But it was not to be so. Even the greatest of Israel's leaders and prophets, Moses, would finally see the promised land only from afar.

Lest you think that this perception of life and faith has been superceded in the coming of Jesus, then consider Luke's account of the Transfiguration. What began as an act of devotion and piety turned out to be an intense religious experience. When Peter saw the glory of the Lord, he wanted to build three booths. It's as though Peter were saying, "Master, let's make this moment of glory last." But, of course, it wasn't to be. The disciples, once again, would have to see the glory of the Lord from afar.

Another New Testament writer underscores this same dimension of the life of faith for Christian men, women and children. The author of Hebrews listed biblical characters who were examples of faith. Then he concluded, "These all died in faith, not having received what was promised, but having seen it and greeted it from afar, and having acknowledged that they were strangers and exiles on the earth."

All testimonies to the fact that our faith involves a certain not having, a certain not yet, a certain seeing from afar. This fact may disturb and perplex us at times, but it also points to the sustaining basis of our faith, namely the faithfulness of God. That, I think, is what Moses recognized. He was permitted to see the fulfillment of God's promise from afar. And it is God's faithfulness which is the basis of faith.

And, you see, it is precisely God's faithfulness which delivers us from the compulsion to possess our own life, to secure it permanently in the here and now. Delivered from all such compulsions, we can finally be at home here, because our ultimate home is elsewhere.

Each of us has a vivid reminder that our ultimate home is elsewhere when we celebrate the Sacrament of Holy Communion. We sometimes call it the feast or the supper of our Lord. But what a strange feast! The courses are limited, the portions are small—a morsel of bread and a sip of wine, hardly enough to satisfy our appetites. No this is certainly not the heavenly banquet.

We see the promised land and the heavenly banquet from afar when we participate in Holy Communion, but we also taste the goodness and faithfulness of God in Jesus Christ our Lord. And through both, the seeing from afar and the tasting God forms God's parish in the world. And you know what a parish is: it's a group of *aliens* who are at *home* in any community.

Morris J. Niedenthal, a minister of the Lutheran Church in America, in 1980 was Professor of Preaching at the Lutheran School of Theology at Chicago, Chicago, Illinois

---

LUKE 9:28-36

TRANSFIGURATION
FEBRUARY 9, 1986

The intentionality of our Biblical lessons for today, the Feast of the Transfiguration, is best summed up for me in 2 Corinthians 4:6, "We have seen the light of the Glory of God in the face of Jesus Christ." Because God has "faced" us in Jesus Christ we can "face" ourselves and "face" the world.

The great claim of the Christian faith is that while we may be in the dark about many things, on the ultimate issues of human life there is light. St. Paul put it in writing to the Corinthians, "For it is the God who said, 'Let light shine out of darkness' who has shone in our hearts to give the light of the glory of God in the face of Christ" (2 Cor. 4.6).

There is light! It comes from God and it shines from the face of Jesus Christ.

It is as if we had been in the dark—lost, confused, frightened—and suddenly a light breaks to reveal the path which leads us home. We do not see everything. But we see enough: enough to know that we have been found, enough to know that we can make it.

God chooses to shine from the face of Jesus Christ. God could have made a spectacular show of it; could have set off cosmic fireworks in the sky; could have illuminated the landscape in a stupendous historical flash; could have found some extraordinary means of showing power. But when God chose to be revealed in the fulness of Glory, God chose a face, a face like yours, a face like mine. And we see the light of the Glory of God in the face of Jesus Christ.

Most of us have seen faces which give us a picture of what St. Paul had in mind. My first stay in the hospital came when I was young. It was nonetheless frightening for being called routine. I remember waking up to see the face of my nurse. She was like an angel, I still remember her name: Miss Cooling. I suppose because that's what she was, a cooling, calming presence in the hot distress of that situation. Ever since then nurses have been special people, and my appreciation for their ministry has grown over the years. That experience was about a quarter of a century ago and I can still remember her smiling face. I saw the light of the glory of healing in the face of that nurse.

Most of us have had experiences like that. In the face of our mother, our father, our teacher, our doctor, our minister, a rabbi, a nun, a shopkeeper, a truck driver, a friend: That face has given us a glimpse of the glory of God. Few of us would be Christians if there were not a face like that in our lives. Someone, somewhere, showed us a face in which there was peace, joy and togetherness rooted in Christ that had we not been a Christian we would have wanted to become one because of the glory in that face. Because that face has turned toward us, we can face life, we can go on living with hope.

The early disciples had that experience with Jesus, "They sat in darkness," as the Gospel puts it. They sat in the darkness of uncertainty, bondage, despair, sin. They sat there, and suddenly there was that face, that fabulous face, full of light, full of love. It beamed with forgiveness and with hope.

Ever since, artists have tried to picture it. Still, everyone has his or her own version. Rembrandt shows Jesus as a sensitive man of great inner strength. His face is capable of expressing intense pain and exquisite joy. You can always spot Jesus in a Rembrandt work by looking for the light. Rembrandt shows that radiance which shone from his face to illuminate and to heal those who came to him. They saw the light of the Glory of God in the face of Jesus Christ.

Because God has faced us in Jesus Christ, we can face God. We can turn toward God with confidence. Because Jesus Christ has shown his face, we do not cringe before some cosmic bully, nor bow before the raw forces of nature. Rather ultimate reality has turned toward us and shown us a face to which we may relate with trust and love.

Because God has turned God's face toward us, we can turn our face toward the world. We can face life with its problems and difficulties. We can face the problems of our globe creatively and redemptively. Consider how Jesus behaved when he found himself in conflict with the law as the Pharisees understood it, as described in the Gospel according to Mark in second chapter, verses 23-38. Jesus was passing through a wheat field with his hungry disciples. As they made their way, they began to pluck at the grain, grind it in their hands and eat it. The Pharisees held that Jesus was breaking the law when he plucked grain and ate it on the Sabbath.

What does this mean and what are we to do? The Jesus who placed the priority with the feeding of the hungry rather than with the preservation of abstract law, leaves us little doubt about what our priorities should be. If we wish to feed the hungry, we must change the economic structure which allows such disproportionate consumption. The United States and the United Nations are now at work on such changes.

However, in addition, each of us must get hold of hunger where we can and do what is best to ease it. We can keep our own priorities. For example, one report suggests that if Americans substituted chicken for one-third of their beef consumption, we could release enough grain to feed one hundred million people every year.

Every Christian in America has, through church channels and principally Church World Service, a means of concrete response to the world's hunger. The Christian can help solve the problem of world hunger, but first you must face it. This you can do because God has faced you in Jesus Christ.

How we face the world may make the difference. If we do so with fear or cold calculation, we will not say much for the world or for our faith. Christians who face the world with constructive confidence are the best witnesses for their faith.

God has not left us in the dark. We don't see everything, but we see enough to know that we have been found and that we can find the way. Because God has faced us we can face God. And we can face the world with a glow of constructive confidence. "For it is the God who said, 'Let light shine out of darkness,' who has shone in our hearts to give the light of the Glory of God in the face of Christ."

David James Randolph in 1986 was minister of Christ Church, United Methodist, in New York City.

MATTHEW 17:1-9

TRANSFIGURATION
FEBRUARY 18, 1996

Nostalgia is memory without the pain. We are all guilty, at times, of wanting to take up residence in the past; to return to a simpler day when innocence reigned and we were not responsible. But as Carlyle Marney said: "We know too much to go back." Proper memory creates a reflective balance between past, present, and future—without neglecting the pain.

The transfiguration was for the early Church an exercise in proper memory. To be sure the faithful looked back—to Old Testament heroes and to the earthly Christ—but in doing so they also took a giant leap forward into God's future. The transfiguration is best understood as an eschatological or end-time event. An eschatological vantage does not rob the story of either its historical or its present power. God is more than a series of past supernatural tricks. A "mighty acts of God" theology can dovetail into rigid historicism. The future for Christians is constantly breaking into the present: "Repent, for the kingdom of heaven is at hand." "*Now* is the day of our salvation." God is not simply a first cause, but a continual cause. Faith liberates us to understand *how* the Gospel makes its own history, not just mountaintop history, but history here below.

Our temptation is two-fold: If Moses and Elijah fade too quickly from the Mount of Transfiguration, we end up setting the gospel over and against Judaism in absolute fashion. On the other hand, if we acknowledge that Jesus is thoroughly Jewish, it may be difficult to pinpoint exactly what we mean by the radical nature of his message. His message, however, is radical. And we must preach the radical faith of Jesus Christ until we believe it!

Why is Jesus radical? He is radical because while he declares the imminent inbreaking of a new age, he does so in the presence of some who are stubbornly committed to 'this present age.' If one kingdom is entering, then another kingdom is crumbling. And here is the rub. The mountaintop experience is often a symbol for the renewal of meaning— a place where we recharge our batteries. The location may be a summer camp, spiritual retreat, sabbatical, or just getting away for vacation. But to paraphrase William Sloane Coffin: 'It is one thing to bark from pulpits: Let justice roll down like mighty waters but quite another, to get down in the valley and help build the aqueducts.

Jesus is radical because he declares the sure and swift in-breaking of 'God's new age.' 'The present age' will no longer do. His message is disparate enough to get him killed. If our churches seem too safe these days, it is probably because we are teaching and preaching 'cleverly devised myths' rather than a cutting-edge Word.

I attended recently a preaching workshop with an African-American colleague. Most of his congregation is below the poverty line. His small salary and expense checks are routinely late. I asked him how the congregation's budget was doing. His reply: "Not bad. But my greatest financial concern is finding enough life insurance to protect my people from the implications of the gospel. If I preach the gospel, they will live it, and if they live it, they will be in danger."

Matthew's gospel does not allow us to separate the glory from the pain. After Jesus and his disciples come down the mountain they are confronted by the need of an epileptic boy. God pushes them, and us, back into life. Howard Thurman once said: "God expects us to come into His presence with the smell of life upon us." We serve a down-to-earth God in ordinary places. God says: "Here is my Chosen One. Listen to him!" This is nothing less than a breath-taking announcement of God's new age.

God's future is a mixed bag. Once Simon Peter glimpses the glory, he is simultaneously exhilarated *and* frightened. Tom Long tells about seeing his daughter one day dancing playfully in their living room. He was on the couch reading the newspaper when her whirling motion captured his attention: "I watched her spin, her arms spread wide and her hair tossing as she twirled across the room. Suddenly the way her mouth was fixed, the manner in which her hair fell across her cheeks, in the play of sunlight through the curtains on her face was created an unusual effect. For one instant she looked not five years old, but twenty-five. There was a single fixed-frame in her motion when I saw her, not as a child, but as the grown-up woman she would become. Then she turned, the light changed, her face broke into a grin, and she was a child again. But I had seen what I had seen, and there was no escaping it. It was a wonderful moment and a frightening one as well" (Long, *Shepherds and Bathrobes*, p. 102).

A new order is bound to be intolerable to those who have invested themselves in what seems to them to be 'time-tested' structures. But look around. Who administers the test? Surely, not God. If weapons are our security, there is no place for a "Prince of Peace." If wealth is our game, anxieties rise proportionately to our proximity to the poor. If evangelism is synonymous with numbers, our churches may soon be filled with nonbelievers.

I serve a downtown congregation with all its challenges and joys. Last week a young mother called me from a lakefront suburb to tell me she was considering moving her children from a wealthy all-white congregation to our downtown gaggle of believers. "Why would you want to do that?" I asked. "You're in a nice church. Good pastor, modern facility, and healthy budget." Her answer: "Yeah, I know, but I've had about all the *nice* I can stand. My kids think the world is all peaches and cream. I feel as if I'm failing them as a parent." There was a disturbing urgency in that young woman's voice. She was both elated and hesitant about the gospel. What disturbs us most about Jesus, says David Buttrick, is his use of two little words in particular: "new" and "now" (Buttrick, *Preaching Jesus Christ*, p. 41). Why do we celebrate the feast of Transfiguration? Because it reminds us that Christ is about more than a tiny baby or resuscitated corpse. Surely, without the resurrection our faith is in vain (I Cor. 15:14). But today on Transfiguration Sunday we find hope for eternal life, we see clearly an open and real future. To ascend the mountain means nothing less than that we hold ourselves responsible for what we have heard and seen: a future where lions lie down with lambs, where tears are wiped away, where fighter jets are beaten into tractors. To be sure, we have, on this road, in this place, our share of trials and cross-bearing. Great encouragement is needed for our trembling hearts. But if we look closely we will see again Jesus' radiant face, shining like the sun—beyond the shame and spiking, beyond the thorns and His bleeding brow—we will not only see but hear the Father's voice again telling us: "This is my Beloved. My Chosen One. Listen. Listen."

Philip N. Jones is an ordained Disciples of Christ minister. In 1996 he was on staff at Central Christian Church in Austin, Texas, and a PhD student in Homiletics at Vanderbilt University.

Season of Lent

JOHN 11:1-45

THE FOURTH SUNDAY OF LENT
MARCH 12, 1978

Mary Travers recorded a song by Bill Taylor and Dick Dallas:
I wish I knew how it'd feel to be free;
I wish I could break these chains holding me
I wish I could share all the love that's in my heart;
Remove all the bars that still keep us apart I wish you could know what it means to me;
Then you'd see and agree, every man MUST be free
I wish I could give all I'm longing to give; I wish I could live like I'm longing to live.

What would it be like to be "risen" in an everyday, tedious, tension-filled and unredeemed world? What did Lazarus feel like when he felt the bindings loosen and drop?

This story has been beautifully set to music and dance in a stirring ballet. Lazarus is seen wrapped and bound by his shroud. He lies cold and unfeeling in his grave. It is silent, empty, void of meaning. He stares with unseeing eyes. He is alone, cold, and still—capable of nothing. Then, suddenly, the stone is rolled away from the opening, and Lazarus becomes aware of light. Gradually, the light grows brighter, and as it does so, Lazarus begins to feel its warmth. And then he hears a sound: a voice calling from the source of the light, calling HIM, and calling him by name! Someone knows him, in person. Someone remembers him and cares.

Now, he feels he can move. He is capable. Slowly, with determination, he gets up and moves toward the light. It's difficult because he is still bound by his death wrappings. But he struggles and stumbles and finally makes it out into the light. Strangely, the wrappings begin to fall away. As they do, he begins to move more freely— tentatively at first because his muscles are stiff. He has to learn all over again it seems, but it gets easier and easier. And finally, he begins to DANCE!

And such a dance he does! It is as though he is no longer bound by the forces and tensions of the world that we all know so well. He all but defies gravity. He is not only capable, he has potential he never realized before. He moves in ways he never thought possible. The world hasn't changed—Lazarus has; his perception of the world has changed. He knows what it's like to feel free.

What would it be like to be free: free from the expectations of all the "others" in the world— parents, children, teachers, preachers, employers, employees, colleagues, neighbors. What would it feel like to be tree to be the person we know we were meant to be, were created to be, and somehow sense that we could be?

In the ballet, Lazarus is seen as the prototype. Unbound, he discovers that the world is pretty much as he had always known it, but in his freedom he could afford to accept the unacceptable, love the unlovable, tolerate the intolerable, and dare to risk living. Who could harm him now? Who could keep him from the Source of Life itself? The breath of life that was breathed into the dry bones of Israel and into the putrid flesh of

Lazarus has been breathed into us. WE have been joined unto the living Body of the Lord Himself— sustained by His flesh, nourished by His blood. The call that beckoned Lazarus forth from his grave goes out continually to us. "Get up! Come out! Go forth to LIVE!"…and know what it is to be free. It is rather surprising that in the middle of Lent we are invited to sing Alleluia. It is surprising that in the middle of Lent we are unbound and set free, invited to join the dance of life. Resurrection is always a total, beautiful, wonder-full, awe-full surprise.

WE…ARE…RISEN!!

David E. Babin, an Episcopal priest, in 1978 was a Professor of Liturgies and Preaching at Seabury-Western Theological Seminary, Evanston, Illinois.

JOHN 12:20-33

THE FIFTH SUNDAY IN LENT
APRIL 1, 1979

I would have liked to have been one of those pilgrims last fall filing in anonymous groups of 100 past that remarkable shroud in the cathedral at Turin, Italy. It would have been an experience standing there like three million other visitors hushed before the altar hoping to glimpse something in those fourteen feet of faded cloth. For me it doesn't matter much what scientists prove or disprove about the Shroud of Turin. Carbon 14 dating or whatever cannot change the impact that it has had on believers for at least four hundred years.

I suppose the thing that grabs me about the shroud and, I suspect, the thing that would grab you too, is the remarkable response people make to it. Believer and non-believer, loyal sons of the Shroud Guild and scientists, patrons and skeptics, sindonologists and students from every land, all seem to be magnetized by this ancient article of faith. And I have to wonder, what is it that draws them? What is it that draws you and me to the shroud—to what could be no more than a very grand hoax?

It is not unlike the way I felt as a Protestant child when a Roman Catholic friend of mine would tell of her first Holy Communion and then pull out of a velvet box a very ugly, yet somehow beautiful, crucifix that her grandparents had given for the occasion. Once or twice she let me hold the treasure and I remember goose bumps going down my spine. How I envied her that crucifix. There was something terribly appealing about its sparse painful portrayal of Christ which touched even my low church spirit.

So it is with the shroud. There is something ghastly, something appealing, something utterly mysterious about burial clothes in the first place, and especially one which under the scrutiny of the camera reveals such horrible wounds of terrific pain.

No matter what the tests may prove, the Shroud of Turin has amazing appeal that the marks of suffering always claim on us. I often notice how in the context of local church groups it is the sharing by one or another person of some hidden personal suffering which always seems to draw the group sympathetically together. We are drawn by the suffering and vulnerability of others because it is so like our own.

In the scripture lesson from John, Jesus pointed to such a phenomenon. He said, "When I am lifted up I will draw all men (and all women) unto myself" (v. 32). Somehow it is the wounds of the cross, the symbols of the suffering of Christ which draw us to him. It is the marks which seem to be blood on the shroud which make it special. Without them it would be a meaningless piece of old scorched cloth. What draws us to Turin and to Christ are the marks of suffering—a suffering not unlike our own.

It is the very fact that Jesus suffered which makes him real to us. We experience the suffering of loneliness, isolation, difficult decisions, family problems, kids that run away, marriages that fail. We suffer with the reality of death for ourselves and our loved ones. We suffer in a world lacking in love for us and for our causes and we wonder if life is still worth living. All these wounds we see in Christ and they draw us unmistakenly to him. They are like the sympathetic movement of soul to soul.

But there is more than this. The observers at Turin say that the face on the shroud bears a smile. It isn't the smile of a fool caught in his own ridiculous actions. It's not the forced smile of the funeral parlor. But it seems to be the graceful smile of a peaceful man. The point is this, you and I are attracted not just by the wounds on the body but by the hope in that smile.

Somehow in the mystery that is Christ there is not just the fellowship of suffering but also the promise of victory. What we find when we seek to see Jesus is not just a man caught in the same mire of life and pain as we are, but someone whose glory comes in that he has victory over all.

Karen Engle Layman, a minister of the United Methodist Church, in 1979 was Associate Pastor, Calvary United Methodist Church, Harrisburg, Pennsylvania

---

LUKE 13:31-35

THE SECOND SUNDAY IN LENT
MARCH 2, 1980

"Jerusalem! Jerusalem!" The first word from God is a name. The first word addressed to us in church, at baptism, is our name. God calls us, and God is specific. Why was God so specific as to pick a certain people (Israel), a certain city (Jerusalem)? It seems exclusive. But then we see: the God who weeps over Jerusalem longs for Ninevah, too (as Jonah discovered!), and therefore also longs for our town, and our church, and our family, and you, and me: loving each one of us as if there were only one of us to love.

But Jerusalem rejects (sometimes brutally) the messengers of this all-too-specific care. Pastors have been hounded from their pulpits when the sword of the Word cut too close. But preachers aren't God's only messengers to us: then God would be so easy to avoid! No, messengers abound. Haven't we turned off the TV when some program about war, or alcoholism, or infidelity, or embezzlement, has come too close to us? Haven't we avoided someone who identified for us some weakness or bad behavior? But our deepest rejection is saved for the messengers of love: For the love of God, and of others, comes too close to our castle gates.

"How often would I have gathered you, as a hen gathers her chicks." Every once in a while, when Jesus spoke, folks realized with a start that the voice was more than human (Jn 8:58, 14:9). This voice comes yearning down through time, from one who repeatedly sent messengers to the holy city, to the chosen people, to the elect nation; this voice comes from One who is now sending his beloved Son. It comes from One who has never given up on God's people, who *repeatedly* sends messengers to us. And how tender God is! As the Spirit brooded over dark and rebellious chaos like a mother bird (Gen. 1:2) nurturing it to life and light and order, so has God, like a mother, often stretched out bright wings, to hide, to hold, to gather and protect us. *This* is what we most deeply reject: embracing love.

We hide from God's tender, mothering love, as Adam and Eve hid in the Garden, as Jonah hid in the belly of the fish: when we cannot hide, we look for stones, to silence the voice that calls us back—as they did with Zechariah (II Chr. 24:20f; cf. Mt. 23:35) and Stephen (Acts 7:58ff.) and Paul (Acts 14:19, cf. II Co. 11:25) and others (Heb. 11:37). Why do we hide, and strike out when we cannot hide, from that loving voice? Because we want to be left alone? or are ashamed? or would keep sinning? or do we fear and distrust God? We offer many reasons, but Christ shows them all for excuses: we "would not." It is just our sinful will, wanting always to get shut of God.

But even when we have done our worst, and the beloved Son is dead, the great stone cannot shut out God's love. Christ lives, and calls us still, by name, specifically, daily, through Bible, pulpit, friend, news, TV, song, teacher, spouse, parent, child. When we hear him call, let us say "Blessed is he—or she—who comes in the name of the Lord." In that moment, what seemed like a hateful, oppressive weight on us will be seen for what it really is: the constant, glorious shadow of the shelter of God's bright wings.

Donald F. Chatfield, a minister in the United Presbyterian Church in the U.S.A. in 1980 was Professor of Preaching, Garrett-Evangelical Theological Seminary, Evanston, Illinois

EXODUS 20:1-17; I CORINTHIANS 1:22-25; JOHN 2:13-22

THE THIRD SUNDAY IN LENT
MARCH 14, 1982

When Jesus began to swing his flail of ropes in the temple, there can have been few who were not alarmed, among all the officials, tradespeople, priests, crowd, and even disciples. Most of us would share that alarm; for we suspect God, sometimes, of harboring a grudge against us, barely holding the divine anger in check. A shift in the old hymn's words will express our fear: "Behind a smiling Providence, He hides a frowning face." And now our worst fears are realized: an outburst of rage from the Prince of Peace himself. We did well to be afraid.

Perhaps we did, but we may be letting our guilt and fear get between us and Jesus like dark-lensed glasses. We may even be seeing in him feelings that are really ours! Do we fear our sins are so great that God wants to break out against us, drive us away? Are we so enraged at life, at others, perhaps at God, that we are convinced that rage will be directed at us? "Whenever our hearts condemn us... God is greater than our hearts, and he knows everything" (I John 3:20). Besides, it doesn't say Jesus was angry. Then what was he up to?

When a friend comes to talk, with something important to say, you will drive people from your door and off your phone who come on lesser errands. Jesus will not have any distraction and noise that we can use to keep us from truth, or self, or God. He does not oppose legitimate work or pleasure; he sets himself against distractions that we are using to try to drown out the "still small voice" (I Kings 19:12).

But contrary to our fears, his arrival is not destructive. It is merciful. The "whip" is only made of cords. Though he is firm, he is strangely gentle, like some surgeons. Yes, he drove out animals and people. Maybe some few coins, rolling, chinked down cracks between the great flagstones and were lost. But no breakage is reported, and no injury. And look: when he comes to the pigeon-sellers, he will not overturn. That would crush or lose the birds. With heaven's courtesy, he only speaks, commanding them to go. At least some of our fears of God are unfounded: Christ enters to still the competing voices, to show us that we are God's temple (I Cor. 3:16, II Cor. 6:16), to supplant our previous loyalties, to bring, not destruction, but life and healing.

He tells us that it is we who destroy: "Destroy this temple, and in three days I will raise it up" (John 2:19). But God's intervention is not to destroy, but to raise up new hope in Christ, in the wake of our destructiveness. After his resurrection, and especially after the Jerusalem temple was razed for the last time, Christ's glorified body became the new temple, and his people who are in him meet God in any place or time. Loss of every kind levels our proud structures. But Christ is not destroyed. He who came to us when we were building, to claim for himself our first loyalty, comes again when all is rubble, comes risen and glorious to lead us out to new hope, new life and trust in him.

"Who can endure the day of his coming?" Those who remember that even in his fiercest zeal he would not hurt a pigeon.

Editor's Note: John Updike's short story "Pigeon Feathers" would be suggestive parallel reading.—C.L.R.

Donald F. Chatfield, a minister in the United Presbyterian Church in the USA, in 1982 was professor of preaching at Garrett-Evangelical Theological Seminary in Evanston, Illinois

---

II CORINTHIANS 5:16-21

THE FOURTH SUNDAY IN LENT
MARCH 13, 1983

Shortly before his death, the psychologist Abraham Maslow described a change in his life which occurred when he suffered a serious heart attack at the pinnacle of his career:

> My attitude toward life changed... everything gets doubly precious, gets piercingly important.... Everything seems to look more beautiful rather than less, and one gets the much intensified sense of miracles.... (There is) a kind of spontaneity that's greater than anything else could make possible.
>
> (as quoted in William K. McElvaney,
> *The Saving Possibility,* Abingdon Press, p. 170)

For Maslow, the heart attack was far more than an illness now past and forgotten, a single moment lost among many in his life. It was an event so central, so shaking, and so profound that it called his life into question, re-shaped his values, altered his perceptions.

In a much deeper sense, this is what it means, Paul tells us, to be "in Christ." To encounter Christ is not simply to have a deeply religious experience, one moment among many in our lives. Being "in Christ" is *the* experience by which all others are measured. To be "in Christ" is not simply to know something about life, God, or ourselves that we did not know before. It is, rather, to see life, God, and ourselves in a way not possible before. Being "in Christ" is a value-changing, perception-altering relationship. In Christ we see what God's future is like; we discover in him how God is making all things new. Thus, to be "in Christ" is to choose God's future over against our past—to "convert," as it were, to the new creation. The miracle is that, in so doing, we are made into new creations ourselves.

What does it mean to be a "new creation"? Does it mean that life becomes free from struggle and pain? To the contrary, it means a confidence that in our struggle and pain God is at work to make us more human. Theologian Letty Russell tells of an experience of suffering in her life in which God's new creation was at work:

> ...I lost the sight of one eye in a freak accident. Out of that experience I discovered a different perspective on reality. Small things didn't matter as

much to me in the light of major issues of sight and health, and partnership with caring people. Yet, at the same time as I was growing in courage, my vulnerability and dependence on God, world and my life was heightened so that my vulnerability and dependence on God were increased. The discovery that I was becoming at one and the same time both stronger and weaker was a small sign that God was patiently helping me to become more human.

(from *Becoming Human*, Philadelphia:
Fortress Press, 1982, pp. 102-3)

To be a new creation "in Christ" means not only that we view ourselves differently, but also that we view others differently, too. Justice becomes more important than personal ambition. Compassion for others is more valued than private power, and mercy is more cherished than self-justification. Having experienced in Christ the values of the new creation, we hunger and thirst for them in the present age. When Julius Nyerere, the President of Tanzania, was asked why he wanted to work for social justice, he said it was because all human beings are created in God's image:

I refuse to image a God who is miserable, poor, ignorant, superstitious, fearful, oppressed and wretched—which is the lot of the majority of those... created in (God's) image.

(from *Becoming Human*,
Westminster Press, 1982, p. 83)

It used to be that we regarded ourselves, other people, indeed the whole world, with weary and despairing vision. No longer. The old has passed away, and the new has come. The Cross overcomes death. Easter is more potent than Auschwitz and Hiroshima. God in Christ has moved over the dark and formless void of our history and said, "Let there be light!"

Thomas G. Long, a minister of the Presbyterian Church, U.S., in 1983 was Professor of Preaching and Worship at Columbia Theological Seminary, Decatur, Georgia.

EZEKIEL 37:1-14

THE FIFTH SUNDAY IN LENT
APRIL 1, 1990

Dostoevsky, in *The Brothers Karamazov* said, "For every hour and every moment thousands of men leave life on this earth, and their souls appear before God. And how many of them depart in solitude, unknown, sad, dejected, that no one mourns for them or even knows whether they have lived or not." Such was the fear of the Psalmist when he said, "Death stared me in the face. I was frightened and sad." Or a valley of dry bones, breathless and lifeless reminds us of the poignant sense of hopelessness. We are faced with the same question the prophet asked in the Old Testament, "If man dies, will he rise again?" The yearning for the penetrating ray of hope.

The graveside mourners walked solemnly back to their cars while the immediate family members remained in quiet solitude and grief beside the bronze casket, which shimmered as it reflected the dancing rays of sunlight, dodging through the leaves overhead. The cars edged their way around the small winding path, leaving the cemetery. The moment was filled with broken hearts and hurting lives.

The waving hands of a funeral director, summoned me from across the grounds. Walking towards the other gravesite, I found myself standing before a grey, compressed, cardboard casket. The unknown person in this casket was a case of the State. No family. Having died and left the world, unnoticed while alive and alienated even in death. I was asked to say a brief prayer. This person was one of the thousands who depart in "solitude, unknown, sad, dejected, ...no one mourns for them or even knows whether they have lived or not."

But to God, this magnified moment of dejection was filled with the truth that He would never leave any of us desolate. We need have no grave doubts about the fact that God's loving embrace was enwrapped around this moment of loneliness. To the believer in Jesus Christ, God made a wonderful promise. Jesus would be the "songbird" on the stone rolled away from the tomb. Who ever believed in Him, whether living or dead, would have eternal life. No grave! Have no grave doubts. God intends for you to have, not a grave, but the warm, loving embrace of God's kingdom. This is the power of the cross. The promise of Easter. Ezekiel 37:12 says, "My people, I will open your graves of exile and cause you to rise again."

Christ rose from the dead that we might have everlasting life. Joseph of Arimathea illustrates to us God's intention that we were never meant to have a tomb. We should not have any "grave" doubts about God's Easter proclamation, that we would have everlasting life through Christ. "When it was evening, there came a rich man from Arimathea named Joseph, who also was a disciple of Jesus. He went to Pilate and asked for the body of Jesus. And Joseph took the body, and wrapped it in a clean linen shroud and laid it in his own new tomb, which he had hewn in the rock for himself, and he rolled a great stone to the door of the tomb, and departed" (Matthew 27:57-61).

Joseph of Arimathea laid Christ, not only in a tomb hewn out of rock, but in his own tomb, a tomb he had hewn for himself. Freshly hewn. Unused. Its purpose? To provide God's new message of faith. We would never know the confinement of the grave. We would not remain a valley of dry bones. The empty tomb which Joseph of Arimathea made for himself was never to be used by him. Christ took his place. He entered the tomb.

Jesus had no need of returning to Bethany to prevent Lazarus from dying. Scripture already revealed this miraculous ability of the Lord to raise people from the dead. His delay was indeed, "to show the Glory of God," through the faith of one who believed in Him as Savior. It was the moment in which faith became the miracle and not Jesus performing the miracle. He provided the promise to what an individual's faith would proclaim (Romans 8:11). If Christ lives in you, your dying bodies will live again by means of the same Holy Spirit, that lived in Him, living in you. "He has saved me from death, my eyes from tears, my feet from stumbling. I shall live!" (Psalm 116:8). Hope is not gone! In Christ there is no grave. No valley of dry bones! How do we know? In seeing the risen Lord we affirm Ezekiel's words, "Then you will know that I, the Lord, have done just what I promised you." You shall live!

Rev. Ronald W. Cadmus in 1990 was the 48th Minister in time of Succession at the Collegiate Church of New York City, the Mother Church of the Reformed Church in America, America's oldest congregation and the United States' first Corporation in America. He is the author of God's Loving Embrace and The Embrace of Grace published by the Thomas Nelson Publishing Company.

EPHESIANS 2:1-10

LENT 4
MARCH 13, 1994

I never really thought of how beautiful two words could be until I saw them that day. Stepping from the train at an underground station in the city of London, having completed my initial trip on that excellent transit system, I found myself - along with my wife and son swallowed up in a swirling sea of humanity. People were coming and going ... all but we three appearing to know how to reach their destinations!

We were to be there a few days. It made sense to claim that means of crisscrossing the city, in order to see the wonderful sights London has to offer. But no one had prepared me for that moment when we stepped out onto the platform, faced with the immediate choice of which way to go, and not a clue as to the *right* way.

It was at that moment that I fell in love, with a sign! There it was, on a wall at the end of the platform. "Way Out" it shouted to me with its lighted letters.

"Way out: that's what I'm looking for!" I thought to myself. And soon the three of us were on the streets of the city again, headed for our next visit.

Over the next few days my affection for that sign deepened. Time and again the scene was repeated: step off of the train, look down the platform, on the wall, a sign, "Way Out" All is well.

And all *was* well until that trip when every sentence of the routine but one was completed: step off of the train, look down the platform, on the wall—nothing!

It didn't take but a moment—a moment that felt like a lifetime—to discover that the sign was still there, but the light had burned out. However, that moment of panic had a strangely familiar feel.

—It felt a lot like one of those moments when I have made a terrible mess in my life and I am desperately searching for a sign—any sign which will announce "Way Out".
—It felt like one of those moments when I have discovered that I have no more tricks in my bag tricks by which I can straighten out the mess.
—It felt like one of those moments when I have had to admit that if there *was* a way out, someone else had it, not me. Have you ever had moments like that?

I saw the handwriting, one day, of someone who, apparently, felt like that. His, or her, words were scribbled on a wall by the side of a road along which I walked. He, or she, had written, "Dear God, set me free from all of the pain." I have no idea what prompted that painful request. I can only imagine that there are many, in bold honesty, who could echo its sentiments today.
—I am trapped.
—I cannot free myself.
—Show me the way out!
If the author of Ephesians was correct, those to whom he wrote could have identified with that sign.

—"You were dead through the trespasses and sins in which you once lived ..." he wrote.
—"... we were by nature children of wrath ..." he continued.
—Dear God, set us free, show us the way out.

Just when it appears that the "no way out" assessment of life is correct, however, that author of Ephesians illumines the otherwise darkened sign. "But God,"—that is the sign which he offers for our "Way Out". In those two words, with which the fourth verse of the lesson begins, there is a magnificent reversal.

—What follows is a story of life, not death.
—What follows is an announcement of mercy, not wrath.
—What follows is the good news of God's amazing grace.
—What follows is the affirmation that there is, indeed, a way out. It is God's way. It is bound up in the remarkable gift of Jesus Christ.

"But God!" Those words radically alter any painful statement we feel compelled to make of life.

—I have made a terrible mess of it...but God!

—I have no more tricks in my bag...but God!

—I have no way out...but God!

Upon entering the large room, in which the annual session of a denominational gathering was to take place for several days, participants noticed that one object dominated the platform upon which the sessions would be led. The object was a giant cross, stretching from just above an altar table to the tall ceiling of that room. Across the face of that cross one word had been emblazoned. It was the word "Yes".

Those participants never entered that room without being confronted by that cross—and Yes. It was a powerful witness to the message of grace which God has lived out, for the world, in the life and death and resurrection of Jesus Christ.

Quite frankly, I have never fully understood that "Yes". Have you? When it was totally logical—from a human point of view—to speak a resounding "No" to sinful humanity, God has spoken a redeeming "Yes". John Newton was correct, wasn't he? God's grace is, indeed, amazing!

In his book *Prayer: Finding The Heart's True Home*, Richard J. Foster reminds us, in speaking of the splendid mystery of the Eucharist, that "As C. S. Lewis wisely quipped, 'The command, after all, was Take, eat; not Take, understand' " (Harper San Francisco, 1992, p. 112).

Foster's words call us to an exciting, life-changing alternative. Instead of staring at that cross-and-Yes with a puzzled "Why?", we can embrace it with the answering "Yes!" of our faith. Thanks be to God!

Jerry Sisson, an ordained minister of the United Methodist Church, in 1994 was the Pastor of Canterbury United Methodist Church, Birmingham, Alabama.

JOHN 12:20-33

LENT 5
MARCH 20, 1994

Mrs. Bixby of Boston, having lost five sons in the American Civil War, received a letter from President Lincoln in 1864. He wrote, "You are the mother of five sons who have died gloriously on the field of battle. I feel how weak and fruitless must be any words of mine which should attempt to beguile you from the grief of a loss so overwhelming." The great challenges come amidst those times and experiences when persons and structures disappear, when things fall apart around us.

Things were falling apart for Jeremiah and his country. The hordes of Babylon were streaming across the borders of Judah. God's holy city of Jerusalem had fallen. The ancient promises of God gone, buried in the rubble of the temple. Jeremiah must speak an optimistic word. Jeremiah speaks God's word and this word is of a new covenant in the future.

When this God acts again in the new covenant, this God will no longer be the God of one people alone. This God will be glorified in a man supremely dedicated, willing, capable of doing his Father's will. Jeremiah's God will reach across race, class, economic station, geographical boundaries, educational attainment, and into the hearts of men and women everywhere willing to follow this man, fully god and fully human, into the hard places of life. "I, when I am lifted up, will draw all people to myself." When Jesus' hour arrives, it is the hour of death, resurrection and ascension. The Fifth Sunday of Lent marks Jesus' journey to the cross as nearly complete, leading us into the reign of God, God's victory over evil, which lies hidden in the mystery of Jesus' cross, the seeming hour of his enemies triumph. Things fall apart in our lives. In this man of God, things will finally stay together for us. For things to stay together, we must be where he is in the hour of glory. "Where I am, there will my servant be also." There we are, at the foot of his cross. Willing to carry our cross too. This is the door to hope when things fall apart around us.

He with us, and we with him, how will we live when things fall apart around us?

God's strengthening hand is experienced through the power of memory. We mull over the question, "What has the past been like with God?" As Jeremiah looked over his shoulder into Israel's past, and as Jesus looked into all his days up to the hour of glory, so we also look. Is God reliable, steady, firm, to be trusted, wise, patient and merciful? God works in our depths, preparing us always for that next time when things again fall apart. With a cross at its center, memory is God's gift. Memory enlightened by the wisdom of God's Spirit. One channel through which God's strengthening hand is known and felt when persons and things are disappearing from sight.

Being part of the extended community of Christ's people, a community that honors the necessary solitude when things fall apart, this too is God's channel of grace. In a Berlin prison in 1944, Fr. Alfred Delp, S.J., waited the fateful call for execution. He wrote in his diary, "If this is the way God has chosen, then I must be willing and without rancor to make it my own way. I will honestly and patiently await for God's call. I will trust in him till they come to fetch me." Of Fr. Delp, Thomas Merton said, we meet a man "who clung desperately to a truth that was revealed to him in solitude." We are made to be in community. When things fall apart, the community's gift comes in honoring the solitude necessary to sense the hand of God.

Give something away when things are being lost. Lydia watched her daughter run a yard sale prior to Lydia's moving to a retirement home. Lydia was losing her home, the accumulated things of her marriage. Across the lawn, a woman held up a tablecloth, talking to Lydia's daughter. The woman came over; Lydia was suspicious. The woman spoke. "It's beautiful! We had one when I was a tiny girl in Poland. My mother did the work herself. I don't know what happened to it. I was sent away for safety. I never saw any of them again." Lydia's attitude changed. "Please take it. I'm so glad you have it. It's been looking for a home." Lydia sat back. She felt better. She placed her carryall on her lap and waited for the people from the retirement home to come and get her. Lydia sensed the power of Jesus in his hour of glory. Jesus who tasted all the losses ever known. Who was strengthened by His Father. Jesus, who strengthens us when things are falling apart.

The Very Rev. Earl A. Whepley is an ordained priest of the Episcopal Church and in 1994 was Dean of Christ Church Cathedral, Springfield, Massachusetts.

LUKE 13:1-9

LENT 3
MARCH 19, 1995

The Bridge of San Luis Rey, begins this way: "On Friday noon, July the 20th, 1714, the finest bridge in all Peru broke and precipitated five travelers into the gulf below."

Brother Juniper, looks at the bridge the instant it breaks. He watches the five people fall into the canyon. And he wonders, "Why did these five die?" And this question sends him on a mission to prove or disprove providence.

But Brother Juniper never discovers why these five people die. Instead, he learns that they are no worse or no better than anyone who would have crossed that bridge ten minutes later.

"Do you think that these Galileans were worse sinners than all the other Galileans because they suffered this way? I tell you, no! But unless you repent you too will all perish."

Jesus turns toward the Pharisees and points at them and says, don't worry about the sins of Pilate, don't worry about the sins of the sacrificers, worry about your own sin. For unless you repent, you will die, just like everyone else.

Jesus points at the church as well and says, "stop running around assessing sin and judgment on people in this world. Stop looking at other people's sins and condemning them. Look at yourself and repent of sin, or you too will die."

Right now, Christians in America need to hear Jesus. A few months ago a man who viewed himself as righteous, because of his position on abortion, killed another man, whom he viewed as unrighteous, because he performed abortions. Paul Hill believed that he was an angel and he believed that Dr. Britton was a devil. And whenever that position is held, death can be justified.

But it doesn't matter on what side of the abortion issue you stand, there are sinners standing with you. It doesn't matter on what side of the euthanasia issue you stand, there are sinners standing with you. It doesn't matter in what political party you stand, there are sinners standing with you. It doesn't matter whether you stand within the church or outside of the church, there are sinners standing with you. All need to repent or die.

Daniel Pinkwater is a children's author and occasional commentator on National Public Radio. For a while, he thought about being a sculptor. So he decided to apprentice himself to a sculptor.

Every morning Pinkwater would show up in the sculptor's studio and say, "What would you like me to do today?"

And the sculptor would reply, "Do? Do anything you like."

And then Pinkwater would search the studio all the rest of the day, trying to figure out what the sculptor wanted him to do. Pinkwater says, "after a while, I would figure out what task he had subtly set for me, and go about doing it."

And then, after a year and a half, Pinkwater finally figures it out: "when you say I can do whatever I like, you mean, that I can do whatever I like. I can work. I can watch you work. I can take a nap. I can look out the window, get drunk, read a magazine, eat my lunch, play your records, yodel, hold my breath. I can discuss Mozart with you, or get you to try to teach me to fence. I can invite my friends in and have a party....So, actually, when you say I can do anything I like, you simply, literally, mean that I can do anything I like."

And the sculptor replied, "I say so every day" (Daniel Pinkwater, *Chicago Days/Hoboken Nights*, Addison-Wesley Publishing Co., 1991, pp. 44-46).

Grace is like that. God says, I forgive you freely. Simply believe. Simply turn toward grace and accept it. Period. That is repentance—turning toward grace and accepting it.

We don't earn grace. We don't receive grace for being on the right side of a political issue or a theological debate. We don't receive grace by making ourselves righteous. We don't receive grace for having the right position on abortion, euthanasia, homelessness, poverty, or any other political issue.

Grace is God's gift. We need not do anything to earn it. We only need to turn toward it and accept it. And then we live.

And to live means, living eternally with God, beginning here and now. And to live also means that all of our relationships, change when grace becomes part of us. All of our thoughts about enemies and conflict change when we turn toward grace and accept it.

One more image. Grace is like sunlight. We may be cold and depressed as we sit with our back to the sun. But when we turn and face the sun. When we shut our eyes and throw our head back so that the rays of the sun strike our face. We are transformed. Transformed only because we have made ourselves open to its power, its presence, its warmth.

Open yourself to the power, the presence and warmth of God's grace and you will be changed. Do? You don't have to do anything. God's grace is already here, knocking at the door. You only need turn toward grace and accept it. Then you will live.

Harry Winters in 1995 was the pastor of the Akron Christian Reformed Church in Akron, Ohio.

Palm/Passion Sunday

PHILIPPIANS 2:5-11

PALM/PASSION SUNDAY
MARCH 30, 1980

One of the most frequent questions asked of college students is: "What are you going to do after you graduate?" That question caused me considerable uneasiness during my college days, because I had decided to enter the Christian ministry. When I would tell someone I was going to become a minister, he or she would say, "Oh, I see, I really must be going now." It got to the point that I would try to avoid telling people about my plans. I began to avoid saying the name of Christ in any way that would identify me as a Christian—in fact I felt uneasy even saying that I was a Christian. There seemed to be a connotation of "thick piety" and "holier than thouness" associated with calling oneself a Christian. It was a connotation that made me uncomfortable.

Over a period of time I became so adept at avoiding the name of Christ that I began to fool even myself. I began to question my plans for ministry and became confused about my personal faith. Through my failure to be honest about what was important to me, Christ in my life, I began to lose what was important to me. Through my attempt to be acceptable to others I began to become unacceptable to myself. I had protected myself from appearing too passionately concerned about anything in the fear that I might be thought a fanatic. I did it well, so well that I was no longer passionately concerned about anything.

So often that's the way it is: we suppress what is most important to us in an effort to present a good appearance. Husbands and wives stop saying they love each other in public because they don't want to sound silly, and then not in front of the children, and then not even to each other. Finally the love that is so important to them starts slipping away. So much of what is important to us gets squashed because we don't want to appear too concerned, too moved, too passionate.

It is frightening to say out loud the things that mean the most to us. It is frightening because to say something out loud places who we are, what we think, and how we feel into the hands of another. When we speak what is most important to us there is a chance that we might affect the life of another or might even be affected ourselves. To affect others and to allow others to affect us is the power of passion, and passion is a power of life. To avoid affecting others or being affected by others is the power of apathy, and apathy is a power of death.

The passage in Philippians says, "that at the name of Jesus every knee should bow, in heaven and on earth and under the earth, and every tongue confess that Jesus Christ is Lord, to the glory of God the Father" (vs. 10-11). To confess Jesus as Lord is to become quite concerned, quite moved, quite passionate. It is in fact to enter into the history of Jesus, a history that is "affected, changed, transformed, and matured by the lives of others" (M. Douglas Meeks, *Passion For Life*). If we do not confess, and confess openly, we run the risk of losing that which is important to us, we run the risk of serving other lords. But if we serve Jesus as Lord, if we confess this One as Lord, we are led to engage ourselves in the lives of others passionately.

David Greenhaw, a minister of the United Church of Christ, in 1980 was pastor of Centerville United Methodist Church while doing graduate study at Drew University, Madison, New Jersey.

MATTHEW 27:11-54

PALM/PASSION SUNDAY
APRIL 12, 1987

In a preview of the forthcoming performance of a symphony orchestra, the director observed that a musical masterpiece has two distinguishing marks: surprise and inevitability. When you hear a masterpiece, you think, "Who would have thought of doing it that way"? and, "It had to be that way."

The drama of the Passion, from the borrowed donkey to the borrowed tomb, is marked by both surprise and inevitability. No other god would have done it that way. On the other hand, "Nothing in his life/Became him like the leaving it" (Macbeth). So surprising is the cross that it continues to be scandalous. Yet all other scripts of redemption wear thin before they end. Nothing rings so true to the depths of human experience as the Passion of our Lord.

Judy Viorst's recent best seller, *Necessary Losses*, is a rich compendium of perspectives and insights on the inevitable losses we experience. Her thesis is that the losses of loved ones, impossible expectations, illusions of freedom and power, life dreams, and youth are necessary if we are to continue to grow until we die. The good news is that in loss and in gain our God is one who has chosen to be with us wherever we are.

Another way of viewing our losses and Christ's cross is given us by Madeleine L'Engle who speaks of the noes and yeses of life, God's noes and yeses. The cross is a resounding and inevitable no from which Jesus had prayed for deliverance. But what a surprising and resounding yes it was, silent though it was. Who standing at the cross could not hear in the dark silence the baptismal affirmation: "This is my beloved in whom I am well pleased"? Even one of the Roman soldiers knew that the crucified one was the beloved of God. Yet it was necessary that he be crucified, and now we live in a Good Friday world. Recall Wallace Stephens' line, "Under every no/ lay a passion for yes." Yes and no. No and yes.

Inevitable surprise, the Passion of our Lord. Who would have dreamt of such? None but God. Yet there is none other name by which we must/need/can/be saved. He rode in on a donkey and reigned from a tree. And as for us, if we suffer with him we shall also reign with him.

Deryl Fleming, a minister of the American Baptist and Southern Baptist denominations, in 1987 was pastor of Ravensworth Baptist Church, Annandale, Virginia.

LUKE 19:28-40

PALM/PASSION SUNDAY
APRIL 12, 1992

Last week Leonard Sweet, the President of United Seminary, was a guest on a television program which I host. When he arrived at the station he told me a bizarre story of an incident that had occurred as he drove to the studio. On the interstate he had passed an old beat up pick-up truck on the back of which was perched a large cage. Inside the cage was a huge active brown bear. The bear was so enormous that he filled the cage so that there was barely enough room for him to move. Yet, the animal struggled pathetically with his prison as he frantically gnawed at the bars of the cage.

The image of that bear has haunted me. Sometimes it reminds me of the Spirit in the life of the church.

By contrast Gary Richmond tells another story in his book, *A View from the Zoo*. Richmond worked as a zoo keeper at the Los Angeles Zoo where he ran into a group of 15 red-tailed hawks. The majestic birds had been illegally trapped and the police had turned them over to the zoo while the perpetrators were brought to trial. It had taken a long time and the hawks had never been returned to the wild. Gary decided one day that they should go free.

So, one afternoon, he slipped into the center where they were housed, took the lock off the cage and set it where they could easily escape. With great satisfaction he went back to his usual duties. An hour or so later he returned to check the cage and to his astonishment all 15 birds were still relaxing in the cage. He decided they needed some "inspiration" so he ran at the cage waving his arms and growling like a bear. Well, they did fly out. But they landed just ten feet from the cage and eyed him with the most pitiful look of confusion. Hey, he yelled, "Don't you see the sky?" He pleaded, "That's what you were meant for. What's wrong with you? You're not chickens. You're majestic birds of prey. You hunt your food. God gave you a purpose, now go fulfill it." But no matter how he badgered those birds they wouldn't budge.

Finally, he realized, "Those birds had long since become satisfied with just waiting to be fed. No famines to suffer. No droughts to survive. No territorial battles to enjoin." To them there was no reason to move from their comfortable perch.

Richmond suggests that true freedom is fulfilling the purpose for which we were created. (Richmond, Gary, *A View from the Zoo,* Word Books, 1987, pp. 47-50).

Sometimes I feel like those hawks and then sometimes I'm more like the bear.

I was sitting in a worship service not long ago and the music about carried me away and the preaching was great and I felt like dancing. Now, I am not the dancing type - the more sedate controlled worship is my style. But I had this enormous urge to raise my hands in praise and dance. But I didn't do it. There were too many bars around me.

Bars of propriety. The words of the old spiritual came back to me. "I'm Gonna Sing When the Spirit Says Sing."

But am 1? Or will 1? I like order and ceremony Would I have risked singing praises with the disciples as they followed Jesus from Mt. Olivet to the Golden Gate? Would I have danced in spite of the ever present critical eyes of the Pharisees?

Sometimes I am more comfortable in my cage though I sense there is a Spirit gnawing at me to be free.

Karen Engle Layman in 1992 was pastor of Hope United Methodist Church, Mechanicsburg, Pennsylvania.

ISAIAH 50:4-9a

PALM/PASSION SUNDAY
APRIL 4, 1993

The text: "*I have set my face like flint, for I know that I shall not be put to shame, because one who will clear my name is at my side*" (Isaiah 50:7f).

I'm not sure quite why, but that text reminds me of Scotland, the country that my namesake Sidney Smith described as "*that knuckle-head of England, that land of Calvin, oatcakes and sulphur.*" Or more accurately, it reminds me of the people of Scotland, memorably depicted in John Kenneth Galbraith's *The Scotch*. "*They were made to last. Their faces and hands were covered not with a pink or white film but a heavy red parchment designed to give protection in extremes of climate for a lifetime. It had the appearance of leather, and appearances were not deceptive. This excellent material was stretched over a firm, bony structure on which the nose, often still retaining its axe marks, was by all odds the most prominent feature.*"

Faces like flint. I think of Hebridean crofters, out cutting hay on land so rocky that Cain would have disdained it; of a great mountain of a Glaswegian tossing the caber in the Highland Games; of bright-faced lassies on the beach at St. Andrew's, wearing bathing suits and panty-hose to protect themselves against the summer zephyrs off the North Sea. Faces like flint reflect lifetimes on paths that have been flinty, they bespeak struggle and endurance, forbearance and grit.

I think of other flinty faces. The face of a marathoner gasping her way up Heartbreak Hill. Faces of nameless refugees huddled together in the transit lounge of the Bangkok airport. My mother's face as she sat on the edge of her hospital bed five days before her death, her illness either undiagnosed or not admitted by the doctors.

And, oh yes, the flinty face of the one riding into Jerusalem on the back of a donkey. All around him the people are cheering and shouting, celebrating the predictions by ancient prophets that Messiah would enter the city in exactly this way.

Can you see his face? Are his eyes taking in the details of the crowd, the riot of color, the sea of faces, or are the eyes distant eyes? Is he having fun, teasing, grinning, clasping his hands over his head like a victorious prizefighter, or is he unmoving, unresponsive to the acclaim?

Luke says in his account that *"as the time approached when he was to be taken up to heaven he set his face resolutely towards Jerusalem."* He does so because he is remembering the words of the Servant, *"The Lord God opened my ears and I did not disobey.... I offered my back to the lash and let my beard be plucked out.... I did not hide my face from spitting and insult.... I have set my face like flint, for I know that I shall not be put to shame, for one who will clear my name is at my side."*

That Jesus should take his cue from the Servant of whom the prophet wrote is an easy thing for us to accept. Things begin to bind, however, when we realize that following Jesus in our time means setting *our* faces like flint! For the way of the servants, in our time, can only be the way of the Servant in his time.

The flinty face tells us that it was not an easy thing for him to ride into the city. The faith that sustained him was not to be confused with knowledge. You don't know for sure that the avalanche won't hit when you're crossing the face of the mountain. You don't know for sure that the security police won't crack your skull open with their billy clubs. You don't know for sure that this is really the right confrontation, or the right time. You don't know for sure if worst comes to worst and they hang you out to dry that you won't crack up, let down, fall apart, cave in, spill your guts all over the place. But you do what you have to do because you trust that, like the Servant, *"I shall not be put to shame, because one who will clear my name is at my side .... The Lord God will help me; who then can prove me guilty?"*

On the night of November 18, 1989 the elite Atlacatl battalion of the Salvadoran Armed Forces spilled onto the leafy campus of the University of Central America, and for over an hour blasted the residence of the rector of the University with rocket and machine gun fire. When they retreated the rector, five other Jesuit priests, their housekeeper and her young daughter lay dead. The crime of the Jesuits was to name as evil in the sight of God the economic and political systems by which the poor people of El Salvador were oppressed.

A year later I was part of the ecumenical group who gathered in the Romero chapel to commemorate the death of the martyrs. The evening was long, the air close, and those of us who had traveled long miles to be present were beginning to flag when Jon Sobrino, the seventh Jesuit who, but for the fact he was out of the country that fateful night would have also been assassinated, came to the microphone. He held in his hands a tray on which rested eight clay flower pots filled with earth. His hands shook as he solemnly planted a single frijole, the bean which is the staple food of the Salvadoran peasant, in each of the pots. He placed the tray before the tomb of the martyrs and turned and said softly the only words he could have said, *"Unless a grain of wheat falls into the ground and dies it remains alone, but if it dies it bears much fruit."*

Would you be surprised if I told you that his face was set like flint?

Robert F. Smith in 1993 was minister of Shaughnessy Heights United Church in Vancouver. He is a former moderator of the United Church of Canada.

LUKE 19:28-40

PALM/PASSION SUNDAY
APRIL 9, 1995

The story of Palm Sunday is one we all know well, too well perhaps. For those of us who have heard this story since childhood from Sunday School teachers, preachers, and parents, it is hard to remember how very unlikely this procession into Jerusalem really is. It is an odd event. Odd because the crowd gets it right, for once - hailing Jesus as the Messiah. Odd because even as they get it right, they also miss the point - wanting him to be a Messiah who leads to victory without pain or sacrifice. But most of all odd because it is an event which is deliberately staged and planned by Jesus himself.

This seems odd because it seems so out of character. Why would Jesus encourage the crowd to worship him without real understanding or commitment? Why would he set the stage to be hailed as the Messiah, refusing to rebuke those who worship and praise him? Jesus surely knew what was in their hearts. He knew the depth of their understanding—or the lack of depth. He knew that within the week this same crowd would be cooperating in his execution. He knew all this, and yet he not only allowed this triumphant procession, he orchestrated it. His subsequent action of cleansing the temple seems more natural. Shouldn't he also be cleansing the road into Jerusalem of these hypocrites who hail him as king but will soon be shouting for his blood?

I have a niece who is still only a toddler. Long before she was speaking clearly enough for me, a mere aunt, to understand her, she was learning how to pray. Before and after each meal, she would fold her hands piously, mumble something unintelligible, and would "Amen!" with great glee. Clearly, she did not understand what she was doing. She was playing at prayer, not yet praying. She was mimicking what her parents did before and after meals, and the jubilant "Amen!" was a part of the ritual which had no further meaning for her.

Yet I think most of you would agree that it is good for my niece to be learning to pray. Even though she does not yet understand exactly what she is doing when she closes her eyes, folds her hands, and murmurs reverently—it is still good for her to play at praying. This is how we learn. Most of us learn to believe things by first acting them out. We learn about being adults by playing dress-up, and school, and house when we are children. We learn to share by being made to act out sharing actions. We learn to be kind by playing at kindness. We learn to pray by pretending to pray.

This way of learning does not stop when we grow up. We, all of us, continue to act our way into new forms of believing. We cheer for a candidate for public office and find ourselves believing in the platform that candidate represents. We pretend to feel affection for a spouse during a dry time when we feel nothing but distance and disillusionment, and over time the loving feelings return. We find ourselves busy on Sunday morning - in need of some extra sleep, or extra time in the yard, or extra time with the family; the habit of attending church is broken, and eventually we find that our prayer life is nonexistent, that our thoughts rarely turn to God, that any belief we once had has faded into irrelevance.

It strikes me that we are not so different from that Palm Sunday crowd. And Jesus, the great teacher, is helping them to learn something important. Even though they do not understand the full significance of the worship and adoration which they offer, still by worshiping they may come to understand. W. H. Auden once wrote: "Human beings are by nature actors, who cannot become something until first they have pretended to be it. They are therefore to be divided, not into the hypocritical and the sincere, but into the sane, who know they are acting, and the mad who do not." On Palm Sunday, Jesus was not concerned with rooting out hypocrisy or with rewarding sincerity, but with teaching the truth. He was helping this crowd of people pretend to be something so that they could then become it. They were pretending to be his disciples, his followers, his worshipers.

The problem was that most of the crowd decided to switch roles part way through the week's drama. By Thursday night, they were acting at something different. They failed to see the play through to its end.

Every Sunday we stage a little drama here in this place. We begin, as this Holy Week begins, with praise. We call each other to worship, and we sing the praises of God—Father, Son and Holy Spirit. "Hosanna!" we cry, though often in other words. But then we also speak words of confession. We act out our penitence and affirm our forgiveness. We share with one another the peace of Christ in a ritualized, dramatic way—extending the hand of fellowship and even speaking the words, "the peace of Christ." We sit quietly and listen—or at least act as if we're listening!—to the teaching of the Word of God. We show our commitment as we place offerings in the offering plate. We sing of our devotion and of our changed lives. Sometimes we gather around the Lord's table and break bread and share one cup. Every Sunday is full of drama.

Some weeks you may not exactly understand what you are saying. Some weeks your heart may not be in some parts of the service. But "human beings are by nature actors, who cannot become something until first they have pretended to be it." Pretend. Act the part. Play at praising, at repenting, at committing. Keep acting until you get it right. Just as my niece learns to pray by praying, we learn to worship God by worshiping.

But we must complete the drama. It's easy to move through the praise section and drop out when it comes to the costly acts of confession, making peace, hearing the Word, giving money, making promises. If you want to become Jesus' faithful disciples, you have to stay in the play to the end. You have to play your part all the way through. You have to keep pretending until someday it's not pretend anymore. You've become what you were pretending to be.

Laura Smit in 1995 was pastor of the First Presbyterian Church of Clayton, NJ, and a minister member of the Presbyterian Church (USA).

Maundy Thursday

MARK 14:22-25

MAUNDY THURSDAY, 1977

pecial night for the church. For not only is it the night when Jesus is betrayed the night before he hangs on the tree, it is the night when our community eats s it was for the twelve with Jesus, it is good for us to be sitting around the table with friends, with persons whose children are as our children, whose laughter is as our laughter, whose tears are as our tears. We are here because we have been drawn into this community. We have felt the warmth and love which grows in response to Jesus.

The church to which Mark addressed his gospel was much the same. It was a church of like-minded, like-living persons. It was a congregation of persons who were both Jewish and Christian, that is they were Jewish-Christians. They observed the Jewish institutions while proclaiming that Jesus is the expected Messiah.

Consequently, when the Jewish-Christian church gathered on Maundy Thursday, they celebrated the Jewish Passover. Had we been in that congregation on a Maundy Thursday evening, we would have been in a room filled with tables and smelling of a great meal. In those days, when they kept the Lord's Supper they had a real supper. It must have been pretty cozy, for everyone was known to everyone else and the community was similar in aspirations, values and lifestyle.

We hear the familiar words of institution: "He took bread, and blessed it and broke it, and gave it to them and said, 'Take, this is my body.' And he took a cup of wine and when he had given thanks, he have it to them and they all drank of it. And he said to them, 'This is my blood of the covenant which is poured out for *many*" (Mark 14:22-24). *For many.* For many? These are strange words for they are a pointed and surprising address to a group of Jews. "The many" are Gentiles, not only people who are different from us but people whom we, often for good reason, by nature avoid.

Who are these people, these Gentiles? The answer to that question depends on the congregation to which these words on the lips of Jesus seem strange. To a well-heeled, middle class congregation, they may be persons whose clothes do not quite fit and are ragged around the sleeves, whose smiles expose decayed teeth which are turning mossy-green around the edges and whose grammar ruptures a trained ear. They may be the unambitious, the less than industrious, the unwitty and unimaginative. To a poor congregation perhaps they are the social workers and junior Leaguers who try to help but whose nonunderstanding comes across as patronizing and impatience; perhaps those coming in from the outside do not know what it is like to receive a Christmas basket. To a black congregation, perhaps Gentiles are whites who impose their cultural norms and expectations on black people.

The strange thing about the words of Jesus in Mark is that they do not come to us as words of comfort and encouragement. They come to us reminding us that God does not simply affirm our communities; when Jesus is nailed to the cross, a new, larger community is created. For Mark, the gift of the supper is not the presence of the Lord, but the presence of the Lord's community. When Jesus died, he died for saints and hucksters, union and management, banker and debtor, housewife and libber, teacher and student. Mark looks forward to the day when Jesus will come again in power and great glory and will gather this strange flock together—from the ends of the earth to the ends of heaven.

According to Mark, the supper of the Lord is an anticipation of what that great in-gathering will be like. Our differences are not ignored. Instead, we are asked to see them from God's perspective and to do what good friends do, join together around a common table. When we open ourselves to the reality which God created, a community of the many gathered around a single table, we share a little taste of the Kingdom of God.

Why talk about these things on Maundy Thursday? Because there is no other night of the Christian year when we are so conscious of our need and inadequacy before God. We have nothing with which to commend ourselves to God. Indeed, the betrayer himself shares our table, yet he is not turned away. Jesus meets our need and accepts us by placing us arm in arm in community.

In a few moments we will gather around the table We will anticipate what it will be like, yet what it is like, in the Kingdom of God. The differences which divide and separate us from one another are broken, nailed to the tree with Jesus, and we drink from the same cup and eat from the same loaf. We, many, broken, divided, in need, stand as one before the one table of the one Lord.

Ronald J. Allen, in 1977 was instructor of Greek at Drew University. Linda McKiernan Allen, was United Methodist Metropolitan Urban Minister, Newark, New Jersey. Both are ministers of The Disciples of Christ.

I CORINTHIANS 11:17-32; JOHN 13:1-17, 34

MAUNDY THURSDAY
APRIL 19, 1984

You're waiting in line at a stoplight, and suddenly a horn honks like a trumpet behind you. Go ahead; the light is green! You had been miles away, and suddenly you remember where you are.

The Lord's Supper gives us a chance to remember where we really are, and especially on Maundy Thursday. Of course we know we are to do this meal "in remembrance of" Jesus Christ, his life and teachings, his washing of our feet, his whip-torn back and splintered death, his unthinkable, unguessable resurrection, his continual presence with us.

But Paul tells us to remember also ourselves: "recollect" yourselves, as one translation puts it. His words can be like the horn sounding behind us, recalling us to reality. Lots of our troubles come because we live in the world not recollecting that it's God's; in our bodies not remembering they're gifts; in our families forgetting what treasures they are; in our world ignoring the news of need and change that now (in God's providence) can touch us from around the globe.

It is foolish for us, as for the person at the stoplight, to ignore our real situation in the world—and potentially even dangerous. What is that situation?

First, *we are part of the Body of Christ.* Together with our sisters and brothers here and around the world, we belong to a great tide of people who believe there's more to life than meets the eye. We are not alone! For instance, when any Christian prays, even in a distant prison, the Spirit joins her prayers to those of a basketball player, head bowed before a game; a desperate father whose child has been missing since breakfast; an old nun before an operation; a farmer facing drought... we are part of a great galaxy of souls whose prayers, though uttered separately, wreathe and intertwine around the Throne of Grace.

Then too, *we all belong to an ordinary, sinful, struggling local limb of that great Body.* The other members are not always those we'd choose; of course not! God has chosen them —and *us*! Look around; how unlikely it seems, sometimes, that these are the saints of God; that we are! Yet even those thoughtless Corinthian Christians of Paul's were called by God. Some people refuse the church because of the people in it: so many of them are sinners. Of course, that's true; Jesus himself admits that he didn't come to call the righteous but sinners. In fact, that's part of the Good News. The church is full of sinners. They're the ones Christ always calls. So I don't have to be "good enough" to be a Christian. I'm a member of the Body of Christ because Christ wants me, not because I can pass an entrance exam.

And of course, *we all are nourished by the Body of Christ.* Jesus himself tells us (Paul vouches for it that it's Jesus as he hands the words along to us), "this is my body." How do I know Christ died for *me*? How do I know *my* sins are forgiven? I can know it because in eating this bread and drinking this cup, I take his death right into myself, proclaiming that this is the food that really keeps me alive; that this is the love that will never desert me, until at last it's sealed forever by Love's return; that this is my hope, my reassurance, my strength. The Bible's words of hope were written so long ago, in the past; a sermon's promise of grace might be for someone else, not me. But this piece of bread I eat, this sip of wine I taste and swallow, these are without any doubt for *me*. Jesus' promise attaches itself to my eating and drinking, and I can let go of my doubts and my sins and my unworthiness. Now without question I am a part of Jesus' body given for the world, and he a part of me; I am cleansed of sin by the blood he shed for all.

We get dreamy, sometimes, like the person waiting for the light to change. We imagine we're isolated, unworthy to be Christians, and stuck in our sins. But Paul sounds the Gospel trumpet behind us, waking us from our deceitful daydreams into the reality of Christ. Let us recollect who we really are: one of a great company anchored in eternity, where Christ prays for and with us to God; called to be one of Christ's sinful, saved pilgrims; cleansed and nourished by Christ's death and resurrection for us.

Don Chatfield, a Presbyterian minister, in 1994 was professor of preaching and worship at Garrett-Evangelical Theological Seminary in Evanston, Illinois, where he also operated an individual sermon consultation service by mail.

Good Friday

JOHN 18:1-19:42

GOOD FRIDAY, 1977

Last night was so pleasant. Eating together, drinking together, God seemed so near, so totally present. We had something to celebrate while he was with us: his love for us, our love for each other. He commanded us to love one another (John 13:34, 15:12)—as if we needed a command to feel what was involuntarily drawn from us by the magnetism of that moment.

Now love is dead. Hate wins. So it seems. God has abandoned his son, has abandoned us, and we keep our distance, isolated from him and from each other. The sheer ugliness and blasphemy of the sight is evidence enough. God has cursed the whole project and has left the scene, giving it over to the sarcasm of Pilate and the blase greed of the soldiers. The cynical equation of Caiaphas (18:14) is resolved: one man dies for the preservation of the whole people.

And yet there is something more. The unknown script is read. The actors move in perfect cadence. The lead seems strangely composed:

> "There is one actor who moves quietly
> instead of milling about as though he,
> of all the company
> understands the script
> and has learned his lines and actions.
> Perhaps if I go on stage and follow him…" [1]

The title is nailed to the cross, on the ground the soldiers toss dice, the dying man calls out in thirst. Event tumbles onto random event, yet something seems to stick—and fit. Perhaps a sense of *deja vu*—or is it a premonition? This sense of things like a rumor in our consciousness: that here God is present beyond all imagining. More than that. Here God is suffering: with him, with us (for us?). Above the mumbling crowd the crucified whispers, "It is finished," and dies. It is over, completed, done. The dice roll snake-eyes. The one-eyed soldier swears with glee and holds aloft his prize. The seamless robe is untorn—perfectly woven, whole, complete; as are all things in this moment. Whole and pregnant with possibility.

There are moments which make a claim on our lives. There are sights too beautiful or too horrifying to simply behold. We are drawn *into* them. Rainer Maria Rilke, contemplating the "Archaic Torso of Apollo," felt himself examined:

> We did not know his legendary head,
> in which eyeballs ripened. But
> his torso still glows like a candelabrum
> in which his gaze, only turned low,
> holds and gleams ....
> …there is no place
> that does not see you. You must change your life. [2]

Looking at the crucified we see not only the last drops of vinegar dripping from his beard but we see ourselves as well: the poverty of our love, the shallowness of our faith, the smallness of our hope, the banality of our living. We hear the challenge: You must change your life. But there is more. This cross and the body hanging on it proclaim beyond understanding: Your life is changed! Nothing will ever be exactly the same. We will never be exactly the same again. Something touches a place hidden deep within us. This death transforms everything. Through all the pain, barely audible in the noise of the crowd, we heard him say, "It is finished." "And it was as though he had said: Everything has begun."[2]

[1] Madelein L'Engle, Passion Play," in *Lines Scribbled on an Envelope*, Farrar, Strauss & Giroux, 1969, pp. 33-4.

[2] M.D. Herter Norton, *Translations from the Poetry of Rainer Maria Rilke*, W.W. Norton, 1938, p.181.

[3] Nikos Kazantzakis, *The Last Temptation of Christ,* Bantam, 1960, p. 387.

Patrick J. Willson, a minister of the Presbyterian Church in the United States, in 1977 was Associate Pastor of First Presbyterian Church, Tupelo, Mississippi.

LUKE 23:33-46

GOOD FRIDAY
APRIL 13, 1979

Ah, what can we say this dark day? What can be said here at the foot of the cross? I think it was Reinhold Niebuhr who said, "society treats its criminals and its saviors in the same way."

And so it should not be surprising for us to climb to The Place of the Skull and find Jesus hung ignobly between two thieves, surrounded on all sides by human criminality. For doesn't the story go to great lengths to remind us that they were all criminals of some stripe or another on that dark afternoon. Some criminals sat in the Roman Governor's palace washing their hands, some watched from the porch of the Temple at the afternoon sacrifice, some thrust the spear in his side or nailed his hands and feet, some pushed and shoved in the mob below the crosses, and some criminals were among his twelve best friends who (says Luke) *all* forsook him and fled.

One of these criminals on the cross, in mockery and in desperation says, "Save yourself—and us. Do what saviors are supposed to do; a little magic, some self-centered miracle, show your glory!" And the other thief, much more penitent, admitting to the justice of his sad fate, cried, "Jesus, remember me when you come in your kingly power." And Jesus replies, "Today, you're with me in paradise." Compassionate, forgiving, loving to the end.

But what strikes me most is how, even here at the end, as he suffers and dies, both of the thieves are asking Jesus for things for themselves. They're not all that different from the crowd, even the penitent one in his admittedly admirable humility, for everybody always wanted something from this savior, right up to the end.

They wanted proof, or healing, rewards without risk, or glory without pain. Right up to the end. Here, up at The Place of the Skull, we see so clearly the image of our self-centeredness, the end result of our self-righteousness, and the final act which comes from our illusions that we can justify ourselves by ourselves and demand our just reward and exalt our petty criminality as the highest righteousness if we have to nail Jesus upon a cross to do it. Herbert Butterfield writes:

> ...Jesus Christ was not merely murdered by hooligans on a country road; he was condemned by everything that was most respectable in that day, everything that pretended to be the most righteous—the religious leaders... the authority of the Roman government, and even democracy itself which shouted to save Barabbas... the Crucifixion... accuses human nature, accuses all of us in the very things that we think are our righteousness... the Crucifixion challenges the prestige and power of the Pharisaical notion of upright living, challenges the old Roman respectabilities, and supersedes the pre-Christian notion of a righteous man.... In the light of it the claim that *our* conscience is clear' is the ugliest pretense of all....
>
> (Herbert Butterfield, *History and Human Relations*,
> London: Collins, 1951, pp. 61-63)

We are not good. Sometimes even our so-called "good" is our greatest evil. What hope is there for such as we?

The cross stands as both judgment upon us and as a sign of our salvation. Our hope is not in ourselves but in God. All else is illusion, petty play-acting, self-deception. All else leads either to despair over our criminality or to other Good Fridays which come as a result of trying to achieve the good on our own terms.

As old Malcolm Muggeridge said, Human beings are only bearable when the last defenses of their egos are down; when they stand, helpless and humbled, before the awful circumstances of their being. It is only thus that the point of the cross becomes clear, and the point of the cross is the point of life.

> (Malcolm Muggeridge, *Jesus Rediscovered*,
> New York: Random House, 1969, p. 109)

The cross points us to not only our sin but also to our hope. Jesus hangs there this day, not only to show our criminality but also to show our salvation. He hangs there to show the way. The way for him and for us is the way of the cross, to cast ourselves upon God's love with nothing more said than, "Father, into thy hands we commit our spirits...."

For what else can we say?

William H. Willimon, a minister in the United Methodist Church, in 1979 was Assistant Professor of Worship and Liturgy, Duke University Divinity School, Durham, NC.

HEBREWS 4:14-16, 5:7-9

GOOD FRIDAY
MARCH 28, 1986

Recent Holy Week rites provide a central and specific place for the cross. My own tradition, for example, suggests that a rough-hewn cross be carried in procession through the church following the bidding prayer of the Good Friday liturgy. Three times the procession stops. The liturgical president announces, "Behold, the life-giving cross on which was hung the salvation of the whole world." The congregation responds to each announcement with the words, "Oh, come, let us worship him." Following a period of silence, two or three hymns are sung. Then the congregation kneels. "We adore you, O Christ, and we bless you," the leader announces. The Good Friday liturgy ends with the congregational affirmation, "By your holy cross you have redeemed the world." All leave in silence.

Such rites as these continue a tradition which dates back to the fourth century. Whether or not we actually use them in our own celebration, these acts of "veneration" or "adoration" suggest the way that we should view the cross on this day. They insist that the cross is a throne. They call us to give homage to the crucified one, homage like that paid to a sovereign at a coronation. They put us on our knees as we declare our allegiance to Christ and to his rule.

Such a perspective does not intend to rob the crucifixion of its horrible reality. It is possible, as F.W. Dillistone has suggested, to view the cross as "the supreme illustration of the divine immunity to the most virulent diseases and infections that belong to the mortal scene" (*Jesus Christ and His Cross: Studies in the Saving Work of Christ*, Westminster, 1953, page 18). But this is not what the Good Friday liturgy calls us to do. The torture of the cross is not to be avoided. The assigned texts speak of sorrows and griefs, wounds and stripes, oppression and rejection. They make us hear the loud cries of Jesus as he offered up his prayers with tears. At the same time, however, the liturgy and its texts insist that the cross was Jesus' throne. It was the final act in a life of unceasing obedience to his Father. By it he "became the source of eternal salvation to all who obey him" (Hebrews 5:9).

The Good Friday liturgy holds fast to both Jesus' death and rule, to both Jesus' crucifixion and sovereignty. Thus it challenges us to remember that God's kingdom can come in no way other than this. Jesus reigns from a cross. The Church which shares his sovereignty will also share his cross. We wish it could be otherwise; perhaps we pray with "loud cries" that it could be otherwise. We cannot help but wish that his rule would be demonstrated through a Church that is successful, influential, or powerful. But Christ reigns by dying and we might pray this day for the power of that vision. It is in the rejected and despised, in the innocent who suffer because of others, that Christ's glory shines forth.

By holding Christ's death and rule together, the Good Friday liturgy also comforts us. The suffering by which Jesus was exalted is the same suffering by which he is able to "sympathize with our weaknesses" (Hebrews 4:15). It is with confidence that we are to "draw near to the throne of grace" and receive mercy. Before the Christ who reigns from a cross we can confess our sins without fear. He is none other than the one who made himself an "offering for sin" and who makes many "to be accounted righteous." To the cross we can come with our fears, our loneliness, our grief, and our failures. He whose suffering encompassed fear, loneliness, grief and failure with "deal gently" with us. To the exalted Christ we can offer our timid prayers, our faltering hymns of praise, and our inconstant love. He can transform them as he transformed the cross itself.

Richard L. Thulin, a minister of the Lutheran Church in America, in 1986 was Professor of Preaching, Lutheran Theological Seminary, Gettysburg, Pennsylvania.

PSALM 22:1-18

GOOD FRIDAY
MARCH 24, 1989

"My God, my God, why have You forsaken Me?" Hear the cry of the psalmist, hear the words of Jesus Christ from the cross. Feel the anxiety of being alone. After all who hasn't at some time or another felt alone, separated even from God? what can be learned in these moments of solitude?

One lesson is that we need Jesus every moment of our lives. Sounds so simple, yet so difficult to always practice. This is beautifully illustrated by Abba Elias, who said: "An old man was living in a temple and the demons came to say to him, 'Leave this place which belongs to us,' and the old man said, 'No place belongs to you.' Then they began to scatter his palm leaves about, one by one, and the old man went on gathering them together with persistence. A little later the devil took his hand and pulled him to the door. When the old man reached the door, he seized the lintel with the other hand crying out, 'Jesus, save me.' Immediately the devil fled away. Then the old man began to weep. Then the Lord said to him, 'Why are you weeping?' and the old man said, 'Because the devils have dared to seize a man and treat him like this.' The Lord said to him, *'You had been careless. As soon as you turned to me again, you see I was beside you'* " (Bendicta Ward, trans., *The Saying of the Desert Fathers*, London & Oxford: Mowbrays, 1975, p. 8).

Today is a time in which we can celebrate the Sound of Solitude and turn to Jesus once again, and accept His righteousness. "The death and the life of the Christian is not determined by his own resources; rather he finds both only in the Word that comes to him from the outside, in God's Word to him. The Reformers expressed it this way: Our righteousness is an 'alien righteousness,' a righteousness that comes from outside of us (*extra nos*). They were saying that the Christian is dependent on the Word of God spoken to him. He is pointed outward, to the Word that comes to him. The Christian lives wholly by the truth of God's Word in Jesus Christ" (Dietrich Bonhoeffer, *Life Together*, Harper & Row Publishing: New York, 1954, p. 22).

The psalmist never gave up his faith and believed that God would continue to work in his life, even when God appeared to be silent. Jesus Christ our Lord, cried in anguish when God was silent. For a moment it seemed that God the Father, turned away and Jesus The Son was left alone. But after that moment the triumphal cry of, "it is finished" was the victory of our Lord and great High Priest. And as we journey through this life, we too cry for God's help and presence. For the world calls us to look away from the love of Christ. It is precisely then, that we feel alone and abandoned, because we have become careless. Careless in our devotion to the One who loves us, the One who gave His life for us, the One who said, "I will never forsake you or leave you." Today, we remember in our solitude of silence that Jesus is next to us always, and His love is always ours if we but listen to Him.

May God grant us His grace and love and a quiet heart and soul!

Donald P. Edwards, a minister of the Evangelical Lutheran Church in America, in 1989 was pastor of Trinity Lutheran Church, McAlisterville, Pa.

JOHN 18:1-19:42

GOOD FRIDAY
APRIL 1, 1994

Today, our focus is on the cross, an instrument of death, that for Christians, is a symbol of hope, of forgiveness, of salvation, of healing, of life. Today, the crosses are veiled in black, reminding us that this is the most solemn and even perplexing day of the whole year. The day that Jesus, our Lord and Savior, carried his own cross to the place of his crucifixion.

The cross. Think of how many times tonight we have been drawn to focus on it. There will be many more times tonight that the cross will be brought into our thoughts, prayers and vision.

The cross. Many of us have one hanging around our necks. Many others have them as casual pieces of jewelry. For those whom their cross has special significance or is a symbol of devotion, the brutal reality of that cross is clearly seen today. The small cross that hangs around our necks springs to lifesize. It is no longer, silver or gold but two separate wooden beams.

When I was in Jerusalem a couple of years ago, we walked the Way of the Cross even though it was January. We walked to the traditional places or stations in Jerusalem where we heard scriptures and prayers traditionally associated with our Lord's passion and death. It was one of the most moving and powerful experiences I have ever had. What made it so powerful was not just the opportunity to be present in the city and to be in places that pilgrims have walked for 2,000 years but it was also the carrying the cross through the streets of Jerusalem. Even though many of the people are used to seeing Christians making this pilgrimage at all times of the year, there is something uncomfortable about carrying the cross in such a public way. We would take turns, one person carrying the cross on his or her shoulder and another person walking behind, supporting it. It was big enough and heavy enough that it took two people to carry it.

I remember my own embarrassment and tentativeness to take a turn. In fact, it took quite a long time for me to do so. Internally, I wanted to be identified as being a pilgrim, of following Jesus but externally, I wanted to remain safe, at a distance, not too closely identified. I struggled with my own struggle, ashamed of how easily I come to disassociate from the cross and yet understanding in a deeper way how the disciples might have felt when they chose to flee and remain at a distance.

I did, finally, take my turn but the feeling of that struggle, that ambivalence, that fear are still very much alive in me. I want to be a disciple but ...I want to follow Jesus but ...I want to walk his walk but ...I am not as willing to carry the cross as I think I am or wish I were.

Herbert O'Driscoll says that "None of us ever share the cross by choice. We are, by nature, onlookers to agony. It both fascinates and repels us because we know that, if it is not ours now, it soon will be. Time and circumstance call us out of the crowd to take up the cross, and we do so only because we have no choice."

What is it that fascinates us about the cross and what is it that repels us? Why do we feel such ambivalence about it all? I can't speak for you but as I thought about it, I found that what fascinates us is the agony and brutality and what repels us is the call of Jesus to take up our cross and follow him. What fascinates us is the way it was all handled, the betrayal, the perjury, the crowd mentality. What repels us is the call in our lives as Christians to give witness to the world of the hope that is in us. What fascinates is the drama, what repels is the cost. From a distance it is safe. We can be observers but still feel a part of it. To stand right in the midst is frightening.

We are caught in ambivalence, even in irony. What actually gives us life both fascinates and repels us. But, the cross is irony too. An instrument of death is actually the vehicle for new life.

As we meditate tonight and tomorrow on the cross, I invite you to meditate on what it might mean for you to sink into the cross. The cross will only be a distant symbol for us if we have no sense of what brings us to the cross and what causes us to fall into Christ's outstretched arms and sink into his cross.

Frederick Buechner has said, "A six-pointed star, a crescent moon, a lotus—the symbols of other religions suggest beauty and light. The symbol of Christianity is an instrument of death. It suggests, at the very least, hope."

The Rev. Charlotte Dudley Cleghorn in 1994 was Rector of St. Ann's Episcopal Church in Windham, Maine.

Easter Day

LUKE 24:1-11

EASTER DAY
APRIL 6, 1980

It was a very odd thing that the women who visited Jesus' tomb were asked to do—very odd indeed. They approached the tomb at the first sign of dawn, laden with spices and with grief. Suddenly an empty tomb, a blaze of light, the presence of angels. They were terrified—too frightened, in fact, even to run away. They simply bowed their faces to the ground and waited for whatever was coming next. What happened next was that they were asked a question, and given a command. The question is the one in which the whole Christian faith turns: 'Why do you seek the living among the dead?' The thrust of that question is so clear and direct that some of the ancient manuscripts cannot refrain from adding the pointed line, "He is not here, but has risen!" The Resurrection of Jesus means that no question of importance can ever be answered the same way again—especially the question, "Why do you seek the living among the dead?"

The command that follows the question is an odd one. They are not told to *go,* to *serve,* to *create a church*, to *pray* or *transform society*.... they are not even told to *rejoice*. All of these would come later. For now, they are told to *remember*. "Remember how he told you, while he was still in Galilee, that the Son of Man must be delivered into the hands of sinful men, and be crucified, and on the third day rise. And they remembered...."

We usually think of the Resurrection bringing in the new age, pointing up with hope toward the future alive with fresh possibilities. Why, then, is the first command of Easter day directed toward the past? What is the purpose of the call to *remember?*

1) *It illumines the Lordship of Christ over all history.* Even those moments of history which seem to be outside of God's control, in defiance of his lordship, are somehow caught up in the victory of Easter. No event in history— not the crucifixion, not the holocaust, no event—can ultimately stand outside of God's redemptive purpose which we see in Easter. The Church lives its life in a world where God's power seems to be overcome at every turn. The Easter command to remember stands for us as a promise that one day we will see how God's power was at work even in those situations that seem to deny him.

2) *It gives us then a new way to view our current situation.* There is a legend that long ago birds did not have wings. One day God decided to give every bird on the face of the earth a pair of wings. At first the birds complained bitterly. Were not their legs small and weak enough without the extra burden and weight of wings. Then one day one of the birds began to try these new wings and discovered flight. That which had seemed a new burden now became a new freedom. So it is with the Resurrection. If it remains at the level of abstract doctrine—or if it is applied only to some nebulous future hope—then the Resurrection is nothing more than a heavy weight to be carried on legs of faith already grown weary. But the command to *remember* calls us to focus the light of the Resurrection—not on the distant future removed from our current

situation—but on history...*our* history, *our* situation—past and present. Every experience of life, no matter how tomb-like it may appear, can now be viewed through the lens of the Resurrection. What looks like crucifixion will lead to God's resurrection victory. Remember....remember...remember!

Only when we view the past through the lens of the Resurrection do we gain the courage to face the future, the courage to tell the world of the Resurrection power even when it seems to them to be "an idle tale."

Thomas G. Long, a minister in the Presbyterian Church in the United States, in 1980 was professor of preaching and worship at Columbia Theological Seminary in Decatur, Georgia.

JOHN 20:1-9

EASTER SUNDAY
APRIL 19, 1981, VOL. 5 NO. 4 (40)

Watching our team on television make all the wrong plays and blunder through the first quarter of the game caused my friend to become so upset and despairing that he turned the game off certain of defeat. In the fourth quarter our team did the unbelievable and won.

Having not seen the live game, I watched the replay knowing only the final score. I saw the same mistakes and blunders that my friend had, but my attitude and perspective toward the unfolding events was totally different. While I did not know what twists and turns might come next in the game, I had a sense of hope and confidence because I knew the final score.

Easter is God's grand announcement of the final score! In Jesus Christ we have seen certain defeat transformed into victory. Death is overcome by Life. Hatred and evil lose in the final tally. Light shines and the darkness has not overcome it.

That was the Word John shared in his Gospel's first chapter. Between there and the twentieth chapter, however, blunders and betrayals and unexpectedly strong opponents had taken their toll. Defeat seemed a certainty. All was dark and lost—might as well turn this scene off!

But in that darkness Mary Magdalene came. Something unexpected maybe even unbelievable had happened. She did not know...Peter did not know... but the beloved disciple as he peered into that tomb in the dawning light saw, knew, believed a new final score had been announced. From that moment the word started to spread. The final score is victory, life. Christ lives! Have you heard the word, the Good News? Do you know the final score?

To be certain there are the times when by our own blunders or the opposing forces of life all seems lost. Defeat seems sure. We wish we could turn it all off!

But, we have heard the Word; the Good News. Unlike Mary and Peter who did not know, we know the final score. There will still be unknown twists and turns and blunders as life unfolds, but knowing the final score is already victory transforms our attitude and perspective into confidence and joy. We dare to stay tuned in to the fullness of whatever comes in life with the risen Christ. As Mary and Peter and the beloved disciple and the growing community of faith discovered after they knew the final score of Easter, it means life beyond birth as well as life beyond death.

Ask Archbishop Oscar Romero who dared to live for Christ's justice and love unafraid to die. He knew the final score. Ask the teenager confined to Children's Hospital most of her life, but expectantly looking forward to each new day. She knows the final score.

One of the players on our team was interviewed following the game. "I know we won," he said. "I heard the score announced. But I still can't believe it."

The strife is o'er the victory won! We have heard the Good News announced. Will you believe it and live in the abundant joy and confidence of knowing the final score.

Peter D. Weaver, a minister of the United Methodist Church, in 1981 was Senior Pastor of Smithfield United Church (United Church of Christ and United Methodist) in Pittsburgh, PA.

LUKE 24:1-12

EASTER
APRIL 3, 1983

Easter is a time for trumpets! There aren't many who would deny that the dominant mood for Easter Day is one of joy and triumph.

Why then do you suppose those women who went to Jesus' tomb to anoint his body were so afraid of Easter? No question about it, for Luke says: "They were afraid and bowed their faces to the earth" (Luke 24:5).

Think of it: afraid of Easter! And clearly they were frightened *after,* not before, learning that Jesus was risen from the dead.

But why were they afraid? Surely it was more than some creepy feelings about the supernatural. There were more than ghosts here in the light of that Easter dawn to frighten them. I believe something deeper may have terrified them and made them afraid of Easter. Something too easily overlooked! It was the hard and terrifying consciousness that not a dead, but a living Christ confronts us in Easter. I suggest that's what frightened those women. It's one thing to come prepared to anoint a corpse; it's something else to deal with a living person. We are pressed as were the women to reckon with our deepest fears. The living Christ confronts us with the question: what are we *really* afraid of—death or life?

I remember reading several years ago about a man who disappeared from his home in Ohio and eight years later was declared officially dead. His wife worked through her grief, remarried, had more children, and then her first husband turned up alive. Questions surrounded his reappearance, but his wife's remarks at the time of his reappearance have special meaning: "I just wish it wasn't true. We had become adjusted to his death."

We can understand what she means at that deeper level of life's experience. Like the women, we can mourn our way through and become adjusted to the fact of a defeated, dead Christ. But the resurrection, this is much more difficult. Indeed, if we take it seriously, it is even frightening.

And this presence of a risen Christ and our need to deal with it in our lives suggests some specific meanings. Because he has triumphed over death, doesn't it challenge us to focus on hope rather than despair as we make our own life pilgrimage?

This focus isn't easy. It can even be frightening. Sometimes it's easier to be despairing. our Black Fridays loom ever clear about us. Sometimes we are so given to hopelessness that we develop a philosophy to justify it. We point to death and disaster and say: "This is reality." But here comes a living Christ in the clear light of Easter dawn embodying life and hope, and saying: "This too is reality." That takes some adjustment, some living with. But the living Christ urges us to deal with life hopefully.

But more than hope, the resurrection puts promise at the heart of things. "Why do you seek the living among the dead? He is not here; he has risen" (Luke 24:5, 6). That's the promise we all need to hear. It is frightening. Yet for those who will dare believe, that promise offers a whole new dimension for living.

A few winters ago I visited Israel and spent a brief time touring the Golan Heights. From that point the Syrian tanks shelled the fertile plains of Galilee. The scars of war were evident everywhere. In one such gun emplacement, barbed wire still punctuated the muddy tank tracks. As we stood observing this symbol of the ways of darkness and death, there in the mud and rusting wire grew a fragile white wildflower. The seed of life had survived, pushing back on that brilliant morning the stark symbols of death.

What a quiet reminder of Easter and our Lord's resurrection! In the rain and mud of Calvary, who would have ever bet on life? Yet on the third day, like a fragile flower blooming, Christ was alive. The promise of life in him. Christ ever on the side of life.

Afraid of Easter? Yes! But for those who will follow the Lord our fears may be transformed and our lives filled with hope and promise.

As Alice Meynell states in *Christ in the Universe*, "No planet knows of this. Our wayside planet, carrying land and wave, Love and life multiplied, and pain and bliss, Bears, as chief treasure, one forsaken grave."

Robert Drew Simpson in 1983 was senior minister, The United Methodist Church, Chatham, New Jersey.

JOHN 20:1-18; ISAIAH 25:6-9

EASTER DAY
APRIL 7, 1985

Consider the movie *Testament,* which has now been widely seen on television and is continuing to be shown around the country. It stands out among art forms treating nuclear holocaust in that it tells in quite straightforward, believable terms what happens to a family in a suburb of San Francisco in the two months after the missiles hit. This movie manifests the kind of realism about our situation against which the story from Mark, the promise of Isaiah, the insistent affirmations of I Corinthians might be heard.

There may be resistance, of course, to a topic so gloomy on Easter morning. I recall sitting, on Palm Sunday, behind two well dressed persons—you could see that they were going from church directly to a nice lunch—who were experiencing for the first time the long reading of the passion story on that day formerly given to children's parades and the picture of the winsome king on the donkey. At the end of the long account of Jesus' trial and death, one of this pair whispered to the other, "Well, *that* wasn't very cheerful." Easter is, to be sure, a day of celebration for which we have been preparing through Lent and this past week. So let it be that. At the same time, our Alleluias ring out all the more where we stand, as it were, in the teeth of death.

In the movie, we are not sure whether it is hope or just stubbornness. On the day the missiles come, Carolyn's husband does not make it home from work—he never does. Soon the comforts of suburbia begin to disappear, people weaken, the children begin to die, all turns gray. Carolyn, for her part, continues to cook dinner, to send Janie to her piano lessons, and even to dance in the living room with her teenage son Brad, the weakness of radiation sickness beginning to show in both of them. One day they close the garage door, Brad and Carolyn, and start the car. But they cannot do it, not so much for fear as, it would seem, for the dogged need to choose life.

The priest is reduced to burying the dead, and that with great dispatch. Toward the end of the movie Carolyn spends the evening watching the fire in which the body of her firstborn is being consumed. She kneels on the earth and throws the poisoned earth toward the acrid sky: "Who did this? Who did this? God damn you." The priest, as if to answer, says nothing but holds and kisses her.

Isaiah writes, in today's lesson: "And the Lord of hosts…will destroy the covering that is cast over all peoples, the veil that is spread over all nations." Some think—and what we are seeing in the arts and the media seem to corroborate this — that we live already under the cloud, that deep in our psyche there has grown since 1945 this pervasive awareness of the approach of the destruction of the earth. Like those Jews (see Elie Wiesel) who cannot shake from their minds what happened in Europe under the Nazis, humankind, and particularly those of us who bear the responsibility for creating this weapon, live daily with the bomb.

The women come to the tomb with the spices of anointing, the signs of both death and love, in their hands. And the story of Easter is that God turns death into life, reverses this situation of the death of the good to the triumph of love.

And so we come to this Easter with death written not just upon our foreheads— we have known for a long time and are reminded every Ash Wednesday that we are dust— but upon the face of the whole earth. We might well endure the thought of our personal obliteration. The teenage boy who spoke to me at the end of a sermon in one of New York's prep schools reassured me: "Don't worry, Mr. Rice. Vaporization takes place in 1/10,000th of a second, faster than the eye can see. So if you are near enough, you will never even see what hit you." That would not be a bad way to go, if one did not have to contemplate the death, not just of oneself, but of humankind, of God's innocent creatures who live close to the earth, of the earth itself.

And so we come to this Easter. Some Christians, of course, refuse to believe that God would *allow* this to happen. What we have seen already—the holocaust, the wars, Jesus on the cross, even one innocent person rotting in jail—offers little reassurance along those lines. We come to this Easter with death in our hands, and we need as much as ever, perhaps more than ever, the miraculous triumph of love.

And we nourish and celebrate this hope, that the one who was, is daily, and by all odds will once again be crucified, God will make finally in our hearts and to the ends of the earth to reign over every vestige of death. They come, these pitiful women with their hopeless perfumes, to find, at the very least, that he is not to be found among the dead. Alleluia.

Charles Rice, a minister of The United Church of Christ, in 1985 was professor of homiletics, Drew University Theological School, Madison, New Jersey.

MATTHEW 28:1-10

EASTER
APRIL 15, 1990

For whom is Christ not risen this day? Is it the prisoner alone in her cell worried about her children? Is it the family in Ethiopia that has just used the last of their food? Is it someone here today who has just lost his job or a dear loved one? For people in the midst of the darkest times it is hard to believe that Christ is risen. Yet it is precisely these same people for whom Christ has most surely risen. Christ was raised from the dead for all those who dwell in the land of darkness that they might have light.

On that first Easter Morning it is no small coincidence that the two Marys approach the tomb while it is yet dark but with the sky already starting to lighten. Christ rises while it is dark and, in a manner of speaking, could only rise while it was yet dark. He comes in risen glory to us in the midst of our sin, in the midst of our pain, in the midst of our grief for all that is lost and all that will not be. He comes to us and says the same words the two women needed to hear back then, and which we desperately need to hear addressed to us: Fear not. Fear not. The worst is behind you. The power of death has been defeated. There is no going back. A new day has dawned."

The resurrection of Christ in history is no resurrection at all, until we have experienced it for ourselves. Christ comes to us and unless we know that Christ is alive we may not recognize him. The risen Christ comes to us each day.

Hard-hearted Charlie is presiding over his dying Lambourghini business in Los Angeles when the call comes through that his father has died in Ohio. Recently watching *The Rainman*, I saw him return to kidnap Raymond, an institutionalized autistic brother he didn't know he had, because Raymond had inherited the entire estate. He had no affection for him. But something happened on the way back to L.A. that softened Charlie's heart, and we don't know what it was. Perhaps it was having to drive back, because Raymond was afraid of flying. Or perhaps it was stopping to buy apple juice and cheese balls for the regular snack times. Or perhaps it was having to stop at K Mart because that was the only brand of underwear Raymond would wear. Whatever it was, as they were driving across the deserts of Arizona at sunset, "Dem Bones" was being sung acapella in the background. "The hip bone connected to the thigh bone, the thigh bone connected to the knee bone...," and on it went. But you had to listen closely to notice that the music stopped before it got to the last line, "Now hear the name of the Lord." But those who had ears to hear it could hear it. Because we knew that what had happened on that journey was not just bone connected to bone, it was blood to blood, flesh to flesh, family member to family member and that can only be the work of the Lord. Now hear the name of the Lord. It is ours to proclaim, even as it was given to the two Marys to proclaim as they rushed forward in joy, in this same resurrection time and in the age to come.

Paul Scott Wilson in 1990 was Associate Professor of Homiletics, Emmanuel College, Toronto School of Theology, and interim minister at Humbercrest United Church, Toronto.

MATTHEW 28:1-10

EASTER 1
APRIL 7, 1996

Today we find ourselves rushing before sunrise with Mary of Magdalene through the Jerusalem market, past sleeping dogs and horses, out one of the gates of the ancient walled city, the Ganneth Gate, deserted at this hour, but for the soldiers on top of the wall. Outside this gate we are suddenly in countryside, except for a large stone quarry off to our left, looking like a huge gravel pit. From this quarry many slaves had provided stone blocks for building the city. To this quarry that Mary Magdalene goes with her grief. She had shared in Jesus' ministry. She was going to the place where her hopes had ceased, her dreams had died, her worst fears were realized. She passes beneath the clifftop. Two men who had been crucified with Jesus still hang there, on wooden crosses where they will be devoured by birds and dogs. She goes to a far corner of the quarry to a garden, where the cliffside has row upon row of handhewn caves, tombs for the dead.

There should be a checkpoint for us along the way to the tomb. Each one of us should answer one very simple question before proceeding. That question is, "Do you have fear in your life? Are you afraid of something?" If you say, "No way," then turn back. We need not trouble ourselves with the tomb and all of this difficult Easter business if fear has not approached and asked us about approaching death. Turn back if, in watching TV, you have not heard the voice of fear as you contemplated the future of this planet or the suffering of its people. For what person in northern climbs finds the pruning sheers in December, or the garden sprinkler in January or the Christmas lights in April? We do not find what we have no use for, even if it is there in front of us.

On the other hand, this path to the tomb is just the path for anyone who has dreams that have ended, hopes that have died. Come with Mary if you know what it means to go unrecognized, or if you lost your job, or if you were not promoted as you should have been. The tomb is there for any of us if our relationship or marriage is not as happy as it might have been, or if we are deeply disappointed by our children, or by our parents. The tomb should be our destination if we are concerned about the poor; or what we are doing to the earth; Lloyd's of London has recently become environmentalist fearing what global warming, melting icecaps, and rising seas would mean in harbour cities and other lowlands. Whatever fears we may hold, come to the tomb.

Kate Sawford is now 14 years old and has a book of photographs in the bookstores entitled *Kate's Story* (Candlelighter's Childhood Cancer Foundation, 55 Eglinton E. #401, Toronto, Canada M4P IG8, 1995). It is her story of having cancer three years ago, when she had to have part of a leg amputated, and the lower part of her leg rotated and reattached. She writes in her book: "Days of my life I'd like to forget: the day the doctors told me I was sick. The day I had to tell my friends I was ill. The day my hair fell out. The first day after my surgery. They're also the days I'll always remember." She once had only a 50/50 chance of a cure for her cancer. Now she has only a ten per cent chance of cancer returning. Young Kate has been to the tomb.

Kate Sawford has been fortunate in perhaps having been cured. Yet even more important than a cure, Kate has discovered what we all need. We need to be able to go to the place of our deepest fear, our greatest sadness, not to have our sorrows mocked, but to have them addressed. Our need is not for some idle hope, nor some casual word of optimism, "Cheer up, everything will turn out all right." We need what God offers: some divine assurance, some blessed reassurance that what in our fear we thought was the whole picture is not the whole picture. What Kate thought was the end was not the end. What you thought was the end is not the end. However large our vision of reality is, it is not large enough to contain God's truth and power. All our fears, about ourselves or this planet, are never the whole story. God is still in control.

I sometimes think that this Easter story is too big to be played in a stone quarry in Jerusalem. How can we catch the enormity of the event by looking in an empty tomb? It is certainly too big for the big screen and the cardboard characters that Cecil B. DeMille used to give us. It is really a drama of the universe. To see it properly we have to be out at night, away from city lights, scanning the entire heavens, amazed that God created all of this out of nothing, amazed that there is life. Once the screen is large enough, then, only then, come to the empty tomb, and ask the biggest question of our life. Ask, "Is this possible?" You may then be able to tell from the echo of the tomb, what a comparatively small question it is.

Yet keep on listening. Listen. Listen to the voice of the gardener, approaching beside you, whatever fear you may have brought to this place. "Why are you weeping? Whom are you looking for?" he says to us as he said to Mary. We may start to explain, "I am looking for hope, my dream, I am looking for my loved one," we would explain with different voices, the same way Mary of Magdalene started to explain. But Jesus speaks, interrupts, names each of us, the same way he said "Mary." In that moment when God speaks to us, and we know that it is God, when we recognize Christ standing before us, we say with all Christians through the ages and around the world, Jesus is risen. Hallelujah!

There was a man in Northern Ontario I used to know. When his wife was dying, he would drive to the hospital. And each day he would go down to the chapel in the hospital to pray. He would pray, "Dear God, please cure my wife." And finally his wife died. Was his faith shaken by her death? He said, "When I prayed alone in that small chapel, I was seeking God. I knew I was not alone. It was Jesus who was with me, and I knew my wife was in better hands than mine. "

Who can count the times Christ has appeared to each of us, and we have not known? Four travelers were recently at a conference in Chicago. They stayed talking too long and were late in arriving at the local train station. Grabbing their bags from the taxi they ran to the platform. One of them in his haste knocked over a table on which a local boy had some apples for sale. Being late, and not wanting to miss their train they ran on, cleared the gate and arrived at the train before its doors closed. As they were about to board their waiting train, one of them stopped, said farewell to his colleagues, and returned to the station. He was glad he did. When he got back to the table, he discovered that the boy was nine years old and blind. Some of the apples he had been selling were damaged. He helped the boy as best he could and then said to him, "Here's $10 to cover the cost of whatever is damaged." As he walked away, the boy called after him, "Are you Jesus?" (This last story is adapted from William J. Bausch, *Storytelling: Imagination and Faith* [1984], pp 177-8). May his question be ours of each person we meet, and may people ask it of us.

Paul Scott Wilson in 1996 was Professor of Homiletics at Emmanuel College of the University of Toronto.

---

1 PETER 2:2-10

EASTER 5
MAY 5, 1996

Christian Herter was running hard for reelection as governor of Massachusetts and arrived late one day at a barbecue. He'd had no breakfast or lunch, and he was famished. As he moved through the serving line, he held out his plate and received one piece of chicken. The governor said to the server, "Excuse me, do you mind if I get another piece of chicken? I'm very hungry."

The woman serving the chicken replied, "Sorry, I'm supposed to give one piece to each person."

"But I'm starved," pleaded the governor.

Again she replied, "only one to a customer."

Normally a very modest man, Herter decided this was the time to use the weight of his office. "Madam, do you know who I am? I'm the governor of this state."

The server replied, "Sir, do you know who I am? I'm the lady in charge of the chicken. Now move along."

That woman had a healthy self-concept. She knew exactly who she was. She understood the power in her identity.

Addressing the Christians dispersed as exiles throughout Asia Minor, Peter writes to clarify the identity question that they faced as a minority community, "Who are we?" In a continent where the majority claim allegiance to Jesus, the identity crisis of the Christian community is evident in our response to these lifestyle issues:

—30% of all Christians claim that nothing is more important than having fun and being happy.

—40% agree that an individual is free to do anything as long as nobody else is hurt.

—70% admit that they love money and possessions so much that Jesus Christ cannot be said to rule their lives.

The real tragedy of our time is not that the world looks less Christian but that Christians look so much like the world.

So, who are we? Peter's answer is clear: You are a chosen race, a royal priesthood, a holy nation, God's own people

To be God's own people means that God has identified with us. We are children of a loving parent. God's love is like that of a father in the front pew of a crowded church, holding his little boy with an illness that would throw him into seizures without warning. One Sunday morning the entire congregation was disturbed by a particularly violent attack. The father picked the boy up in his strong arms, carried him to the back of the crowded sanctuary where he rocked him, whispering words of love to help his boy through the problem. What most struck the congregants was that the father showed no a trace of embarrassment, only love for his hurting son.

God loves that way. Our problems are often self-imposed moral lapses, but our suffering is as real as that of the boy. God is not embarrassed to call us daughters or sons. God cradles us through those times when we would distract the world around from hearing the message of God's love.

As God's people, we are also a holy nation. We are cut out from the world. In 1 Peter 2:11, Peter goes on to call the church "aliens and strangers." We don't belong to this world.

In the last century an American tourist paid a visit to the renowned Polish rabbi, Hofetz Chaim. He was astonished to see that the rabbi's home was only a simple room filled with books, plus a table and a cot. The tourist asked, "Rabbi, where's your furniture?"

Hofetz Chaim replied, "Where's yours?" The puzzled American asked, "Mine? I'm only a visitor here. I'm only passing through." To which the wise rabbi replied, "So am I."

A holy nation no longer belongs to this world. We don't aim to carry the luggage of the social system. We belong to a new colony, a beachhead, an outpost. We have transferred citizenship and have a whole new loyalty. The values of this world are no longer controlling us.

What does characterize the church? What do we do with this new identity? As believers in Jesus, we are called to be active in the world, changing labels. In the world labels divide, separate, and exclude. In the church we are called to be an open society which though it does not belong to this world, invites the people of this world to belong to us. Christians are "label-changers."

In the Korean war, triage referred to the policy by which medical assistance was given. In one MASH unit, it was up to the doctors to "color-tag" the wounded with green tags indicating the patient would survive without immediate treatment, yellow tags indicating that survival depended on immediate assistance, and red tags which meant that the patient had no chance to survive. With the limited medical supplies, only yellow tags were given help in times of heavy casualties.

Lou came in badly blown apart. The doctor who examined Lou made the decision that his case was hopeless, tagged him as such, and left him to die. A nurse noticed Lou was conscious and stopped to talk. They discovered that both were from Ohio. Getting to know Lou as a person, the nurse just couldn't let him die. She broke all the rules and changed his color tag.

Following treatment, a long trip back to the base hospital, and months of recovery Lou made it. He met a woman in the hospital who later became his wife. Even minus one leg, he led a fully, happy life, all because of one nurse who broke the rules of triage and changed the tag.

As a holy people in this world, the church is called to change tags. We are called to invite those rejected by the powers of this world to join the new colony of God's people.

As people who have received the gift of a new, powerful identity as those claimed by God, we are called to throw open the doors and invite others into God's new people.

Franklyn Jost in 1996 was a PhD. candidate in homiletics and Hebrew Bible from Vanderbilt University, a professor on leave from Tabor College in Hillsboro, KS, and an ordained minister of the Mennonite Brethren Church.

Season of Easter

REVELATION 5:11-14

THIRD SUNDAY IN EASTERTIDE
APRIL 20, 1980

"It's not in the hymnal, but we all know it, let's sing together..." and the song leader invariably announced some hymn I had never heard of and the voices of one of Atlanta's most cosmopolitan churches would join to sing of fountains flowing with blood and the lamb slain for our sins. With the melody came memories of church camps and tent meetings and the words were sung nostalgically but with tongues only halfway in cheek. Never having gone to camp or revivals and not knowing the words, I would stand awkwardly by myself, smiling helplessly until the Wednesday night singing was completed.

I suppose it didn't matter anyway—I don't sing at all well. My singing is a standing joke with the choir. When the public address and radio microphones simultaneously failed, our choir director suggested the uncommon virtues of my voice had been too much even for modern technology. Though I sing terribly, I love to. Some mornings, after my wife and daughter have left for work and school and I am alone, I turn the stereo up to listen to Luciano Pavarotti at full blast while I shower and shave. Mentally, I sing along. And for the rest of the day my mind is filled with that glorious voice, and arias accompany my work. The voice and the words trace so clearly through my mind— but when I open my mouth to sing....

So it's difficult to imagine myself in this heavenly chorale. I suppose the imagery of Revelation should seem strange and foreign to me, a modern man and all, but I find this scene rich and enormously appealing. The symbolism communicates a lushness and exuberance absent from other heavenly visions. But even so, it is hard for me to imagine myself or anyone I know well gathered around the "Lamb standing as though it had been slain" and singing such an utterly new song.

My friend Jim Ingram loathes new songs. Jim was a linebacker in the glory days of Ole Miss football teams and still stands head and shoulders above most of our congregation on Sunday mornings. He's a dedicated Christian and devoted elder but whenever we sing an unfamiliar hymn in worship I dare not look at Jim. He scrunches his face into an overly tolerant smirk to catch my eye and we both wind up chuckling through the song. We would indeed be an awkward, self-conscious pair in the company of those elders so gracefully and spontaneously singing that new song.

But the vision of John is insistent: we'll be there in that heavenly ensemble. Along with myriads of angels and elders and the four living creatures and gosh-knows-who-all-else, we'll be there and we'll lift our voices and belt out a song of praise we can't even imagine yet. All the national anthems, military marches, college alma maters, commercial jingles and any other hymns of praise you can think of will be melted down and forged into something utterly different and completely new— into a new, new song of praise to love that is powerless before it is strong, humble before it is exalted, crucified before it is triumphant, to love that gives itself as a sacrifice for many, love that transforms everything it touches. Our repertoire doesn't include many paeans to weakness, selflessness, humility, suffering, death. We know other tunes to different tempos. However the words might go to a song honoring "the Lamb who was slain," we don't know them. Perhaps the song hasn't been written yet. But it will be. Before history is all over, this song will emerge from God's composing and will astonish us all in its freshness.

A new song, and we'll sing it, every last one of us, "every creature in heaven and on earth and under the earth and in the sea and all therein," because the choir won't be complete until everybody knows the words and each of us is singing with that voice that echoes in our mind, the one we dream we have, the voice that even now prompts us to praise God with whatever it is we have been given.

Patrick J. Willson, in 1980 was Associate Pastor of First Presbyterian Church, Tupelo, Mississippi.

ACTS 13:14, 43-52

FOURTH SUNDAY IN EASTERTIDE
APRIL 27, 1980

A modern "Saint" once said, "There are two mysteries: the mystery of faith and the mystery of doubt!" Here in the Gospel of John both mysteries appear. Some folk believe in Jesus while others do not. Faith and doubt are mysteries, at the center of which is Jesus Christ.

Well, Jesus does provoke faith and doubt! Though nearly twenty centuries have passed since he strode the earth, still he is a controversy. What are we to make of Jesus? Apparently he did do miracles of healing, and according to a few witnesses did rise from the dead. Moreover, stories of his power continue to be told. When Hugh Price Hughs was challenged to debate an athiest, he showed up not armed with arguments but leading a long line of men and women willing to testify that Jesus is Christ had changed their lives. We read the scriptures or hear the stories and face the figure of Christ. Some believe and others doubt. Jesus is still a controversy.

Well, there are always doubters. Like Jews in Jerusalem, there are folk today who hear of Christ's "works" but can't believe. Their doubt is understandable: claims of Christ are not easily credited. Must we actually admit that a hill-billy Jew from a hicktown in Galilee was God in Flesh? "I do not believe that Jesus was God," announced a young Walter Kaufmann to his clergy father, "It's silly!" Well, to be honest, it does sound far-fetched. Jesus proclaimed, "I and the Father are one," but it's tough to accept his say-so in a Jerusalem temple or in the Twentieth Century.

Of course, there are people who *won't* believe: their doubt is not doubt but resistance. Perhaps that's the way it was with the leaders of Jerusalem. If it were true—if Jesus of Nazareth was Messiah—then what would become of their temple, their sacrifices, their legal righteousness, their power? Perhaps with them the issue was not doubt or faith but, "Who's in charge?" For if we insist on holding on to our own lives, our sovereign self-determination, we can't offer house-room to Jesus Christ. Like Dostoyevsky's Grand Inquisitor, we must reject the Christ: "Go, and come no more..." in the name of our religion. For some, Christ hardens opposition. With them, doubt is a last defense. They *will* not believe!

But what of those who do believe? Even in Jerusalem there were people who heard Christ's word and followed him gladly. Perhaps they had been broken by their sins, perhaps they yearned for meaning or freedom or hope, whatever their need, they needed him. Like a young Pakistan student who heard Christ preached for the first time, and exclaimed, "All my life I've longed for a God like that, now I know his name!" Longing and fulfillment meet in Christ, and faith is born. "My sheep know me," said Jesus, and even in our skeptical age it seems true. For some folk, faith is as easy as meeting and following: their trust is instant.

Well, can we claim credit for faith? Hardly. Faith is never reason for pride. Again and again, Christians look back at their journeys into faith and spot the grace of God. "I came around," they may say, and quickly add, "by God's good grace." Faith is always gift. "The father has given!" said Jesus, acknowledging the dear, deep mystery of Grace. In all, both doubt and faith, we bow before the plottings of Grace!

David G. Buttrick, a United Presbyterian minister, in 1980 was Professor of Homiletics at The St. Meinrad School of Theology, St. Meinrad, Indiana.

JOHN 14:15-21

THE SIXTH SUNDAY OF EASTER
MAY 24, 1981

His aide was ill that September evening—springtime in South Africa—so I drove my host Selby Taylor, the Anglican archbishop of Capetown, out into the wine country where the "coloreds" have been living for generations among the vineyards they tend. They are people of mixed blood and, for the most part, the color of strong honey. They have the art of pruning in their fingers, many of them.

It was a colored church, simple and very neat. As I unloaded the trunk of the small car—the case I learned later contained a large staff, in sections and even a mitre—the quiet clergy came out to meet their bishop, who took a moment to stretch his tall frame after the ride. He seemed unusually reflective, almost grave.

The church was full. More than one hundred young people, all dressed in white and sitting at the front, were to be confirmed, and their families banked the church to the doors. The singing had in it the rhythms of Africa and the words of my own forebears, and there was about the service an indifference to time and a great sense that this was a time for which everyone there had waited and which would not come just in this way again. They were savoring each word, each movement of the liturgy.

At the right time, each confirmand approached the archbishop as he sat before the altar. He cupped each small head in his hands—the ancient symbol of the gift of the Spirit—and spoke the familiar words: "Defend, O Lord, your servant with your heavenly grace, that she may continue yours for ever, and daily increase in your Holy Spirit more and more, until she comes to your everlasting kingdom." One by one, as if this were the most important thing that might ever happen to these children.

When all had been confirmed, this tall English gentleman spending a Wednesday evening in a backwash of southwest Africa—with an American low-church minister at his elbow—laid aside his tall hat, took his shepherd's staff, and stood among the newly confirmed who were crowded to the chancel steps. He spoke for about ten minutes, and I have wished many times that I had written down what was said. I remember best *how* he spoke to them, in the tone of someone who sees out of the window a storm approaching, who wishes neither to frighten the people around him nor to hide from them what is coming. The gist of it was: "It will be very hard for you to keep, in South Africa, the promises which you have made to God, to be at all times and in all places a loving person. That is what I call on you, nonetheless, to be, and to do. And I know, and I promise you in the name of Christ, that as you try to be a Christian in a hard land, God will help you." It seemed, for that moment, enough. We drove—it was late by now and very dark—without many words back to his house by Table Mountain.

Or go to Grace Cathedral in San Francisco. I saw a dozen adults baptized at the big font at the church's entrance. There was a procession for the whole congregation, following those white robed initiates on whom the bishop used plenty of water and some oil to boot. We were all called back to the waters of our own baptism, and the Spirit invoked for one and all. The sermon which followed was not so far from—and no less needed—Selby Taylor's words in that other city by another bay: "You will not find it easy to be a Christian in this land, but I can promise you...."

Charles Rice, a minister of the United Church of Christ, in 1981 was professor of homiletics in the Theological School of Drew University, Madison, New Jersey.

ACTS 1:15-26

THE SEVENTH SUNDAY OF EASTER
MAY 23, 1982

This gathering of the nominating committee at First Church Jerusalem doesn't appear, at first, to bear much resemblance to our church meetings. But a closer look may surprise us.

The meeting opens with a sermon. It probably has much the same intent as the opening prayer has at our meetings. Still, it's a weighty start for a business session with only one item on the agenda. We could do it by meeting for a couple of minutes after church while the children wait outside in the car. Of course, we've never had to nominate an apostle, nor do we expect to. It's really not the same thing as replacing a church treasurer or a member of the board of trustees. In spite of the magnitude of the vacancy, though, this meeting in Jerusalem was still a business meeting. If the business of the early church seems to be in a different category from our own it may only be because we hold a different attitude toward church work.

There are more similarities, too. The vacancy was created when a faithful old member fell away from the church. Does that sound familiar? And after the sermon the chairman of the committee describes the qualities that will be needed by anyone chosen to fill the office. The names of two members are then placed in nomination, and the selection made. Someone named Matthias drew the long straw, by the way, and Barsabbas got the short one.

So, if we could transfer our membership across time and distance from this church to that one, we might be surprised by the similarities in church life. Just one thing stands out as being different. The Christians in Jerusalem didn't separate their activities into two categories, one labeled "devotion" and the other "business." The nominating committee meeting proceeded with the same reverence as the Sunday service. And no doubt the weekly worship was a celebration of common life. Sunday morning wouldn't have been a fantasy journey into the realm of the holy.

We could try that, I suppose. We might create rituals to give our church meetings a more sacred atmosphere. And we could write litanies for Sunday worship that allow us to thank God for the parish newsletter, or the accomplishments of last week's board meeting. Those ideas might work, but there is a much simpler way to recapture the integrity of the Jerusalem church. All we need to do is change the following cherished assumption; "We built this church so that people would have a place to come and worship." Where did we get the feeling that the church is a building and that it belongs to us instead of God? Making worship our only holy purpose is part of the problem too. That's what makes other ministries seem mundane. When we encounter God only on Sunday, everything else we do together becomes housekeeping or charity work.

The church we hear about in Acts, though, operates with different assumptions. Something like the following statement might describe it; "God created the church to represent God in the world." Not only does that return the church to its rightful owner, it places our church upkeep and outreach at God's disposal. Church offices need not be mere jobs. We too can elect apostles to minister according to Christ's teachings. And their specific duties will be determined in love by the Holy Spirit.

Daniel Bryan, a minister of the United Methodist Church, in 1982 was pastor of the Charlton Heights-Glen Ferris United Methodist Charge in West Virginia

---

JOHN 21:1-19

THE THIRD SUNDAY OF EASTER
APRIL 17, 1983

When I was seven years old our family billeted two young women who were visiting our city to attend a young people's conference in our church. I still remember their names: June and Frances. June was a beautiful blond; Frances was a shy, loving brunette. Our guests spent two nights with us, and shared breakfast with us on Sunday morning.

During their stay, several adjustments in our household affected me personally. Since June and Frances were sleeping in "the boys' room," my big brother had to sleep on the couch in the living room, and I was relegated to the floor of my sister's bedroom. The bathroom became a hive of activity, especially on Sunday morning when all of us were getting ready for church. Because I didn't require a mirror for shaving or grooming, I washed up over the laundry tubs in the basement. The mood of our home was noticeably lighter too, as the daily concerns of the five Bacons were displaced by a common concern to make our guests' stay as pleasant as possible.

It was Sunday breakfast, however, that I remember best. Breakfast, especially on Sundays, was a routine and rushed affair for our family. More important than the food and the fellowship were our obsessions with getting to church on time, and keeping our dad moving so that he had all things ready for his Sunday School lesson. On this Sunday, though, breakfast was served with elegance and taste, and was something of a feast as we shared the extravagance of a "Variety-Pack" of cereals, bacon and eggs, and mother's fresh-baked bran muffins. And to top it off, all of this was consumed not in the kitchen, but in the dining room on a starched linen tablecloth! I was "some impressed!"

No doubt June and Frances appreciated the "extras" which were bestowed upon them, but they could not have appreciated fully the effect which their presence had had on our household in the way a seven year old boy did. I knew they were special and that something exceptional had transpired. I knew they were special, and knew they were guests; but they were something more—they were royalty. And their royalty evoked the royalty long dormant in our family.

I wept when June said goodbye, and smiled winsomely as Frances walked down our front steps and along the sidewalk. I wept not only because I sensed I would miss them, but even more because of a deep awareness that our family would quickly forget its own royalty, put away its finery, and succumb to the routine of rushed, silent breakfasts, served in the kitchen; we would forget that we were bearers of crowns and coronets and become servants to a "lord" who confined our attention to clock, costs, and kitchen. Cinderella's gilded coach was changing into a pumpkin too quickly.

Easter Day is a time of wonderful stories, of sumptuous breakfasts in the dining room, of radical changes in our expectations and priorities. Too soon, however, we feel compelled to return to the tensions of nine-to-five work days, and instant breakfasts grabbed on the run, and of the immutability of certain "powers that be." But on the successive Sundays of the Season of Easter (i.e., the fifty days after Easter Day) as we gather with our "other" family (dare I suggest it is our true family) to sing and pray and dine with our elder brother Jesus (cf. Romans 8:17), we recall for an instant that we, like Him, are royalty, heirs of God, the true Monarch of all Creation. I think the church leaders knew what they were doing when they gave fifty days to Easter, ten more than the sobering forty days of Lent; they knew it takes longer to grasp the grace of our being "royal" than it does to accept our status as sinners. Through this happy season, we need to remember that we are a royal household, called to extend extravagant amounts of hospitality and service to all children of our Creator God in all places and at all times.

Douglas Bacon, a minister of the United Church of Canada, in 1983 was the senior minister of St. Margaret's United Church, Kingston, Ontario, Canada.

1 PETER 2:2-10; JOHN 14:1-14

THE FIFTH SUNDAY OF EASTER
MAY 20, 1984

In Tidewater, Virginia, they're called F.F.V.'s. In the San Francisco area they're referred to as the Old Settlers. In Hawaii they're known as *kamaainas*. All over the nation we have Descendents of the Mayflower and Daughters of the American Revolution. One of the hottest items in the mail order business (and frequently one of the greatest frauds) is family trees, genealogies, and coats-of-arms.

Everyone is looking for their roots these days, and for most the tracing of family ancestry is an interesting and harmless hobby from which one can gain a better appreciation of history and geography. For others, however, there is a strong need to establish descendency from one of the F.F.V.'s, or the Old Settlers, or the Kamaainas, or whatever is the local equivalent—and there is always a local equivalent. For it seems to be that only by proving their worthy ancestry that some people feel they can claim their own identity and proclaim their own worth. Others want to know another's pedigree before they fully accept them as friends.

There are still not only individuals, but whole pockets of society for whom the crucial question is not, Who are you? but, Who were your parents and grandparents? There are still people whose chief asset, they believe, is a distinguished lineage.

This isn't a new phenomenon. Both St. Luke and St. Matthew were at some pains to trace the human genealogy of our Lord himself. Of course, the two evangelists were out to make two different points and not unexpectedly came up with two different ways of tracing Jesus' descent through the generations. And yet both these authors, whatever their identity might have been, knew that this was a fruitless game when it came to our Lord's ancestry—he who was conceived by the Holy Spirit, who was the Son of God himself. Jesus had no grandfather.

In his final conversation with his disciples, Jesus makes it quite clear that it isn't their human fathers that matter for their salvation—it's their heavenly Father. This is the meaning of the mansion with many rooms—their home in the kingdom—provided by the Father, made ready by the son. They can look forward to a great homecoming!

If Jesus is the Son of God—and he surely is—and that is the same God that is our Father—and he surely is—then Jesus is our brother, and we are brothers and sisters of one another. The heavenly relationship that matters is our relationship to our Father; the earthly relationship that matters is with our siblings—not with our human ancestors.

The author of this morning's reading from the Epistles says that once we were no people—we had no common heritage. Now, by the grace of God, we are Christ's people—chosen and formed into His people, His family.

Our baptism is both the sign and the seal of this relationship. In it, we are made a part of his body, share in his resurrection, and quite suddenly find ourselves in a sibling relationship with some of the strangest people—some of—whom don't even know who their human parents were, many who don't know who their grandparents or great-grandparents were, and countless numbers who really don't care. But if you want to know who your brothers and sisters are…look into the next pew, and the next block, and the next county, and places with strange, exotic names that we never expect to see.

The Rev'd Alice Babin and the Rev'd David Babin are Episcopal priests, married to one another, and in 1994 were sharing the position of Rector of Christ Church, Kealakekua, Hawaii.

I JOHN 3:1-8

THE FOURTH SUNDAY OF EASTER
APRIL 28, 1985

It could have happened to any one of us on this campus at this time of year, only it happened to happen to me. I got so overwhelmed with all the work that has to be done, all that needs to be accomplished before classes end and reading period begins, end of the year evaluations, programs completed, student recommendations, liturgical preparations, infirmary visitation, students fall through the doors down at McCosh at this time of the year, I got so overwhelmed with all the work that has to be done that I almost missed spring busting out all over the place, the great clouds of lilacs bordering Stockton Street, the dogwood coming into their own, Prospect Garden. I almost missed it until one spring night last week I was walking across the campus and the air was an exquisite fragrance, deep, pure, fine. I slowed my pace down, took a deep breath of spring air in and thought to myself—how long am I to be part of all that is creation.

> See what love the Father has given us, that we should be called the children of God, and so we are.

They were friends, fishing companions ever since they were old enough to hold a rod and bait a hook, summer in and summer out, and though one was raised in Cleveland and one in Pittsburgh, and one went to Dickinson and one to Dartmouth, through the years they remained closest of friends, were best men at each other's weddings, and came to love each other's kids. By some quirk of fate they shared the same birthdays and always got together for what they dubbed the National Holiday. They laughed at each other's bad jokes, and worried with each other when the steel business was bad; they lied to each other about golf handicaps and always they fished. So it's not surprising that when one lost a first-born son from a grim cancer, it was only the arrival of the other, his companion's appearance at the back door, that let him know he could survive.

> See what love the Father has given us that we should be called the children of God, and so we are.

In a little coastal stretch between Kegaska and Blanc Sablon, in Quebec, a sparsely inhabited two hundred mile strand, lived native Canadians, strong, independent and trusting, who for generations had lived intimately with land and sea. Virtually untouched by the 20th century until this last decade, the villagers wondered how they could ever relate to the world that was beginning to invade their stretch of coast, with Coca Cola and Twinkies, with lures for the children and with television and also with a fearful drain on their economy. Until they began meeting as a community and formed the Cooperative Canneries, so the fishing and canning could provide the people with a product to be exported, a product widely sought by those further south.

See what love the Father has bestowed upon us, that we should be called children of God, and so we are.

Sue Anne Steffey Morrow, a minister in the United Methodist Church, in 1985 was Assistant Dean of the Chapel, Princeton University, Princeton, New Jersey.

REVELATION 7:9-17

THE FOURTH SUNDAY OF EASTER
APRIL 20, 1986

There is power in being able to name and use names. In the story of Creation, in the first chapter of Genesis, God calls the world into being by naming it. Let there be Light, Sky, Dry Land…. The power to create and the power to name were one. The animals were led to Adam to name. In naming the animals Adam orders his universe. Creation is the naming of chaos, the defining of the empty space, the establishment of limits on the great Void. Naming is an act of creation.

When we meet new people we are invariably tempted to play the "do-you-know" game. We each trade names back and forth trying to reorder our individual universe that has been disturbed by the entrance of a new creature. Like Adam we name the creatures. If we can name and use names we have control. Order is established.

"How long will you keep us in suspense? Can we call you by the name Messiah?" Those gathered in the portico of Solomon sought to order their universe, to know, to control their destiny, "Tell us plainly, does the name Messiah apply to you?"

Those gathered in the portico are not alone in their desire. Moses asks God, "What shall I say when they ask 'What is his name?'" Jacob wrestles with the angel for a name. The crowds ask John the Baptist whether his name is Messiah, or Elijah, or the prophet. Even Jesus' closest disciples wonder who he is.

In Jesus we see the revelation of God's name and identity so we may know who and what it is that has a claim on our lives. The claim of love's endurance, of purifying truth, of suffering righteousness, of terrifying justice becomes intertwined with our name, our lives. Being Christian or carrying the name of God does not become an insurance policy, far from it. God in Christ took on our hunger, our thirst, our scorched lives, our tears, our death. To live as one whom God knows and names is not a life without death but a life filled with the promise of the resurrection—that death will be transformed, that God will wipe away tears, that no one will snatch us from God's hand.

We learn what it is to be called by our name gradually. At first we just turn our heads but gradually we assume greater responsibilities and live with its claim. To be called a person of God, a disciple of Christ is not different. At first we are not sure we have heard it correctly among the hosts of competing sounds and noises but in time our discernment grows and our willingness to live by the claims of the name is nurtured.

As a good shepherd knows the sheep and can call them by name, so God knows us, has named us, has claimed us as God's own. Whether we live or whether we die we are the Lord's. Our name is known.

There is a lovely passage in Faulkner's, *The Sound and the Fury*, where Dilsey is talking with Caddy, an older woman, about why Benjy changed his name.

> "His name's Benjy now," Caddy said.
> "How come it is," Dilsey said. "He ain't wore out the name he was born with yet, is he?"
> "Benjamin came out of the Bible," Caddy said. "It's a better name for him than Maury was."
> "How come it is," Dilsey said.
> "Mother says it is," Caddy said.
> "Huh," Dilsey said. "Name ain't going to help him. Hurt him, neither. Folks don't have no luck changing names. My name been Dilsey since fore I could remember and it be Dilsey when they's long forgot me."
> "How will they know it's Dilsey, when it's long forgot, Dilsey?" Caddy said.
> "It'll be in the Book, honey," Dilsey said. "Writ out."
> "Can you read it?," Caddy said.
> "Won't have to," Dilsey said. "They'll read it for me. All I got to do is say Ise Here."
>
> (Vintage Books. 1954.)

Jesus is God's promise that our name is known. The Good Shepherd knows who we are. God's claim to our life overpowers all competing claims. They are but shallow graves. In times of tribulation and despair, of doubt and destruction, of suffering and death, we can remember who it is that knows us. We have been claimed, our name will be called, and all we got to do is say, "Ise here."

Richard Edens, a minister of the United Church of Christ, in 1986 was co-pastor with his wife, Jill, of United Church of Chapel Hill in Chapel Hill, North Carolina.

PSALM 23

THE FOURTH SUNDAY OF EASTER
APRIL 24, 1988

It was my very first day as a student chaplain at Roosevelt Hospital, a huge sprawl of a city hospital in the section of New York's called Hell's Kitchen. We had been introduced to our supervisor, who then introduced us to various administrators. We had a guided tour of the hospital, though I was certain I could never find my way back to the cafeteria, the chaplain's office or even to the closest visitor's bed room. I was twenty-two years old, wet behind the ears, a first year seminarian, when I was told by our supervisor that I was assigned to the female surgery ward and to the Intensive Care Unit and "Oh yes, by the way, there was a patient in intensive care who has asked to see a chaplain. The nurse has just left a message, why don't you start there?" "There?" I thought to myself, "Where was there?" "Where was this patient of all the seven hundred and fifty plus patients of this hospital." I struck out, somehow got myself back to the ICU, took a deep breath, went through the door and introduced myself to the nurse at the desk, who led me to the bed of what looked like an ancient mariner. I've forgotten his name but not his face, unshaven, frail in some sense from all he had suffered, but deep strong eyes. He had had a heart attack and his lungs were failing. So he had a tracheotomy. He was attached in a manner that with every heartbeat of his there was a beep beep beep. Oh, I'm not certain I have all these details true to memory, but I do remember his long, thin fingers, writing out shakily, "Please," on his little hospital pad, "please say the twenty-third psalm ."

"The Lord is my shepherd, I shall not want, He maketh me to lie down in green pastures, He leadeth me beside the still waters, He restoreth my soul. He leadeth me in the paths of righteousness for His name's sake. Yea, though I walk through the valley of the shadow of death I will fear no evil. For thou art with me; thy rod and thy staff they comfort me. Thou preparest a table before me in the presence of my enemies, thou anointest my head with oil, my cup overflows. Surely goodness and mercy shall follow me, all the days of my life, and I will dwell in the house of the Lord forever." We both needed to hear the psalm. We both, the ancient mariner who lay dying, and I, wet behind the ears and shaking in my shoes at his bedside, both needed to feel the power of the psalm, its familiar verses that calm us, its promise of God's care that enfolds us. We both needed to hear the psalm for very different reasons, and at the end of the psalm we were one in our need, and in some manner that is much a mystery, one in our trust that we were dwellers in God's house.

And how about for you…can you recall times when in dark hours our shadowy valleys the words of the psalmist have surfaced from some deep recesses to help get you through…?

Sue Anne Steffey Morrow, a minister in the United Methodist Church, in 1988 was Assistant Dean of the Chapel, Princeton University, Princeton, NJ.

JOHN 17:11b-19

THE SEVENTH SUNDAY OF EASTER
MAY 15, 1988

The bombing of civilians gathered for the 1987 Remembrance Day service in the town of Enniskillen, Northern Ireland, has colored my reading of today's lessons. Though violent death is not new to this island this act seemed particularly barbaric, striking as it did children and old-age pensioners. The IRA claimed responsibility for the bomb, but the group's announcement that it "regretted" what had happened gave no comfort. Student Nurse Marie Wilson was trapped in the rubble with her father, Gordon. After she asked him if he was all right she clutched his hand and said her last words, "Daddy, I love you very much." She died later that day in hospital. Gordon Wilson, grieved for his 20 year old daughter, and yet he testified that he felt no ill-will; he would pray for the people who planted the bomb. In the midst of a situation that usually results in sectarian reprisals, Gordon Wilson's spirit of grace and Christian hope defused the community's anger. Truly, this is what it means to be in the world but not belonging to it.

Until Jesus Christ comes again we will continue to live in a world of "regrettable" circumstances. People will continue to go their own way, making betrayal and hate and death all too common experiences. But through it all we are promised the presence of Jesus Christ, whose work continues through those who know Him. Our circle of support will be broken, but not abandoned. This is not something we just believe, it is something we can know from personal experience and, more reliably when we're in the depth of night, through God's Word.

A witness to this truth is the lifestory of an 83-year-old Irish gentleman, Dick Bryan. A survivor of the Irish Civil War, Mr. Bryan quietly tells inquirers what it was like living in the Republic with houses being burned, pedestrians shot, and the constant uncertainty of what would happen next. "Our ministers told us to get out now if we weren't going to help to make the new Republic work. I remember my parents committing us to the Lord in prayer, and then getting up and going back to the fields." Mr. Bryan lived to see peace come to the Republic, and he credits "those who walked daily with Jesus" for being God's instruments of change.

If we are fortunate, we will not personally witness the terrors of war, either of "freedom fighters" guerrilla tactics or of declared battle. But there will be "fighting without and fear within," as the old hymn goes. Whatever our lot may be, we can experience the assurance of God's presence and guidance. For the promise of God's work continuing does not rely on our faithfulness but on God's. Just when we'd rather hide, God gives us the ability not only to stand firm for righteousness' sake but also to continue the daily walk.

A few years ago my husband and I were in a situation that we were sure God had called us to. The work and the environment were harsh but the knowledge of being in mission would carry us through, or so we thought. We threw ourselves in the work while also suffering the culture shock and guilt feelings that come with working in the Third-World from a First-World background. Many important things were getting done, there were fruits of ministry readily seen, and yet I was unhappy. In the middle of one night I started to pray, feeling totally unworthy of this call, knowing I was not the willing missionary of my dreams. In that desperate moment God's peace and assurance came to me, not in words but in a calm that came from nowhere. It was then I realized that we are promised joy, not constant happiness. Morning came, with all the problems still there, but I knew then that the work of Jesus Christ would continue even through me, even me.

Cheryl Jane Walter, a minister of the United Methodist Church, in 1988 worked through the Board of Global Ministries as co-pastor, with her husband David Range, on the West Cork Circuit of the Methodist Church in Ireland.

JOHN 21:1-19

THE THIRD SUNDAY OF EASTER
APRIL 9, 1989

I would like to know how to get from where Simon Peter was the night he denied Jesus three times to where he finds himself in today's Gospel reading, restored to fellowship with Jesus and given a job to do. I would like to know how to move from those moments when I feel I have made an absolute mess of things, relationships, tasks, parenthood, to a time when I could feel strong and purposeful, forgiven and accepted and responsible for my own life. Are there any clues in our scripture story as to how this could happen for you and for me?

First clue: Where was Simon Peter when Jesus appeared? He and the others with him had returned to the place and work where they had been when Jesus first came along. They did not remove themselves from the secular world in order to experience the Risen Christ, in order to be commissioned to be his messengers. Their new beginning was right back in the fishing boats. Ours may be right where we struggle to live day by day and deal with our relationships in the best way we can. Certainly running away from them is not the answer. When the disciples ran away during those dread dark hours before Jesus' death, they were utterly alone, scattered, isolated. Now, they are together, back in their world of work, in the most mundane of situations, and it is there that the Christ appears.

Second clue: Jesus appeared to the disciples when they were in community. John mentions that at least seven of the twelve were fishing together. Even in our spiritually down times we need to remain in fellowship with our fellow Christians. A woman who was going through a difficult time with an alcoholic husband found a sense of help knowing that the church, its minister and people were there to listen if she needed to talk. In fact from her front window she could look out when she was feeling low and from there she could see her church across the river and she knew she was not alone.

There is something to be said for placing ourselves in the midst of the Christian community even when we don't expect anything to happen. The role of the church in Paul's conversion (Ananias, *et. al.*) is not to be doubted. The Risen Christ appeared to the disciples when two or more were gathered in one place, a room, a boat, at a meal. Here he appears cooking breakfast on the beach. My Lord, what a morning!

Third clue: In this story the future collides with the past. The disciples try to go back to the past, thinking there that they may discover the meaning of all that has happened. In fact, there is a real sense that Jesus is coming into their lives now from the future. He knows what lies ahead for Peter, that he will face martyrdom; he helps them catch so many fish that they symbolize the universal proclamation of the gospel. Our faith is in one who holds not only the past but the future in his hands. We are too often bound by the past, we think of communion with Jesus as a remembrance, a memorial meal only. It is also breakfast on the beach, it is the heavenly banquet invading the present time, invading our mundane existence, experienced in ordinary bread and wine.

J. Allan McIntosh, a minister of the United Church of Canada, in 1989 was minister of Sydney River United Protestant Church, Sydney, Nova Scotia.

JOHN 15:1-8

EASTER 5
MAY 1, 1994

There are many people who when hearing this Bible story about God the vinedresser who uses pruning shears to discipline and cleanse and keep things in order, hear nothing else. It seems there is too much evidence in life that proves the experience of God's blade is all-powerful.

Many have said similar things:
—When the car was towed away during an extra long Church meeting.
—Another, deep in grief, said it when a young man of 26, full of promise, was struck down with Hodgkin's Disease.
—Another spoke it about the nightly news when we see places in the world where war and corruption and severe drought seem to conspire to destroy entire tribes and nations.

How can we trust God's loving when there is so much evidence of God's judgment? We experience life's pain and suffering as punishment. It doesn't take much before we conclude that our own sins or those of others are more than we or God can bear. It seems only reasonable that our failures and short-comings cause the branch of our family or Church or community life to be unproductive. The strong and beautiful and powerful and rich seem like they are the vinedresser's favored branches. They are the ones who have kept their jobs during the recession, who have wonderful homes and successful children and thriving businesses.

Could it be that we stopped listening to the Gospel too soon? Jesus was giving a larger picture of the love that God, our heavenly Gardener has for us, and it was too hard to hear. Jesus is the vine. Jesus is the one who provides our strength and nourishment and connectedness to life. The Gardener has depended on the vine to feed and care for the branches that includes all of creation and those who dwell in her. That true vine lived and produced fruit, but as all who are gardeners and farmers know, vines need to be pruned back in order to be even more productive. God brings forth the fruit. God is bringing forth rich harvest from us, even when we may feel cast off.

Sydney Carter captured it in his wonderful hymn "Lord of the Dance." Christ, the Lord of the Dance, claims: "They cut me down and I leap up high: I am the life that'll never, never die; I'll live in you if you'll live in me...." Christ's death on the cross was an ending of his earthly relationships, but a beginning of something vastly more powerful and meaningful for human existence. God's love is more powerful than human pain and suffering. God is in the midst of our life to nourish and sustain our life and to bring forth new vision and understanding even in the midst of death.

Where is this new life? In relationships with God and with others. In community with those who abide in Christ, the community of those who know that all love comes from God, that our loving of one another and of ourselves is the source of real life and being truly human.

In Margaret Craven's novel *I Heard the Owl Call My Name*, a young vicar is sent by his Bishop to serve the Anglican Church of the Kwakwatl tribe on British Columbia's Pacific Coast. He does not know that he is dying. But he learns from his people how to love well, how to give himself to the beauty and power of the created order of trees and water, and birds and fish and how to trust the rhythms of life and death that are in God's merciful care. When he hears the owl call his name, the sign that death is coming, he knows of God's abiding presence and gives himself in love to the community.

Sometimes the experiences of the vinedresser's pruning shears can take over your life and affect every relationship and dominate your attitude to choices and risk and daily routines. It can be present for a season or for a lifetime. It happened for me over a period of time to the point of exhaustion and it was clear a rest was needed. A change. During this time I began to visit weekly a community of faith that lives in the Christie Gardens Nursing home in Toronto. Most of the community are well over 75 years old, many travel using their wheelchairs. A number spend their entire days, weeks, months, like a "wandering tribe" through the halls. However varied and productive and exciting their life experience, now a majority speak or shout only in fragments that seem not to relate to who they have been as sons and daughters, husbands and wives, parents and grandparents, leaders in Church and business and community. Often they do not seem to make any sense. This community of faith gathers for worship twice a week, every week. And it was there I heard through the fragments with a clarity that moved me to the core of my being, the familiar old hymn as they joined in singing every line and every verse ... "Jesus loves me, this I know; For the Bible tells me so."

I heard then beyond the experience of the vinedresser's blade. The love of Jesus Christ connects us with God and with one another in a relationship so profound and important that it alone helps us to understand all of life's experiences.

Deanna L. Wilson is an ordained minister and in 1994 was serving St. Stephen's-on-the-Hill United Church in Mississauga, Ontario.

ACTS 9:1-6 (7-20); JOHN 21:1-19

EASTER 3
APRIL 30, 1995

Don't you think that after three years of tough ministry, the pain of the cross and the darkness of the tomb the Risen Jesus would take some time off? Maybe hole up in some heavenly hideaway, kick back on his throne and take it easy for awhile?

But, no. No sooner is Jesus raised from the dead than he's hard at it, bringing the hope of Easter right into the middle of people's lives. Look at him working in our Gospel text. Jesus has already appeared to the disciples several times in Jerusalem, John tells us. But now they're back home and what are they doing? Spreading the good news? Getting the word of Easter out? No, they have gone fishing! Didn't they drop their nets a long time ago to follow Jesus? Why are they fishing now? Maybe, they are scared by the road ahead of them. For three years they have just watched Jesus do his thing and now it's time to do their thing and it's probably scaring them to death. Because it's the unknown and sometimes when you're scared by the unknown you fall back on something you know and they know fishing.

So, Peter says, "I'm going fishing" and all the rest say, "Yeah, and we're going with you." But they catch nothing—they come up empty. Sometimes no matter how hard you try and how much you know you still come up empty.

But Jesus comes again to them, meets them right where they work. They didn't even see him arrive (often we don't see him either when he comes to us in the midst of our busyness). He calls out to the disciples, "Children, you have no fish, have you?" "You are empty aren't you?"

And to their credit, they don't lie. They make no excuses. They just say, "No, we haven't caught a fish." And then he tells them, "Cast your net to the right of the boat." They do and they get so many fish they couldn't haul 'em all in. When they were coming up empty, Jesus met them where they were and gives them an abundant catch.

And maybe it wasn't just about fish, maybe Jesus was letting them know that on the hard road ahead, that he was going to be there, and that no matter how things fell apart, how empty "their catch," that he would see them through. Well, the disciples finally did get going. They started spreading the good news and were baptizing people by the thousands. So then, do you think Jesus would finally take some time off? No, the Risen Jesus keeps on working.

He even works with those who are out to do in his church like this guy named Saul in our first lesson who breathes threats of murder against the Lord's disciples. Saul is dangerous and what makes him dangerous is this: He *knows* he's absolutely right and he knows that his will is God's will. And so, in his self-righteous zeal, he is out to do God's will by destroying the church of Jesus Christ, no matter who suffers, no matter who dies. He is blind to the possibility that he might be wrong, to the possibility that his will may NOT be God's will. This Saul does not fall to his knees to pray, "Lord, not my will, but thy will be done." No, if Saul is going to fall to his knees, he's going to have to be driven to his knees. And the Risen Lord does exactly that. He goes to meet Saul as he's on his way to do his self-righteous business and knocks him down with a blinding light. And why? To punish him? To rub him out? No, the Risen Jesus comes to this self-righteous, murderous, threat-breathing fanatic—believe it or not—to give him a new beginning, a new start. He blinds him only to help him see like he's never seen before:

to see who Jesus really is,

to see what God's will really is.

And you don't need me to tell you "the rest of the story." This Saul is given a new start, a new vision and becomes the Apostle Paul proclaiming the Gospel from Damascus to Rome.

So, then, that Jesus has Saul (a.k.a. Paul) straightened out you think he would take a break? No, he did not, has not and will not take a break until kingdom come, until the promise of Easter arrives in all its fullness, until the day when there are no more empty catches, or murderous threats, or cancer, or AIDS, or betrayal, or bullets, or violence, or death the day when the lion finally lies down with the lamb, and when all God's children get along as brothers and sisters.

And until that day this Risen hard-working Lord will not rest no matter how hard and bloody the work. And he's been hard at it lately.

(When I first preached a version of this sermon it was the time of the L.A. riots and I talked of Christ's willingness to be in the midst of the violence to do two things: bear the violence in his wounds and to, even in the midst of hopelessness, work for a new beginning. I also stressed how Jesus would stick it out long past the time CNN moved on to another story. Unfortunately, at the time of your reading there will no doubt be current examples of horror in which the Risen Christ is nevertheless present.)

Yes, busy and hard work for him, but not too busy in whatever examples we find and all kinds of other places to be hard at it with us as well. (Here I name some places in our local community life where Jesus is hard at work.) He is hard at work where we work and where we live. Some of us are coming up empty at work, at home, with struggles in our hearts, and with our faith. And in the midst of our emptiness, he comes to fill us with his abundant promise and to give us a new start.

And sometimes he comes to knock us off our feet. When he does it is not to make us crawl, but help us walk with a new vision and real freedom.

Yes, a busy Lord, still hard at it with all his brothers and sisters, including you, including me.

But now, he takes time out from his busy schedule to invite us to breakfast, his Holy Breakfast where he offers the abundant gift of himself. Come and be filled.

Larry Henning in 1995 was the Pastor of Messiah Lutheran Church in Twin Lakes, Wisconsin.

Ascension Day

ACTS 1:1-11

ASCENSION DAY
MAY 20, 1982

I once saw a small boy try to fly a kite on a windless day. He stood on a long grassy stretch, laying out the tail, adjusting the bow of the cross pieces, and seeing that the guide string had the right amount of slack. Then he bolted over the ground as fast as he could. The brilliant red kite climbed and climbed. The boy got to the end of the grass and stopped, and the kite fluttered to the ground. The boy wound his string around a stick and returned to study the kite. Again he checked the tail, the cross pieces, and the guide string. He hefted the kite in his hand, decided it was too heavy, and made the tail half as long. Once more he took off across the field and the kite began to soar. But as soon as he stopped it fluttered back to earth. Still not discouraged, he went through the same examination as before, this time increasing the bow in the cross pieces. He was bound and determined to get that kite up, and he obviously was an expert at how to adjust the thing for better flight. Yet again he poised himself on the edge of the grass, then charged across the field at full speed. The kite lifted higher than before and when he stopped it seemed for a second to lift higher! Then it made a papery jiggling sound and swished to the ground. Another boy who had been watching called out, "You've got to wait for the wind."

"I know, I know," said the child winding up his string. But I could see in his face that there was great disappointment because he had to wait and because all of his skill could not compel the kite to stay in the sky.

"You've got to wait for the wind"—those are hard words for a child and hard words for us adults too. They were hard words for the disciples and for the early church. Jesus "charged them not to depart from Jerusalem, but to wait for the promise of the Father, which, he said, 'You heard from me, for John baptized with water, but before many days you shall be baptized with the Holy Spirit.'"

But when they came together, the very first question they asked Jesus was, "Lord, will you at this time restore the kingdom to Israel?" They wanted to get on with it. And the early church for whom Luke wrote his ~~gospel~~ *these words* did not want to wait any longer either. They had been expecting the return of Jesus for more than half a century, and still he had not come.

Today, Ascension Day, we recall the frustration of the disciples and the first century church, waiting and longing and yearning for the kingdom of God. Most of us know something of that same frustration in our hearts. Like the first disciples, we have given ourselves to Jesus Christ, and what has followed has been the same mixture of defeat and triumph that they knew. We keep wondering when the pieces of life will come together in some whole and enduring pattern. ~~We look at the world about us and we know the truth of Yeats' famous lines, written earlier in this century:~~

Things fall apart; the center cannot hold;
Mere anarchy is loosed upon the world,

The blood-dimmed tide is loosed, and everywhere The ceremony of innocence is drowned;
The best lack all conviction, while the worst
Are full of passionate intensity.
("The Second Coming," *A Pocket Book of Modern Verse*, ed. Oscar Williams, NY: Washington Sq., 1962, p. 184.)

Wearied by the chaos of the world, Yeats reflects, "Surely some revelation is at hand; Surely the Second Coming is at hand."

Listen now to what Luke told the early church when they felt the same anguished yearning in their hearts: "It is not for you to know the times or seasons which the Father has fixed by his own authority." How hard those words must have seemed to a church that for more than half a century had expected Christ to return any day. How hard they sound to us who still look for some instant salvation from the turmoils of soul and state that plague our daily life. How tempted we are by every movement that promises the kingdom—be it a quick fix for the economy or a self-help program that will heal our deepest wounds.

If it is not for us to know the day of the kingdom's coming, then where does that leave us? Luke leaves us with the belief that Christ reigns, and Christ will send the Holy Spirit to us so that we can live as we must live here and now. We can no more conjure up the Spirit than the child could force the wind to blow his kite. But if we wait, the Spirit will come.

Thomas H. Troeger, ordained by the United Presbyterian Church in the U.S.A., in 1982 was Associate Professor of Preaching at Colgate Rochester Divinity School/Bexley Hall/Crozer Theological Seminary in Rochester, New York.

EPHESIANS 1:15-23

ASCENSION DAY
MAY 28, 1987

The Ephesians epistle makes me feel small. Much like those times when I put my foot in the ocean, swim fifteen yards from shore in six feet of water, and say "I've been in the ocean—what power!" Obviously, I have been in the ocean only in a manner of speaking. I know only its faint edges, its fringe energies, the barest display of its depth and force. The Ephesian author is praying and he asks that we shall be given "a spirit of wisdom and of revelation in the knowledge of him, having the eyes of our hearts enlightened." He knows the smallness that I am (and feel) in the ocean we call "theology, the knowledge of God." I have been through Church School, confirmation, college, and even seminary. I have spent years of concerted, disciplined, pressurized seeking after the knowledge of God. And now this ancient letter writer asks God to involve me in life-long continuing education! That makes me feel small. But it does not make me feel ashamed. The writer's prayer is not a sign of my poverty. It is rather a sign of God's wealth. No matter who we are, we have touched only the faint edges of the finally unfathomable "Father of glory." Greater discovery always lies ahead. God and God's work are never less than we know. Our "inheritance in the saints" is more glorious than we ever imagine.

The Ephesian epistle makes me feel carried forward. Much like a "drift dive" in Bahamian waters, where one slips over the boat's side into the fast-moving Gulf Stream and is picked up several miles down current. An exhilarating ride, marked by effortless speed and sheer inevitability, in which one is propelled toward a destination with both ease and finality. The magnificent vision of the epistle writer causes word to tumble upon word. It is a vision of the flow of all things created toward an ultimate unity in Christ. He sees the risen and exalted Lord as the integrating power of the universe and he claims that all things are even now being gathered toward that center. So often the Christ we proclaim is a pre-ascended Christ. We are good at talking about Jesus as master, rabbi, companion, friend. We are not very good, however, at talking about Jesus as the cosmic and universal sovereign. Our author is coaxing us out into the drift, past the point of our attained knowledge, into the full flow. The cosmic function of our ascended Lord may well stagger our imaginations. All things are destined to become a part of the Christ and made tributary to his fullness.

The Ephesian epistle makes me feel supported by unbelievable power. Much like the ocean, whether one swims at its edges or drifts at its center. The ocean water, whose power can be awesomely fearful, is put at our disposal. Simply put, we float. That which can reconstruct whole beaches, wear away rock and hurl ships at will, gently surrounds us, cradles us in its strength and urges us toward our destination. The ancient letter writer sees a strength compared to which ocean strength looks weak. Here his words pour forth faster than ever and there do not seem to be enough words in the Greek vocabulary to express all that he wants to say. "The immeasurable greatness of his power," "the working of his great might." It is this "immeasurable power," our author claims, which is at work in the Church. It supports, cradles, maintains and carries forward. Here the writer coaxes us even farther beyond the limits of our practical knowledge. We have many definitions of the Church and most of them are inadequate for the vision set in front of us. The Church is nothing less than the first stage in the gathering of a divided humanity into one. It exists as a sign that all the world is God's property and that God upholds God's claim upon all. It is through the Church that God's purpose is being worked out.

Our letter-writing theologian has been teaching us while on his knees in prayer. This is the right posture for us who celebrate this great Festival of Christ's Church.

Richard L. Thulin, a minister of the Lutheran Church in America, in 1987 was Ulrich Professor of the Art of Preaching, Lutheran Theological Seminary, Gettysburg, PA.

EPHESIANS 1:15-23

ASCENSION DAY
MAY 28, 1992

My youngest child, Christopher, aged 8, knew exactly what he wanted for his last birthday. He wanted his room painted all black. By this he meant all walls and the ceiling! When I heard it I was appalled. So too was my older son David. My wife, Louisa, perhaps did not fully encompass what this all meant for us (the sane ones). She said that we should pursue Christopher's wish. Friends in upstate New York, old enough to return to second childhood, when told of Christopher's birthday wish, agreed. They even told us how they transformed their basement into a cave bedroom for their two kids many years ago.

We eventually arrived at a compromise. Christopher's room was to be painted with a light shade of blue walls and a matt-finished black ceiling.

Christopher then directed the decoration of the room. Luminous stars were to be purchased and stuck on the walls and ceiling. Some were to be put on the ceiling fan. Our friends in upstate New York sent a luminous planet. We purchased a wall chart of the universe for one of the walls.

When all of this was done, we gathered in Christopher's small room one night. The door was closed behind us. He switched off the light. The room was miraculously transformed. It was like being in the universe itself, amongst the stars and planets.

Christopher was thrilled. No one wanted to leave. Even David said he wanted to spend the night in Christopher's room! Louisa my wife tried hard not to say, 'I told you so.'

Christopher loved sleeping high upon his bunk bed, amidst the little universe in his room. Above everything, with the illusion of being so high, he found a sense of tranquility and security.

The letter to the Ephesians has something of the idea of the church being exalted with Christ in the heavens. All divisions and all barriers are broken down by the effective reconciling work of Christ, through His death on the cross. Christ, who is raised high, raises all peoples into newness of life. All peoples are one divine society. Christ, being lifted up, draws ALL unto Him. Before the cross there is only level ground. Child-like tranquility and security is guaranteed by the knowledge that Christ died, is risen and transcendence. Exaltation belongs to God alone.

Those who misunderstand Psalm 47:3, without regard for Ephesians 1:22, do a disservice to the good news of justice before peace. History demonstrates this. Independence Wars, civil wars, world wars and freedom wars today are specific examples. Recent movies like *The Mission, Romero, Cry Freedom* clearly depict exaltation of power (i.e. being seated in the heavens) for the twisted *'adult' purposes of sovereignty, authority, power and dominion*. The violence and atrocities that have been and continue to be unleashed, is too ghastly to contemplate.

Repentance is the answer for us as individuals. Repentance is the answer for us corporately. This can be costly. In the situation of Southern Africa, this repentance means giving back the stolen cow (or whatever else has been stolen). Repentance does not mean that the thieves now sit with owners to share the milk of the stolen cow. When all is set right, righteousness will kiss peace and peace will be the outcome of justice. This is the way of Christ, the One who made the costly sacrifice by dying on the cross.

Praised be to God who raised Jesus from the dead! The same God, through the effective reconciling work of Jesus' death, makes available to us the Church, the Body of Christ, the same power of reconciliation. The eyes of our mind are enlightened. We can see the hope that his call holds for us, what riches he has promised that saints will inherit and how infinitely great is the power exercised for us believers.

In this power Sovereignty, Authority, Power, and Domination gives in to servanthood in love. In this power the church are the ambassadors for reconciliation through repentance. In this power the church hastens the Coming of the Lord by fulfilling the divine command of mission. In this power Christ will fill **ALL.**

Errol L. Narain in 1992 was Rector of Trinity Episcopal Church in Chicago, Illinois.

ACTS 1:1-11

ASCENSION DAY
MAY 12, 1994

They gathered in the Temple to worship their God. If we could understand their language their words would not sound strange in our ears. We know their hymn book quite well. "Clap your hands all peoples! Shout to God with loud songs of joy! God is a great king over all the earth; God subdued peoples under us. God reigns over all the earth. Even the princes of the peoples will gather to honor our God."

You can look it up. It's selection number 47 in their hymn book, psalm 47 in our Bibles. And you can find the same ideas in our hymn books too.

In fact, the big problem is that it all sounds so ordinary that we miss how strange this whole business is. If there had been a foreigner present to hear them sing the foreigner would know right away how very peculiar this hymn really was.

You would think that this hymn was sung by people riding high, by people who could claim with justification, "This is the greatest country on earth, maybe even the world's only superpower!" But no, that's not the way it is at all! The people had been conquered many times; their land was reduced from the size of a good-sized modern county; they were politically, militarily and economically insignificant. To call them second-rate would be a compliment.

In their world, depending on the year, Persia mattered or Babylon mattered or Egypt mattered... but not the Jews. And if anybody's god was in control it was not the God of the Jews. All this looked like willful delusion and the worst kind of national hysteria.

But the Israelites knew themselves and how weak they were. They knew how very hard it would be to prove to a hard-headed, bottom line, observer that their God reigned. But still they sang and still they shouted. They trusted that what they could not see was true, that their God who showed a special care for the weak and the down-trodden was, despite all appearances, really in charge. As they sang they created for themselves a new world of hope. And perhaps they even began to live in that world. They trusted in the sovereign rule of a God they could not see.

At some point after Easter the appearances stopped. People didn't see Jesus anymore. This would be easy to explain for the hard-headed bottom line observer. Jesus had, after all been crucified. If the appearances had stopped it was because these crazy followers of Jesus had come to their senses. It wasn't too difficult to say where Jesus was; he was peacefully rotting somewhere in a criminal's unmarked grave. In the meantime it was not too hard to see who was in charge—Caesar, and his governor, Pontius Pilate, and of course some wealthy collaborators in the Jerusalem establishment.

But those followers kept insisting that their master was not dead; he was risen. Challenged to say where he was, they would claim that he had ascended to the right hand of God, the seat of all authority. God had put all things under him and he ruled, over all. They had made up for themselves an alternative world in which Christ ruled not Caesar. In the meantime they would try their best to live as if, as if this were reality. They would obey Christ's word rather than Caesar's command. They trusted in the sovereign rule of a Lord they could not see.

They were crazy, of course, those Jews, those early Christians. It just doesn't do to create for ourselves alternative realities. It's pretty close to mental illness. But today we need a little craziness, to believe that a crucified carpenter rabbi sits at God's right hand and bears the rule over our much more complicated universe. To believe that ultimate authority is not in the hands of Clinton or the corporations but of Christ, that's what it is to be a Christian—to trust in the sovereign rule of a Lord we still can't see. It's crazy. But then, we haven't heard much lately from the Caesars, or the Babylonians, or the Persians. Keep trusting.

Stephen Farris, a minister of the Presbyterian Church in Canada, in 1994 was Professor of Preaching and Worship at Knox College, the Toronto School of Theology.

Pentecost

ACTS 2:1-21

PENTECOST
MAY 25, 1980

In a small town near a South American border, there once lived a little boy by the name of Angelo. One day he crossed the border and came back with a wheelbarrow full of sand; and when the customs inspector asked what he was smuggling in the sand, Angelo quickly replied, "Nothing." So all the sand was poured out and sifted through before he was permitted to go on.

The next day the same thing happened, and so on through the third day and the fourth day and virtually every other day besides—and each time, the sand had to be poured out and Angelo interrogated before he could move on. "I know you think that someday we'll be careless, Angelo," said the inspector, "and that's when you'll smuggle something across. So as long as you bring sand across, we're gonna make you put it through a screen."

The process took place for five years, each day Angelo appearing with his wheelbarrow and each day the customs people pouring it out, sifting through it, and then permitting him to go on—until one day, it came to an abrupt halt. Soon after Angelo began to shown signs of prospering; and then he purchased a big home in the little community and opened a thriving business. One day, years later, the inspector who had retired met Angelo on the street. And so he asked him how in the world he had become so prosperous when he had spent so much of his time hauling sand across the border and never once was anything in it.

Angelo smiled and then said to the inspector, "My friend, during those five year, when you were paying so much attention to the sand, I smuggled 1,593 wheelbarrows into this country!"

The little story is surely apocryphal, but in a humorous way it makes a point that lies at the heart of the Pentecost experience: namely, we grow so accustomed to thinking of God in a certain way and to looking for God in a certain form that often we're completely caught off guard as to who God really is and where God can actually be found. The disciples who gathered in the room on that first Pentecost had no idea that God would come upon them in the way he did. They had their preconceptions, their ways of relating to God that were very familiar and patterned, and undoubtedly they were shocked beyond words when the strange Spirit began to come in such an ominous way. But The God of Pentecost is the God of Christmas and the God of Easter—that is, the one who appears unexpectedly and who at first is not recognized for who he is. "Behold, I am doing a new thing," he said through the prophet Isaiah and again through John on Patmos, and in effect that's what he was saying and doing on that first Pentecost as well.

In his book, *The Wounded Healer*, Henri Nouwen suggests that the community of faith shouldn't seek to eliminate pain, but to deepen it to a level where it can be shared by all. What a curious thought! God is in the pains of life as well as the pleasures, in strange and ominous experiences as well as familiar and customary ones, in events and occurrences where we never expected to find him at all as well as in where we have found him again and again. The God of Pentecost speaks all the "languages" of the human heart, and the miracle of Pentecost is that each person hears God in his or her own tongue—however disparate this "tongue" might be from the many different "tongues" of others.

Norman Neaves, a minister of the United Methodist Church, in 1980 was senior minister of Church of the Servant, Oklahoma City, Oklahoma.

ACTS 2:1-21

PENTECOST
MAY 22, 1983

Perhaps the birthday of the church would be better celebrated with balloons and presents and cake and candles and ice cream and games and streamers and banners. Surely we should not be sitting like this, as on a bus with everyone's eyes to the front and so little contact between us. That first Pentecost must have been different. Truly inspirational. I suppose if we acted like that they would think we were drunk, too. Too much wine for communion, they'd say. After all, who ever heard of a party in church? Who ever heard of having a good time at church?

Everyone knows church is not supposed to be a party. We are supposed to sit quietly and attentively, and be serious. Sing a few songs left over from 100 years ago, say a prayer, hear the scriptures, give our offerings, listen to a sermon. Who can make a party out of that? Certainly, no one could accuse us of being drunk so early in the morning!

Things had been quiet for the disciples and other believers for the weeks following Easter. The dreams and visions of the followers of Jesus had just about faded after the initial enthusiasm, and Easter was beginning to seem like a cruel joke, an idea whose time had not come. Where was Jesus, now that we really need him? He said he'd return. He promised us an Advocate, a Comforter, a Counselor. Then the new age would dawn; the promise would be fulfilled. But each dawn brought another day just about like the last one. No more dreams and visions for them. The crucifixion had made realists of them all.

And then it happened. On the Day of Pentecost. How appropriate! Pentecost, the celebration of the giving of the Torah, the birthday of the Torah which began the old Israel; the day of the celebration of the harvest of first fruits and the offerings of thanksgiving to God! Maybe it was just a neat bit of editing on Luke's part to place the birthday of the church, the new Israel, alongside the birthday of the old. But there it is. The Holy Spirit comes to the community of faith in the rush of a mighty wind and in tongues of fire with such power that others around are drawn into the community. And they, too, receive the Holy Spirit by participating in the covenant community.

But there are always those crass cynics who toss off the good news, who refuse to participate, who say, "they're drunk," or, "they must be crazy," or, "who needs it anyway?" To them Peter recalls the words of the prophet Joel to remind them of the possibilities for life that had been spoken of a long time ago. And now the dreams and visions are coming true. The Spirit is being poured out upon us in new and exciting ways.

We all had dreams and visions once upon a time. Remember when you used to dream about how it was going to be when you would finally be a teenager, when you finally got your driver's license, when you graduated from high school, when you would be 21, when you got married, had kids, retired? What will it be like when...? What would it be like if...?

As a runner, one such dream keeps me going sometimes now. Every run is a marathon. I've won the olympics 15 times, and Boston 25 or 30 times. Maybe that's a fantasy rather than a dream, but it has sustained me on those particularly cold days when the wind was blowing and I was tired to begin with.

And I've had dreams and visions for the church, but with a difference. Those dreams and visions are possible, perhaps inevitable, because they do not depend on the strength of my legs, or on me at all, but they are born out of the promise and purpose of God. And, if I'm lucky, I can participate in it.

Martin Luther King had a dream that described and defined the direction of his life. And the movement toward the dream helped to make it a reality. I—we—have a dream of a church alive and moving and growing, not for its own sake, but in commitment and love and faith and stewardship, and excitement. Of a church making a difference in our community and our conference and maybe even in the world. Of a church alive and well, serving the people of the community, and being witnesses, because we have been there from the beginning.

The Church has a dream expressed in the early prayers of the Church, when it said "Thy kingdom come, O Lord," and when it proclaimed, "Amen! Come Lord Jesus."

Terry Immel in 1983 was a minister of the Christian Church (Disciples of Christ) serving Community Christian Church in Marana, Arizona.

GENESIS 11:1-9; ACTS 2:1-21

PENTECOST
JUNE 4, 1995

One of the hardest things to cope with is not being able to communicate. And there are so many ways to suffer communication breakdown—all of them frustrating:
—I have laryngitis.
—Your ears are plugged.
—We are too far apart to hear each other.

—We are well within hearing range, but everybody else is making a racket.

—I am deaf, and you don't know sign language.

—Your native tongue is a Mayan Indian dialect, and I have never bothered lear anything but the English I grew up with.

—I am being perfectly clear, but you just aren't listening.

—You are trying to say something important, and I just don't get it.

It is mighty frustrating when we can't communicate. Frightening too. It is a lonely feeling to stand all by yourself in the circle of your own language. What do we do when the circles of our languages don't intersect? Try again; try harder—getting progressively more desperate with each succeeding failure. Desperation sometimes drives us over the edge:

—"Who needs this? I'll just talk to myself!"

—"I'm going to drag you inside this circle, if it kills us both!"

If we do manage to make connection, the sense of relief is so great, we may just hunker down in the space where our circles overlap. Why go outside anymore? Everyone inside understands each other. What do the other folks know, anyway?

Today we have heard a story about people who went to monumental lengths to keep from having to break outside language circles in which they had finally managed to get cozy. It's hard to blame them. What they intended was very impressive, and made good sense. But God came down, so the story goes, and busted up the circle. Why did God have to go and do that?

Perhaps it was mercy, not meanness. The more time we spend talking only to ourselves, the less time we have for talking with others. Sights and sounds that are new and strange become inconsequential; irritating, threatening—positively evil—so it seems. That is a great pity, because what is new and strange can also be fascinating, energy-generating, community-creating, life-giving. At least, that's the way God saw it.

"Spread your circles wide," God commanded the earth's inhabitants when the world was young. "The circumference of your language needs to stretch. It will not shatter if you hit the boundaries of circles in which others stand. Your language games don't have to be less fun, just because the games that other folks play follow different rules."

But the people were far too serious, insecure, and self-absorbed. "Our game will be the only game," they said. "Since other circles are threatening, we will ignore them, declare them useless, destroy them if we must."

"Not on your life," God responded, and promptly put right next to their ears the very strange languages they refused to go out and listen to. "You will be much better off engaging lots of languages," God said. "Trust me on this. Or live with the chaos until you learn to trust each other."

Well, they didn't trust God. And they didn't trust each other. We are their children; and we are still having trouble.

God has, however, given us mercy upon mercy. Not by going back on the original game plan of many dancing, sparking circles; but by coming into the center of all the mass confusion. In the flesh, through Jesus Christ. In the Spirit through the release of many tongues that, somehow, can talk to each other without shouting each other down; or shutting down, because they cannot get a hearing.

We heard another story today—of wind, and fire, and strange prophecies fulfilled—where young men, old men, daughters and sons, women and even slaves speak God's Word. Competition and chaos dissolve into celebration and communion—everyone dancing and singing the grace of God. People partly understanding each other, and partly not. But, wonder of wonders, they are patient with what they can't follow. Eager to hear things about God and the world that they never imagined. And humble enough to recognize, in the languages they just can't make sense of, that God is much bigger by far than the largest circles their own language can draw. And you know what? That doesn't seem to threaten them! In fact, everyone is relaxed, even though the party gets wilder by the minute! After all, the Spirit is in the middle of things; and promises to stay there for good.

God's Pentecost project is far from finished. You and I are in the thick of it. It's still scary when you're in it up close. So here is another story to help us make the best of it—because frightening and frustrating though the language circle game often is, God thinks it's well worth playing.

David Schlafer in 1995 was Interim Director of Studies at the College of Preachers in Washington, D.C., and also teaches preaching at Virginia Theological Seminary.

Trinity Sunday

MATTHEW 28:16-20

TRINITY SUNDAY
MAY 21, 1978

The Apostles' Creed begins, "I believe in God...." The Nicene Creed begins, "I believe in one God...." The United Church of Canada affirms, "We believe in God...." And, Article I in The United Methodist church is "Of Faith in the Holy Trinity"—"There is but one living and true God, everlasting...in unity of this Godhead there are three persons...The Father, The Son, and The Holy Ghost." Those are the words used traditionally to refer to our triune God Father, Son, and Holy Spirit. I want to look at three other words used to refer to the Trinity: Creator, Redeemer, and Counselor.

God is Creator. Next to the view of God as Father, the belief in God as Creator is more deeply implanted than any other. The "Paley argument" makes real sense to me. (Simply put: If you find a watch, there must be a watchmaker.) In 1954, Albert Einstein said, "I cannot believe that God plays dice with the cosmos."

Popular magazines now have articles about biology's most recent discoveries, telling us that God the Creator is not playing dice, that there truly is plan and order in creation, particularly in the most celebrated chemical of our time, DNA deoxyribonucleic acid— "The master choreographer of the living cell and carrier of the genetic code." The intricacy and complexity of creation is seen in genes, cells and DNA.

A gene is the basic unit of heredity, a bit of bio-chemical information which tells the cell what to do. A human cell, one of them, has some 100,000 different genes linked into strands. These long strands of DNA are intertwined in the core of living cells. DNA is so narrow and tightly coiled that all the genes in a human body would fit into a box the size of an ice cube. Yet if all this DNA were unwound and joined together, the string could stretch from the earth to the sun and back 400 times!

But, long before we knew about genes, cells, and DNA, the Hebrew writers were telling us, "In the beginning God created...." The Psalmist was exclaiming, "Who am I that thou are mindful of me and who are we that thou dost care for us?" God is Creator.

God is Redeemer. "God in Christ as Redeemer" means it is the Christ who renews our broken relationship with God, who renews our own sense of worth, and who renews our awareness of the Holy in our neighbor. James Stewart puts it in these words, "I cannot do without Thee, I cannot stand alone: I have no strength nor goodness nor wisdom of my own. But Thou, beloved Savior, art all in all to me, and perfect strength in weakness is theirs who lean on thee." St. Augustine wrote, "I have read in Plato and Cicero sayings that are very wise and very beautiful; but I never read in either of them 'Come unto me all you who labor and are heavy-laden.' " God is Redeemer.

God is Counselor. Jesus said to his disciples, "It is for your own good that I am going, because unless I go, the Counselor will not come to you..."

Henri Nouwen, in *The Living Reminder,* writes, "The great mystery of the divine revelation is that God entered into intimacy with us not only by Christ's coming, but also by his leaving. This idea becomes clear in the lives of people like Dietrich Bonhoeffer who experiences Christ's presence in the midst of his absence. Bonhoeffer writes: 'The God who is with us is the God who forsakes us (Mark 15:34).... Before God and with God we live without God.' "

I do not understand the Trinity, how there are three persons in one. I know some of the analogies given: The Trinity is like water, which is one element but has three forms - frozen, liquid, and vapor. Or, the Trinity is like a person, who as a woman may be mother, wife, and daughter. I know of the analogies. I still do not understand. Intellectually, the Doctrine of the Trinity is perplexing. Philosophically, it is mysterious. Experientially, it seems, is the way to know.

It may be that Kolya's word in Dostoevsky's *The Brothers Karamazov* is right—"Oh, I've nothing against God.... I admit that he is needed...for the order of the universe and all that.... And if there were no God, he would have to be invented." Has God been invented? Can the creature create the Creator, the child, the parent? Can the axe vaunt itself against the handle or the clay against the potter?

I do not understand the Trinity. But, if I wait to understand every experience in life before I enjoy or am blessed by its benefits, then I may never fly in an airplane, never use electricity, never take an aspirin, never enjoy a rainbow or sunset, never experience the love of my wife or my children. All these, and much more in life, I do not understand. I simply believe, accept, and am blessed by them. Thus, I believe, accept, and am blessed by "the grace of our Lord Jesus Christ and the love of God and the fellowship of the Holy Spirit."

Robert T. Young, a minister in the United Methodist Church, Duke University, Durham, N.C.

JOHN 3:1-16

TRINITY SUNDAY
JUNE 1, 1980

When asked to draw God, children often scrawl a saintly Santa Claus without the red trim or the reindeer. A long white beard accompanies a long white robe. But the Trinity causes more problems. What to do with Jesus? Shall he be a babe in a cradle, or that tall, dark handsome bearded one we see on the wall in every Sunday School class. And then there is the Holy Ghost. Well, a ghost is a ghost. Something like Casper with more dignity, maybe. The people in the Middle Ages made attempts, too. A thirteenth century miniature symbolizing the Trinity and the heavenly choir caught my eye recently. Here a heavenly choir surrounds Christ holding a dove and sitting on the lap of God the Father—yes, an old man with a beard.

How simple, we say, and how simplistic. Surely God is more complicated than that in this threeness. We are more sophisticated, more aware of the theological distinctions. After all, we've been Christians for a while. Every week we sing "Glory be to the Father, and to the Son, and to the Holy Ghost, as it was in the beginning and is now and ever shall be, world without end, Amen." How could we sing it with such vigor without understanding its meaning? We say the Apostles' Creed ("I believe in God the Father almighty, etc." Yes, I know it by heart.) Or sometimes the Nicene Creed. Yes, we believe in the Holy Spirit, Lord and Giver of life, who proceedeth from the Father and the Son. We listen to the leader of worship close with, "The grace of our Lord Jesus Christ, the love of God, and the fellowship of the Holy Spirit be with us all." We know all about the Trinity, don't we?

Maybe not. Maybe we don't know so much. The fact is it's still a mystery to us. With all our technology, we're still fascinated by its complexity, and secretly yearn to be unitarians. With a knowledge explosion that puts other centuries in the shade, we still stare at the stars and wonder and marvel at God's coming to us. We feed the problem into the computer, but every time 1+1+1 comes out three. More than that, we thought we had all the answers, but our lives remain unfulfilled. Something's still missing at home, at work. We look for more than intellectual stimulation, more than a theological lesson.

So we come like Nicodemus—proud, smart. We come to church searching, gleeful secularists outside, but underneath, a shambles. We come asking the wrong questions, expecting Jesus to be only a teacher when he comes as a savior. We come curious but surprised by the depth of the encounter. To understand God and what he's doing in his three-ness, you need rebirth, says Jesus. Back to the maternity ward? Not quite, but almost. It comes with the Spirit. It comes with being open to God's action in your life, and once you make that turn to new life that only comes with the Spirit, you can hear afresh, "For God so loved the world...." "Therefore, since we are justified by faith...." Then we begin to understand what it is to "have peace with God through our Lord Jesus Christ," to see how God's love has been poured into our hearts through the Holy Spirit.

So understanding the Trinity comes with experiencing God in God's fullness. It's almost unexplainable, certainly illogical by standards of worldly wisdom, but our faith rests not "in the wisdom of people, but in the power of God." As Jesus says in verse 12, "If I have told you earthly things and you do not believe, how can you believe if I tell you heavenly things?" So 1+1+1 = 1. It may be bad math, but it's good theology. "Praise, praise the Father, praise the Son, and praise the Spirit, three in one!"

William J. Carl III, a minister of the United Presbyterian Church USA, in 1980 was assistant professor of homiletics, Union Theological Seminary in Virginia.

ROMANS 8:12-17

TRINITY SUNDAY
MAY 26, 1991

The action, or movement of God is always threepronged, close, yet distant. The action is three-pronged as God confronts, engages and causes participation. God is uncanny, alien, not at home with us, yet assertive in our sphere. A dark invader shedding light, a wild lion, a fierce wind storm, a descending dove or a voice from the clouds. God speaks of purification, passion and the chasing after truth, seeking and saving our generation who, that same God has already decided and told us will turn a deaf ear to us, until God's disaster gets their attention, or our own passionate suffering.

The people touched by the wind/breath of this roaring lion of heaven cry out to God freely, joyfully, as to a warm and loving, close parent. They leap at the opportunity to love a hated person, to bear with a burdensome, difficult person, to counsel a tangled, frightened, hostile person, like lion cubs!

Martin Luther realized how foolish it would be for him to try making up something to call the Word of God. He found it difficult enough to try repeating what the Bible attests is the Word of God! On the day of judgment, God will ask Luther if he preached the Word, and ask the generation of Luther if they heard it. He guessed that they would say they had not because they took it to be the word of a poor, simple pastor! Luther said that we have a fear of falling, a case of vertigo, which can be solved by putting on a blindfold, or hood and submitting to being led over high bridges, and up on high towers. Jesus is our blindfold and our guide! Have no fear. Calvin wrote that the Baptism of the Holy Spirit is more necessary for salvation than that of water. Luther speculated that if he were God and knew about the world as much as God knows, he would submit it to hell fire and be done with it. But from the Word of God Luther had to learn that God does not do that, but does the opposite: God loves the world so much....

We are tempted by our earth-bound determinisms to do the wrong thing. Our genetic codes, our sociological ways, and our cultural/racial situation tempt us to erect barriers of legalities, moralities, and seriously rational hatred. It feels so good to stand on one of our barricades and hate the other side! There is a troubling side to human nature that is so afraid and anxious, that loves to hate, kill and destroy others!

God loves, frees and gives life to us by confronting us, by giving us experiences of warm, tender loving and caring, and by participating with us in suffering like ours. The people of Isaiah's generation had no time for it. They were too busy in a furtive quest for wealth, power and self-sufficiency, for international exploitations, all of which finally backfired and destroyed them in the disaster seen so clearly by Isaiah, Amos and Hosea.

The people of John's time had no time for it, either. They were afraid and anxious, sordid and hard, rigid to the point of self-destruction. The earthy, warm love of God made no sense to them. Paul's Romans resisted his invitation to become free, loving and joyful as children, finally mature enough to leap out to others in love of God.

The Great Britain of Kipling's time in India, oppressed and suppressed others in the name of a cold Christ and a tangled, confusing Trinity! Is religion really any different in 1991?

One could speak of the struggles for civil rights, peace instead of war, equal rights for all oppressed majorities (women!) and minorities, but would anyone have time for it? We could speak of our refusal to elect leaders willing to focus on domestic disasters, but would anyone have time for it?

Perhaps the task of this sermon is to communicate something about the deity behind the storm, the ultimate lion, the blowing wind to whom the preacher may only point unable to speak, and to point to the suffering savior/judge with his great, eternal love. The Trinity is, after all a great mystery before whom we all face a terrible dilemma: the closer to this God we come, the more alien to our time we become; the more at home in our time we become, the more alien from God we are. Anselm, of course, put it another way: the closer to God I think I am, the further away from God I really am, and the further away from God I think I am, the closer to God I really am. Since God even has to invade as an alien the space we dedicate to God, and to overcome fear by love, and anxiety by faith and hardness by hope, perhaps in our sermons on these texts, maybe we should have one of the youth dress up like an outer-space alien and have a surprise entrance after the lessons, and carry on a dialogue sermon?!

The final focus has to be on the practical relevance of the Trinity, and the chain of love manifested by the Triune God (Jeungel does a fine job of this in his book). The personal nature of this experience is a key to transforming our generation, providing that experience is radical and earth-shaking enough. Of course, "This revelation of the secret, this apprehension of God in suffering, is God's action in us" (Barth, *Romans*, p. 301).

Ralph Clingan, a Ph.D. candidate at Drew University taught preaching and worship at The Interdenominational Theological Center, Atlanta (1980-88) and in 1991 was a minister in Paterson, N. J.

Sundays after Pentecost/ Ordinary Time

MATTHEW 6:25-33

THANKSGIVING DAY
NOVEMBER 24, 1977

Undue anxiety is wrong because it underestimates God's power to provide. The birds of the air and the lilies of the field witness to their Father's care. Their life support system is in their Maker rather than themselves. God knows our needs.

Undue anxiety is wrong because it is fruitless. By no amount of worry can we add a cubit to our span of life. Our years are circumscribed by God. Freedom operates within the perimeters of destiny. It is irony of a high order that those who seek to save their life will lose it; while those who are willing to lose their life for the sake of Christ and the gospel will find it!

Undue anxiety is wrong because it blunts our witness. For "the Gentiles seek all these things." Those "outside" are burdened with excessive concern for the preservation of the self. Those "inside" are to show the others a more excellent way. One fears that much evangelism is ineffective these days because those who belong to the church and those who do not frequently want the same "things." The only discernible difference in many cases is that those who profess faith in Christ sprinkle their cupidity with prayer. Where there is no difference there is no market!

Undue anxiety is wrong because something else is better—single-minded pursuit of the Kingdom of God and God's righteousness. We seek God's kingdom first or not at all. The expulsive power of a new loyalty is what is offered here. Worry is not weeded out but crowded out! Temporal necessities fall into place when God becomes the soul's predominant desire.

All of God's commands are for our good, even the command to seek the Kingdom first. That God has a plan for this world, that this plan is shown to us in Jesus Christ, that this plan is invincible—these form the cause of our thanksgiving.

Ernest T. Campbell, United Church of Christ, in 1977 was teaching and preaching at-large out of New York City.

GENESIS 18:1-10a

THE THIRD SUNDAY AFTER PENTECOST
JUNE 4, 1978

Funny how time passes when you're waiting for something important. After the something comes, the waiting seems unimportant. But before the something arrives, time is like a slow drip from the faucet, using its long moments to fill, to drop, and to fill again.

Time passed slowly for the old one, his head nodding aimlessly in the noonday heat which seemed to seep up in eerie waves from the burning earth. Only the shade of his tent provided any relief from the simmer. Beads of sweat formed on his forehead, on the back of his neck, and around and under his gray beard. His skin like parchment, thin, yet weathered, dark, and furrowed was scarred from much work and much waiting. Occasionally, the flies would swirl away from the cow dung, buzz his ears, and disappear. Behind him, his wife, equally old, gave in to the afternoon heat and slept; her mouth open and breathing heavily with an occasional rasp.

Be alert, old man. Awake, old woman. For in a moment, in the twinkling of an eye...dinner guests. Three, in fact. And salvation will draw close. Close. Not yet, but soon. A son. As promised before. In the spring. Covenant—come quickly—come as you are—come if you can. Come on! Bake the bread, spread the cloth, put out the best napkins, pour a drink. God's messenger stands before you. Be alert, old man. Awake, old woman.

The old man, Abraham, of course, the bearer of the covenant of land and children had never come so close to seeing the dream realized. He had done too much to make it happen, to force it to happen, perhaps delaying it all the more. And on this lazy afternoon when the sun bent its fury, God lent God's mercy. All the moments of doubt, of worry, of wondering, of taking Hagar to force a son, a bearer of the promise, became history—forgiven and redeemed. For soon, not yet, but soon—a son.

Living in the hope of the not-yet realized promise was the story of Abraham's life. Of Abraham's life, and of ours too. For we live in a time of in-between. Of talents and willing hands idled by unemployment. Of human potential stifled by discrimination, and poverty, and limited education. Of peace broken by crime, and war, and violent acts.

We are waiting, too, for better times, and retirement, and true love, and children, and a raise, and truth in advertising, and a cure for cancer, and even, even the coming of One whose kingdom is not yet in sight, a kingdom of lambs and wolves lying together, a kingdom in which there are no tears and no pain anymore.

We have ached for such. We have worked for such. God forbid! We have even killed for such, with wars to make the world safe, with SALT talks and peace treaties, with electric chairs, and antiseptic test tube babies. We have tried to bring your kingdom with whatever crosses we could construct, with whatever Hagars we could prostitute. And yet, your kingdom has not come.

Here we sit. Waiting for some sign of promise, of renewal, of hope, of beginning again. Your way this time? Some of us have given up. We are too old now, or too young. We are too broken. Too tired. And too involved in today to remember tomorrow.

And yet, the promise. Not now, but soon.

Behold! God's messenger stands before you. Be alert, old Man! Awake, old Woman!

Jon M. Walton, a minister of the United Presbyterian Church, in 1978 was associate pastor of the First Presbyterian Church of New Canaan, Connecticut.

MATTHEW 16:13-20

THE FOURTEENTH SUNDAY AFTER PENTECOST
AUGUST 20, 1978

"On the file folders in its biographical morgue, *The Washington Post* identifies famous people with a single vocational notation ('home run king,' 'motion picture star'). One of these...is marked 'Jesus Christ (martyr)'." [1]

How do you classify him?

Jesus, for some reason, indulged himself in that human question, "What do people think of me?" or "Who do [people] say that I am?" (Mark 8:24).[2]

Like most friends the apostles do not tell him immediately what *they* think. Rather, they repeat the rumors, what the grapevine says. One version had it that he was John the Baptizer. Others, with more insight, thought he might be Elijah or Jeremiah. Interesting guesses all: John the Baptist, fiery-tongued denouncer of spiritual complacency and self-righteousness; Elijah, fierce critic of false worship; Jeremiah, the most Christ-like figure in the Old Testament.

Now, however, Jesus turns away from the "they" question to the "you" question. He asks Peter, "who do *you* say that I am?"

Fosdick helpfully suggests the process through which the young church grew in its certitude about the identity of its leader as Lord: "At first they may have said, God sent him. After a while that sounded too cold, as though God were a bow and Jesus the arrow. That would not do. God did more than send him. So...they went on to say, God is with him. That went deeper. Yet, as their experience with him progressed, it was not adequate. God was more than with him. So at last we catch the reverent accents of a new conviction. God came in him." [3]

W. Russell Hindmarsh, professor of atomic physics, has written of his responses to studying the thought of Einstein. He says that the sheer power of the mind of Einstein, and the depth of his understanding, was simply overwhelming. It produced the same effect as one's first sight of England's Durham Cathedral or as hearing again Beethoven's Ninth Symphony. To this observation he added, "It is something to belong to the same race of beings as Einstein."

Think what it means to belong to the same race of beings as Jesus Christ.

Professor Merrill Abbey has pointed out the delightful ambiguity in the phrase "conceived by the Holy Spirit."[4] Conceived can mean "to become pregnant with." But it can also mean "to think or to form an idea." So Jesus was God's idea. I am not suggesting that this way of putting it is equitable with what the early church meant when it said that Christ was "conceived by the Holy Spirit." I am suggesting that this way of putting it is consistent with their way.

The entire New Testament agrees that Jesus is the Christ, the Anointed One, the Messiah, the Long-Awaited One. Peter's words to Jesus, "Thou art the Christ" (Mt. 16:16 KJV) are a shorthand summary of the very heart of the primitive Christian faith. Whatever else the New Testament writers disagreed about, however variously they phrased it, on this issue they were solidly united. Jesus, the executed rabbi, is the Christ. [5]

The Hebrew word for *salvation* means "to free," "to break the bonds," "to give room." Christ has taken "captivity captive" (Ephesians 4:8 KJV). *Jesus Christ, my savior, has led the greatest prison break in history and has invited me and you and every one to follow him over the wall.* The important thing is not the cell he broke us out of but the world he sends us into.

It was Ireanaeus, in the second century, who spoke of Christ as the prediction. He is the prediction of the freedom and the brightness and the hope that can be yours and mine. "Beloved, it does not yet appear what we shall be, but we know that...we shall be like him" (I John 3:2).

[1] Martin E. Marty in a book review in *Saturday Review*, Sept. 16, 1967, page 46.
[2] Here and following I have adapted some material appearing in my *Seven Questions Jesus Asked*, p. 58ff.
[3] *Living Under Tension* (New York: Harper, 1941), p. 156.
[4] *The Shape of the Gospel* (Nashville: Abingdon Press, 1970), p. 26.
[5] In this and the following two paragraphs I have adapted some material appearing in my *Are You the Christ? And Other Questions Asked About Jesus*, (Nashville: Abingdon Press, 1978), p. 64, 71.

R. Benjamin Garrison in 1992 was Senior Minister of St. Paul United Methodist Church, Lincoln, Nebraska.

MARK 8:27-38

THE SEVENTEENTH SUNDAY AFTER PENTECOST
SEPTEMBER 30, 1979

One of my priorities when I visited Jerusalem was to walk where Jesus walked when he was a cross carrier. I walked that narrow street, the Via Dolorosa, and tried to imagine as I pressed through the crowd and avoided the hawkers in front of the shops what carrying a cross in that first crowd would have been like.

But the walk was interrupted by a visit to the Church of the Flagellation. Under this present day church is the ancient guard room where Jesus is supposed to have been flogged. A stairway leads from that pavement to a souvenir shop in the church above. I walked the way that Jesus walked and came away with a souvenir cross.

This experience has remained a kind of parable for me. It offers a disturbing contrast to the words in Mark's Gospel (v. 8:34). Here Jesus says: "If any man would come after me, let him deny himself and take up his cross and follow me." How he turned over the tables of conventional values and standards of success! This is evident in his shunning the title of "Messiah." He was more comfortable with a title more representative of life's realities, "Son of Man," or as the Hebrew suggests, "The Man," one acquainted with grief and suffering. "The Man" was not sent into the world to market souvenir crosses, but a way of life stained with persecution, rejection, and suffering. Nonetheless, it is the only way of life that lasts.

That's where "the Man" meets us today. But what a disturbing meeting it is, for we are inclined to be Christian creatures of comfort, attracted by easy-payment discipleship. We hear more eagerly the popular Christian advertising which tells us that life is to be enjoyed without cost. Jesus is telling us that it costs to follow him. "Deny yourself and take up your cross and follow me."

But there is something undeniably personal in that word. Jesus doesn't say: "Take up an armful of crosses." He says: "Your particular cross." Cross-carrying requires us to be discerning. What concern, or issue, or person needs to be supported in the face of popular opinion, or, worse yet, public apathy? As it was for Jesus, every cross we make ours is wrapped in the element of risk.

Cross-carrying isn't a matter of shouting the name of Jesus in safe places. It is a matter of shouldering a cross in tight places. I remember years ago an A.A. member taking an alcoholic into his home in order to give him support, and how his neighbors raged. The neighborhood would be in jeopardy with a "drunk" in that house. Quietly a young Christian neighbor stood beside him and risked rejection. A cross was being carried!

I think of a church that offers weekly dialogue on controversial issues—homosexuality, racism, right-to-life, abortion, gun control, business ethics—risking ridicule from community and it's own members. A cross is being carried!

Carrying the cross costs, whether it is as a personal follower of Christ or as a community of believers. When we wonder about what this cross-carrying means, Edward Sim's words are worth reading. Sims points out that Jesus, "promises only what a latter day realist promised: blood, sweat, and tears. No quick victory, no easy conquest, no instant paradise. Instead: Leave self behind...take you your cross...let yourself be lost for my sake. He will usher in a new era. Oh yes, but not an era of easy irresponsibility, of careless, effortless nirvana; he promises no rose garden at least none without the tilling, the planting, the feeding, the pruning" (*A Season With the Savior*, New York, The Seabury Press, 1978).

If we can believe our Lord, cross carrying is the only way to go; all else eventually ends in death and meaninglessness. "The Man" sets us free to choose. And we will choose. We do choose all the time!

Dr. Robert Drew Simpson in 1979 was minister of the United Methodist Church,
Chatham, New Jersey.

LUKE 10:1-12, 17-20

THE SEVENTH SUNDAY AFTER PENTECOST
JULY 13, 1980

There are formal similarities between the commissioning of the Seventy and what the church calls evangelism. Whenever Christians are looking for a handy rationale for their evangelism they often turn to the words of Luke 10:2: "The harvest is plentiful, but the laborers are few; pray therefore the Lord of the harvest to send out laborers into his harvest." Truthfully, this commission has left me cold, frustrated and with feelings of inadequacy. It sounds more like an impersonal edict than a dialogue of Christ, and it is not out of place at church conventions and world evangelism congresses where it is often read in triumphalist tones, as though Jesus wanted to make us winners rather than witnesses. But how is it in the local parish where with a few brave volunteers our field is not the world but the neighborhood?

Those who have banded together for witness are invariably called a committee, the "evangelism committee," as though the business of speaking about Christ is just another job in the congregation, like the property and maintenance committee, the kitchen committee and the scouts coordinating council—and not a holy vocation from God. My congregation has an evangelism committee and through it I relate enthusiastically to the surprise and joy of the Seventy, for God often surprises us with God's presence.

The Lord sends advance teams out two-by-two. What an insignificant assault on the world! They are sent out in teams not to prevent boredom or to shore up one another's arguments with the unbelievers, but because together they are the church in mission (*co-mission*), the church is never isolate. If they are to do what the church always does, they must be in teams so that they can love one another, pray with and for one another, suffer together and rejoice together. In my parish I have seen the closest bonds of friendship formed between unlike personalities only because they have supported one another in a witness to Christ.

The whole effort hinges not on the slickness of the church's program but on the authority of Jesus which He gives to his people. Without that authority they would be goodwill ambassadors but not messengers of the Kingdom. They would be preachers of themselves and not God. But because they have received the authority of Christ no special skills or equipment are required.

The Seventy return elated by their successes. "Yes," says Jesus, "while you were out there, I saw Satan fall like lightning from heaven." "Your ministries are meeting with success. Do you know what that means? It means that you are participating in the overall defeat of the Evil One. It means the Kingdom is coming!" I saw Satan plummet to earth! Where? When? I saw Satan fall when a child entered God's kingdom through baptism. I saw Satan fall when a young man turned his life over to God at an A.A. meeting. I saw Satan fall when an inner-city congregation re-committed itself to the poor. I saw Satan fall when a husband and wife learned to trust one another again. Are these only private visions of God working in the world? Or when they are added and multiplied do they appear as signs of the Kingdom of God? Are we open enough to the presence of the Kingdom that, when we see the little epiphanies of God, we are brave enough to abandon ourselves to joy?

But even the littlest victories may be far and few between. Jesus tempers our enthusiasm for our own spiritual prowess and turns us to the certainty of our election in him: "Nevertheless do not rejoice in this, that the spirits are subject to you; but rejoice that your names are written in heaven."

Richard Lischer, a minister of the Lutheran Church Missouri Synod, in 1980 was Assistant Professor of Homiletics, the Divinity School, Duke University.

LUKE 10:25-37

THE EIGHTH SUNDAY AFTER PENTECOST
JULY 20, 1980

The Scene: The little girl from next door softly knocks. As I open the door I see she is crying again. There is a fresh bruise across her cheek bone. Her alcoholic mother has struck again. Should I call the mother. Maybe I should talk to the school counselor or report this to the authorities But they live right next door. What reprisals might they take? What legal entanglements would I be caught in?

In each of these scenes, for at least a fleeting moment, there is in each of us the urge to care, to be the "Good Neighbor Sam." But then we catch ourselves realizing that caring is not as simple as it seems in our complex world. We have our business which doesn't include other people's business. That's a virtue in a complex world— isn't it? People may not appreciate my intrusion. Dare I risk finding out how they will respond. Maybe simple caring is no longer appropriate to our complex world.

The Scene: The steep, winding, desolate road from Jerusalem down to Jericho that drops 1300 feet in seventeen miles. A man bleeding and beaten lies crumpled by the road. Would anyone dare express simple caring in this complex first century world with its busy city of Jerusalem, its growing crime rate, its complex social prejudices and rules.

The Priest passes by. Maybe he is late for the Social Concerns Commission meeting on crime. Surely it would be embarrassing to have mud or blood stains on his new Pierre Cardin robes.

The Levite passes by. He is wise to the ways of this complex world and may assume that this is just another trap to rob him. Beside this, the law forbids him to touch a corpse.

Then comes the Samaritan, tolerated on this road by the Jews as a matter of commercial expediency, but certainly not respected more than the others. He knows this to be a complex world of prejudice and dangers and tight business schedules. But in his response we have the model of the ages for simple caring in a complex world. He is the "Good Neighbor Sam" because of three things that relate to each letter in the name SAM.

HE SAW. He did not see a dirty, bloody clump or an intrusion on his schedule as did the Priest and Levite—he saw a human being like himself. What if I were the victim? What if I were the abused child, or lonely widow? "Love your neighbor as yourself".

A tourist visiting Hong Kong who prided his photographic skills spotted a thin, malnourished child pressing her face against a bakery shop window, a tear running down her cheek. He took her picture using it as the grand finale of his slide show for groups in his American home town. One evening after showing his slides a man in the audience asked what had happened to the little girl after the picture had been taken. "Oh, I don't know," the photographer replied. "I just went on my way." In looking at that child what he saw was a prize winning photograph, the shot of a lifetime, another trophy in his collection. Not a hurting, hungry human being akin to himself. Simple caring in a complex world begins with really seeing.

Secondly, the Good Samaritan "Sam" *ACTED.* Action, not on the basis of calculated duty required by law to be a good man, but because of his goodness a spontaneous outreach motivated by love. Simple action with oil and wine and bandage and beast...those resources immediately at hand.

The questioner at the slide show pressed his concern with the photographer. "Didn't you do anything for that child?" "You don't understand," said the photographer, "it's more complex than that one child. On every side there were hungry children." "But you could have done something," came the reply. To overcome the apathy, paralysis, and perplexity of complexity and act to feed and clothe and visit and care with the resources at hand is part of simple caring in a complex world.

Finally, the Good Samaritan "Sam" *MOBILIZED* other resources. He knew in the complexity of his life and world he could not help the victim alone. He turned to the agency of the inn and supported its operation and held the innkeeper accountable for caring on his behalf. Sometimes there are ten along the road who are brutalized, or one hundred who are hungry, or a thousand who are lonely, or a whole race that is oppressed. We then must mobilize to influence and support the systems and institutions of our society that can translate our simple caring into effective programs of service and justice.

The scene closes on the Good Samaritan who saw, and acted, and mobilized other resources in trying to be neighbor to his neighbor. Jesus said, "Go and do likewise."

A New Scene Opens: A summer Sunday afternoon where there may be a girl softly knocking, a lonely widow staring, or just a figure crumpled by the side of the road. See, Act, Mobilize, "Go and do likewise."

Peter D. Weaver, a minister of the United Methodist Church, in 1980 was Senior pastor of Smithfield United Church (United Church of Christ and United Methodist) in Pittsburgh, PA.

LUKE 18:1-8

THE TWENTY SECOND SUNDAY AFTER PENTECOST
OCTOBER 26, 1980

You probably have heard of the church as the bride awaiting her groom but today I wish to speak of a more pertinent image provided by Luke—the church as a widow, a person who is abandoned, defenseless, without wealth, with influence, having only persistence as an attribute.

Do you remember the movie, *Alice Doesn't Live Here Anymore*? Unlike the television sitcom, the movie wrestled with the serious issue of a woman who has been dependent on her husband all her life only to be suddenly widowed. Immediately, her world changed—how will she live? How will she support herself and her son? After being married for so long how will she adjust to being single? Adjustment becomes the central issue. Probably all of us have known widows and widowers, young and old, who have adjusted both admirably and tragically to being alone.

The early church was forced to adjust and the church today is still adjusting as Christ's promised return and the coming kingdom of God is postponed. We pray 'thy kingdom come' as it has been prayed by millions of Christians for thousands of years and still no kingdom, at least in its fulfillment.

The early disciples, intimate with Jesus, expected the end of history and the birth of the kingdom to be imminent, so when Jesus did not reappear to them it was much like Alice being suddenly widowed, their worldview changed — how will their faith live? How will they nurture their faith and the faith of those who have joined them? After being with Jesus for so long how will they adjust to living without him?

We, as the body of Christ, are still adjusting, still trying to remain faithful. We would prefer a more triumphant view of ourselves—the beautiful bride, the gorgeous raiment, jeweled and radiant. And so we attempt to live this role many times at the expense of our calling as servants. The image of a bride is exciting and addicting but it can also be presumptuous. And it is here in our presumptuousness that we are in constant need of reform. Through the scripture of the church we need to hear the words of humility over and over. In the traditions and teachings of the church we need to learn once again to abandon our assumptions of superiority and self-love. For while the church waits for the kingdom, we wait not as a bride but as a widow—defenseless, without wealth, without influence, dependent on God, persistent in our prayer and our service.

In the classic story, *The Odyssey*, Odysseus returns home to Penelope after many long years of absence. Penelope remained faithful to Odysseus though many had given him up as dead. She lived as a widow sustained by the hope and conviction of his return. So despite the many suitors in his absence she remained true.

And so, we as Christians have many suitors in the absence of the kingdom, many opportunities to give up hope and become a bride again. But Luke records that our calling is not to embrace another hope and become another's bride but our calling is to be the widow—humble in our life and persistent in our faith, aware of presence even in absence.

J. Richard Edens, a minister of the United Church of Christ, in 1980 served the United Church of Chapel Hill, Chapel Hill, North Carolina.

MATTHEW 13:24-43

THE NINTH SUNDAY AFTER PENTECOST
AUGUST 9, 1981

The yellow ribbon is a simple, insignificant thing. The color yellow in fact, has been associated with cowardice. Yet, in 1980, Penelope Laingen helped provide a positive focus for a nation's hopes for the release of 52 hostages with the help of a yellow ribbon. By tying that ribbon around a tree in her front yard, she invited America to pull out of their memories a hit song from 1973. In that song the yellow ribbon signaled the joy and acceptance waiting for the person returning home. You know the rest. Yellow ribbons became our symbol of care and hope. We saw a yellow ribbon in the hair of Kathyrn Koob on the Christmas broadcasts. The hostages knew of America's concern. Floods of yellow ribbons and balloons greeted the hostages when they returned in January.

The kingdom of God is like a yellow ribbon? Well, maybe in 1981 folklore. It communicated to us the hope that love and liberation (the rule of God) were still possible even when the powers of evil in the world looked greater. The insignificant yellow ribbon became an explosion of relief and joy when liberation came.

Jesus' parables are better but just as mysterious. Matthew uses the parables about the kingdom to tell us that we should not despair when things look hopeless by worldly standards. We should not lash out or withdraw. Instead, we should stay vulnerable with all of humanity and live the joy of the rule of God.

It is very tempting to despair. Any of us could add up a huge list of the woes of the world. On every side, we see traumatic evidence of war, famine, unjustice and despair. In individual lives there are struggles for relationships that nourish, for success, for self-esteem against the abundant evidence of our own failures.

But, the parables of the weeds in the field, the mustard seed, and the leaven urge us to "keep the faith." In the parable of the weeds in the field, the presence of weeds alongside the good grain is tolerable in light of the good harvest at the end. Like the leaven, the power of God is steadily working. The upper hand is that of God rather than that of evil. In the promise of the sprouting mustard seed is our hope.

Just as tempting as despair is the temptation either to lash out at those we see as evil or to withdraw into a protected environment. How often we lash out at others in the name of right! Purging those who do not share our religious convictions has even become a political force. Human logic tells us that our world would be better if the "good" sod defeated the "bad." The lesson for us is in the parable of the weeds. We learn that in uprooting the weeds, we inevitably will uproot some of the good grain. The desire to purge can consume and destroy.

Withdrawal from evil is probably more common. The separation of religion and social action that confronted the church in the 50's and 60's is a sad commentary on our desire to withdraw. We are content to let our own lives go along comfortably. We bemoan the state of the world, but we do little because we have insulated ourselves from the downtrodden and oppressed. It is the same action as pulling out the weeds. We pull these very legitimate people and concerns out of our lives by ignoring them. Our parable says our lives are less because of it.

If despair, lashing out or withdrawal are not the responses the parables urge, what is? The answer lies in vulnerability. Openness to all of life may put us in contact with the glimmers of the kingdom—the yellow ribbons. Jesus' images are the mustard seed and the leaven, small in the present, but promising much. Jesus' scandalous openness to all people earned him the hatred of the religious establishment. By purging, they missed the kingdom. By including Jesus was part of the kingdom. The way of Jesus, the way of reaching out to the despised, the small, will often incur the wrath of those in power.

But, the one who accepts the challenge lives in joy, according to Jesus' parables of the treasure and the pearl. There are no specifics. The parables are frustrating that way. Openness is frightening. But it promises joy.

Let the one who has ears to hear, hear.

Judith Beyler, a minister of the United Presbyterian Church in the United States, in 1981 was Assistant Pastor at Westwood Presbyterian Church, Los Angeles, California.

MATTHEW 18:21-35

THE SEVENTEENTH SUNDAY AFTER PENTECOST
OCTOBER 4, 1981

Why does the servant who has just been forgiven a debt of ten million dollars turn around and treat so harshly the one who owes him only twenty dollars? I have seen such harshness in myself and others when we discuss welfare recipients. Rarely is such discussion even tempered. Usually the statements are heatedly expressed, "These welfare recipients ought to work for what they get!"

In a discussion group of our progressive upper class and upper middle class church, a wealthy liberal heatedly said, "If the parents don't work, we should take their children away!" His expression shocked even him. And many of us confessed that our tempers flared when we stood in grocery lines behind those using food stamps. We became angry even though we knew the food stamp program was passed to benefit farmers more than the hungry poor using stamps.

Discussion group members then began to tell when they became most angry at welfare recipients. The wealthy liberal noted that his anger flared most strongly when his mother visited him and asked him what good he was contributing to the world. "Earning over a hundred thousand a year with my own company, no one asks me that question except mother! Frankly, the novelties my company produces do not help anyone; and I would contribute more to the world if I stayed home and did not go to work. Then at least I would not be polluting up the freeway." Another person, an architect, found that his anger at welfare recipients flared when his mother-in-law visited his house; for he could overhear her ask his wife, "When is he going to work," His wife explained again that his office was at home and that he was working. But his mother-in-law said, "He looks like he's just in there enjoying himself." Another person's father regularly chided him for getting full time pay for less than half time work; for a thirty hour work week struck the father as only half a work week compared to the sixty hours he had worked in his own youth. And he also mocked the idea of "paid vacations" and "paid holidays."

As the work week shortens and the "paid holidays" increase, the difference between welfare recipients and those who work is that the working people receive more money and are angrier. As working people receive more for shorter and shorter work weeks, we may expect to see more and more anger expressed toward welfare recipients. Of course some of us work seventy hour weeks but thoroughly enjoy it and would want to do the work whether we were paid or not.

The anger is a subtle effort to assert that we deserve our pay and that we make a positive contribution to society when we are none too certain. The parallel is most obvious with those who have inherited huge sums and have never worked. At a tea party with several such grand dames who reminded me of my very wealthy grandmother whom I loved very much, one grand dame said angrily what many such wealthy persons say as a favorite topic of conversation, "These welfare recipients ought to work for what they get! I do not believe anyone should receive money without working for it!" The senior pastor turned and asked her, "And when are you going to work?"

We would like to assert our self-sufficiency by saying, "These welfare recipients ought to work for what they get as I do!" But we do not dare add the last three words; for others (like that senior pastor) may be around who know all that has been done for us. So, our anger (like the anger of the unmerciful servant) asserts those three unspoken words. But in truth, we are all God's welfare recipients.

Doug Adams is ordained in the United Church of Christ and in 1981 served as Associate Professor of Worship and Preaching at Pacific School of Religion, Berkely, Ca.

MATTHEW 22:1-14

THE TWENTY-FIRST SUNDAY AFTER PENTECOST
NOVEMBER 1, 1981

Elie Wiesel tells a story about a just man, who came to a sinful town, determined to save its inhabitants from destruction. Night and day he walked the streets preaching against greed and theft, falsehood and indifference. At the outset the people listened and smiled condescendingly. Then they stopped listening; he no longer even amused them. The killers went on killing and the wise kept silent, as if there were no just man in their midst.

One day a child, puzzled by the unfortunate preacher and feeling sorry for him, asked, "Poor stranger, you shout and you wear yourself out. Don't you see that it is hopeless?" "Yes, I see," answered the just man. "Then why do you go on?" "I'll tell you why. I am not sure to what extent, if any, I can change these people. But if I still shout today and if I still scream, it is to prevent them from changing *me.*"

The Parable from Matthew 22 brings to us the immediacy of the claim of the Kingdom of God. But such a claim seems to be in conflict with the assumptions of the world, even to be silly and polarizing and divisive.

After all, salvation is available on any street corner in the United States, offered by a variety of screaming voices. If religion can be described as a consensus about the nature of life which binds people together, then there is certainly a tendency to ascribe to institutions, large and small, salvational powers. Many seem more immediate than some vague claim about the Kingdom.

For example, some believe in salvation through education. If you just get smart enough, possess a college degree, an MBA, Ph.D., whatever, you will have the ultimate in life. David Stockman, Ernest LeFever, and a host of other former ministers now preach salvation through the free enterprise system and social Darwinism. Many others have joined the consensus that our last best hope is through the proper use of science and technology.

It is very easy to listen to a multiplicity of voices and miss the invitation to the Kingdom of God. Some of the most confused people a pastor encounters are those who have moved from one system or fad to another. We live in a time when what is "in" is important. As soon as we try to catch up to what the chic people have decided is important, they change the fad, make new rules. It's hopeless.

I think of a friend who in the five years I have known her has moved from transcendental meditation (to the point that she bought a special license plate for her car to let others know that she had reached the ultimate level of consciousness) through the charismatic movement into est and is now caught up in special forms of healing through diet.

So, how does one try to find Christ's invitation to wholeness in the midst of such confusion and voices? How does one know the immediacy of the claim when so many other demands are pending?

Halford Luccock's story of the three-year-old child who was learning the Lord's Prayer is to the point. The eager child—living in New Haven, Connecticut, and experiencing difficulty with the sounds of words—prayed: "Our Father, who lives in New Haven, how did you know my name?"

That's the point of today's lesson: God calls us whether we are worthy or unworthy, rich or poor, intelligent or mediocre, whatever our sexual persuasion, to the Kingdom. We can respond to a God who knows our names, who says to us: "I have called you by name—you are mine."

One morning in 1888, Alfred Nobel, the inventor of dynamite, picked up a paper which gave an account of his death. The reporter had made a mistake, for it was Nobel's brother who had died. But the death of the munitions manufacturer was reported, and in the account he was called the "Dynamite King." When identified as a merchant of death, and realizing that was what he would be remembered for, Nobel decided to give his life a new direction. He did it through the disposition of his fortune. So, we remember him today not for his invention, but for the Nobel Peace Prize.

It is to such a decision that we are called in the parable.

This God who keeps promise, who remains faithful, offers the invitation to us. Our response cannot be delayed.

Eugene H. Winkler, a minister of the United Methodist Church, in 1981 was pastor of Community United Methodist Church, Naperville, Illinois.

DEUTERONOMY 6:1-9

THE TWENTY-SECOND SUNDAY AFTER PENTECOST
OCTOBER 31, 1982

Three years ago the community in which I live experienced the nuclear accident at Three Mile Island, and still not a day goes by when TMI is not in some way in the headlines here. We are all very much aware of the technological and human dimensions of the nuclear power issue. Yet as a preacher I am conscious of how little has been said from the pulpits of our community in an effort to interpret this event (and other technological phenomenon) in the light of faith.

Shortly after TMI, Dr. Daniel Bechtel, Professor of Religion at Dickinson College, some fifteen miles from the plant, surveyed the surrounding community to determine what religious or faith issues had been raised by the accident. His findings, as yet unpublished, are now in final form and they are astounding. Even among persons who daily practice strong Christian faith there was a tendency to disassociate the events at TMI from religious concerns. Some interviewees suggested that since the reactor was made by humans, it was a human problem and such things as prayer to God to help in repairing it were useless. The concept that God was somehow effective in dealing with a crisis in human technology was difficult for people to grasp.

A prominent United Methodist layman in my community when asked, "Was there anything concerning TMI in your prayers at the time?" responded with some distress; "No, since you bring it up, it does seem strange that TMI was divorced from prayers and such. I don't know why."

The survey revealed other startling dimensions of the faith/culture split. "The overwhelming majority of people interviewed could not think of one Biblical image or ethical injunction which came to their minds during the crisis. Only 9% made any reference to the Bible at all." As Dan Bechtel has concluded perhaps the "Bibles in American homes are closed; that is, they are either literally never opened or never read in such a way that the stories, images, or ethical teachings become part of the resources people use in responding to a crisis or interpreting its meaning." Those who did suggest a Biblical image related a text of punishment or destruction rather than ones which could bring comfort or aid in decision making.

For some reason the way people of faith responded to technological crisis was different from the way they normally approached other crises in their lives. Dan Bechtel's conclusion is that, "Religion and the churches were largely unprepared to help people deal with this technological crisis because many had not then and still have not dealt with the relationship of religious beliefs and practices to technology" (Dr. Daniel R. Bechtel, unpublished paper, Dickinson College, Carlisle, Pennsylvania, 1981, used by permission).

Now, as a preacher this data suggests to me that in my community at any rate there is a real need to address the scope of our religious faith. Is the God we worship big enough to include TMI? I believe so. On the Sunday afternoon during the nuclear emergency I preached at the Dauphin County Prison in Harrisburg. It was a tense time as the prison officials were making plans to evacuate the inmates to a Federal penitentiary upstate. Those who came to the service were jumpy, feeling "penned in." We sang, "He's Got the Whole World in His Hands" including a verse, "He's Got Three Mile Island in His Hands." The response was stupendous. Such a release of energy as inmates and staff alike affirmed a truth beyond the tense realities of their situation.

The texts for this day affirm that our God is One God over all. The command is to respond with the whole self—not just some part labeled "religious." Today, we face a peculiar challenge to integrate faith into our experience of a vast technology which is so much a part of the world around us. The challenge for the preacher is to help people to see the issues of faith in all areas of life, making the Gospel live in the practice of daily living.

Karen Engle Layman, a minister of the United Methodist Church, in 1982 was Pastor of the Mt. Rock United Methodist Church, Carlisle, Pennsylvania.

RUTH 1:1-19a

THE TWENTIETH SUNDAY AFTER PENTECOST
OCTOBER 9, 1983

The year before I was born my brother and sister, aged fifteen and eleven came down with rheumatic fever and my parents in an effort to help them and to escape the bone-chilling cold of a Western Pennsylvania winter packed everyone up and went to Florida for a vacation. But the trip went haywire. The children instead of getting better, only seemed to get worse and my Dad who had long suffered with peptic ulcers suddenly became acutely ill—almost to death.

It was then that my Mother began to have trouble with oranges—or so she thought. It didn't take long for her to realize that her indigestion was not oranges at all, but a pregnancy beginning. It was not a happy realization. Years later she confessed to me how she had complained bitterly to God and how she had prayed again and again, "I can not have this baby! I CAN NOT have this baby!" The pregnancy became an enormous spiritual struggle. Home again she spent many hours with the wise women of our family wrestling with the Biblical message of faith. Finally, a peace came that transformed the rest of her life, and when I was born she gave me the middle name of Faith.

My Mother's choice to accept faith amid forbidding circumstances has had a profound effect upon me too, both historically and spiritually. Yet I could not have blamed her if she had chosen otherwise. She was forty years old, and not a well woman at that. As it was she did not live to see me grown. Abortion was not an available option for her, but she had the choice of whether my birth was to be a matter of faith and promise or an angry moment of despair. She chose faith and for obvious reasons I am eternally grateful. It is of no small significance to me that my Mother's name was Ruth.

Again and again in the course of living you and I are faced with choices of faith. Sometimes the choices involve dramatic changes. In 1918 before the First World War had ended my Aunt Margaret Marsh went to Africa as a missionary and teacher. She was an ordinary person with extraordinary faith which took her from teaching in a one room school in Pennsylvania to service for almost 50 years in East Africa. She married a safari missionary; delivered her first baby herself, matched wits with medicine men, survived famines, and patched up villagers mauled by lions. As I was growing up she was fond of writing me, "Let Philippians 4:19 be your strength. It has been mine. 'But my God shall supply all your needs according to his riches in glory by Christ Jesus.' " When she left for Africa my grandparents thought that she was crazy. But with a half-bushel of home grown apples and twenty-five dollars in her pocket she sailed off in a world still smarting with war.

I often think of Aunt Margaret when I am trying to decide little matters in my life and her faith gives me strength. Thank God for the foremothers in my life whose witness of faith gives me strength.

Praise God for the mothers named Ruth and the Aunts named Margaret and all the others whose witness lives on in us. Amen!

Karen (Faith) Engel Layman, a minister of the United Methodist Church, in 1983 was pastor of the Mt. Rock United Methodist Church, Carlisle, Pennsylvania

PHILIPPIANS 2:1-13

THE SIXTEENTH SUNDAY AFTER PENTECOST
SEPTEMBER 30, 1984

A woman in our church, together with a team of medical personnel from across the United States, went on a special eye mission to Ecuador recently. They established a small clinic in a little wooden building high up in the mountains of Ecuador. They dispensed glasses, performed surgeries, and did all sorts of ophthalmological procedures and treatments in a period of less than two weeks. Unbelievably, they worked with almost 11,000 Ecuadorian Indians in that little clinic in that brief period of time!

Finally, it was time for the team to return to the United States. Since Genie spoke Spanish so fluently, she was given the responsibility of telling those outside the clinic that the team would be leaving and that they were sorry that they would not be able to take care of everyone's needs. Almost a thousand very poor people had been waiting in line for several days and nights outside of the clinic to be served.

When they saw the team packing up their supplies in boxes and loading the boxes on trucks, they began to panic. They started swarming the clinic, pounding on the walls and pressing through the doorway, desperately trying to get in to receive help before the team left. And Genie stood there trying to let them know how sorry the team was, but finally it was to no avail. She became exasperated at the utter futility of it all—and then, she just broke down and began to cry.

And then it was that a beautiful thing took place. A few of the small peasant people who were near her at the front of the mob noticed that she was crying. They began to whisper one to another, "She's crying! She's crying!" And in a very brief period of time, the word passed from one person to another and another all the way through that huge mob of people. And then, almost unbelievably, that unruly mob began to get quiet and become still and soon there was a profound hush over the entire group. Some of those poor people began to cry as well and they reached out to Genie and to touch her cheeks and wipe away her tears and to console her. And Genie said that never in her life had she ever experienced anything so desperate on the one hand and yet so profound and beautiful on the other.

Dietrich Bonhoeffer once said:
> People go to God when God is sore bested,
> Find him poor and scorned, without shelter and bread,
> Whelmed under the weight of the wicked, the weak, the dead.
> Christians stand by God in God's hour of grieving.

The profound revelation of the Gospel to the world is that God suffers in our midst! God is in the world as the lowly one, the one who assumes the form and posture of a servant and stoops to be among the least, the last, and the lost of the earth. And therefore, the Gospel invites us to consider that perhaps human suffering is not a sign of the absence of God as the old argument of theodicy would have it, so much as a sign of the *presence* of God.

And maybe, too, this is what the cross finally means: that the suffering of God stands at the very heart of the universe, and that it is in and through God's suffering that we are somehow mysteriously redeemed in the midst of our own suffering.

EDITOR'S NOTE:
(In the parish church in Landshut, Bavaria, is a statue, "Christ at Rest." He sits slumped and bone-tired, his head in his hands, utterly exhausted. The young German woman standing with me said: "I never even imagined him like that. He looks just like the way I feel sometimes." C.L.R.)

Norman Neaves, a minister of the United Methodist Church, in 1984 was Senior Minister of Church of the Servant in Oklahoma City, Oklahoma.

PHILIPPIANS 4:4-20

THE EIGHTEENTH SUNDAY AFTER PENTECOST
OCTOBER 14, 1984

Not so many years ago, Presbyterians sat around fretting as to whether they were "the chosen" or merely those who were "called"—only to be rejected in the end. Methodists, by contrast, stood up and lustily sang, "Blessed Assurance! Jesus is mine!" So who was right: those who were uncertain or those who were sure?

The truth is that we need elements of each in our faith. On the one hand, we can affirm with assurance the promise of Isaiah that God, "will make for all peoples a feast...and the reproach of his people he will take away from all the earth." On the other hand we have the sober warning of Matthew that participation in the feast is no matter to be taken for granted. For the church is a mystery; it does not follow the conventional rules.

Often the church is trapped in cultural confines—a congregation serves a particular ethnic group or draws members almost exclusively from a neighborhood that is homogenous in age, economic and educational levels. That may be an accommodation to the reality of human narrowness. But God does not share our narrowness. God insists instead on opening the doors to all. Thus Isaiah envisions the great banquet in which those from every people and nation share with joy in God's goodness.

It is this vision of the future that draws us and challenges us. We are called to model the church on earth after that dream of God's great banquet when men and women of every sort will come from East and West and North and South and share the joy of God's goodness. This is what it means to ask that God's "will be done on earth as it is in heaven." We are to be now, in some measure, what we one day expect to become a perfectness. Our life as Christ's people on earth is a dress rehearsal, a practice session, a scrimmage game, for our life with God in heaven. That is why we cannot take anything for granted.

But isn't that an impossibly romantic dream? Certainly it was not for the church in the first century. Witness Paul's words to the Philippians read today. A group of one-time strangers had become, in effect, Paul's family, who shared his hardship and made personal sacrifices in order to help and encourage him. Paul founded cosmopolitan congregations composed of quite diverse persons—many very different in background and outlook from the Apostle himself. Of course this produced problems and tensions. Christian congregations are not magically freed from conflict. But mutual affection in the service of Christ is evident everywhere in Paul's letters—as much when he is scolding the Corinthians for their waywardness as when he is commending the Philippians for their faithfulness and generosity.

How can we begin to attain this diversity-with-love that characterized the New Testament Church and that anticipates the great banquet of God? The starting point is the mystery of our own inclusion in Christ's household. We are not included because we are worthy, but because God is good. It is our unworthiness which causes us, like the earlier Presbyterians, to wonder that we can be included at all. It is God's grace which allows us, like the earlier Methodists, to have assurance. It is our unworthiness which prevents us from trying to exclude those we deem unfit for the Kingdom; it is our gratitude which makes us want to share with everyone the goodness God has made known to us. Thus we are the church on earth, and the image of that which we expect to become.

Laurence Hull Stookey, an ordained elder in The United Methodist Church, in 1984 was professor of preaching and worship at Wesley Theological Seminary, Washington, D. C.

LUKE 18:9-14

THANKSGIVING DAY
NOVEMBER 11, 1984

Ernest Campbell, speaking to a group of preachers at the Fosdick Convocation on Preaching at the Riverside Church in New York said that he has always felt that the important days in the church and civil calendar are the most difficult for preaching. Thanksgiving is a prime example. "You have twenty minutes to preach," Campbell says, "and you start out by saying, 'Beloved we ought to be more thankful than we are.' Okay, you've used fifteen seconds, now you have nineteen minutes and forty-five seconds to go. So you go on, 'As I was saying, we ought to be more thankful than we are.' "

What do you say about thankfulness? That it's rather silly that we only have one day in the year to stop and give thanks to God for all the blessings of our lives? That we ought to give thanks to God every day? That all things come from God as a gift and we are only stewards? That we are especially fortunate in this land of ours, America, with its rich earth and bountiful crops and diverse people? These seem so obvious. And yet they are exactly the reason that we celebrate Thanksgiving. We are fortunate. But our tendency is to take our many gifts for granted. So Thanksgiving Day is celebrated as a way of reminding ourselves not only *what* our gifts are but also *whose* they are.

If we have made a custom of only setting aside one day each year, saving up all our thanks to God for one special occasion, we are obviously out of practice on how to do this. Some clues as to how to offer a prayer of thanksgiving might be in order. Fortunately, Jesus gives us a memorable example.

The pharisee who goes up to the temple does so with every justification. He is an admirable elder of the faith. He not only tithes and fasts but also avoids the likes of sinners. Who of us might be able to say the same? I fast only one day a year, Good Friday, and my spare pledge is barely 3% of my income. This pharisee had some reason to brag. In fact, he would be an ideal vestry member or elder today, just the right sort to have as an example to others. Unfortunately, the outward trappings of the pharisee's religiosity would be all that you might want to have the congregation see. Because once he opens his mouth, his words betray the vacuity of his faith.

The publican, however, offers a prayer of penitence that is a stark contrast to that of the pharisee. He beats his chest, lowers his eyes, and offers a simple prayer asking for mercy and forgiveness.

What does all this have to do with Thanksgiving? Only everything. The pharisee's prayer is a prayer of thanksgiving. He has his own goodness to be thankful for, if you listen to his prayer. In the great scheme of things it does not add up to much perhaps because whatever sincerity is there is countered by the self-satisfaction and sense of worthiness that the pharisee brings to his thanksgiving. The publican, on the other hand, displays no sense of deserving or due from God, only the hope of forgiveness. Jesus tells his disciples that it is this humility that finally makes all the difference. The publican goes down from the temple justified because, Jesus says, "everyone who exalts himself will be humbled, but he who humbles himself will be exalted."

At Thanksgiving there is a great danger. The danger is believing that all of the bounty we celebrate, the good land which comes as a gift, the grain which fills our silos, comes as a sign of God's favor to us, God's favorite nation and special people. Are we then to infer that the people of Southern Africa, suffering from drought, are cursed? Are the street people of our cities, homeless and hungry, frowned upon by a divine countenance? That's the implication.

The truth of the matter is that we are fortunate, blessed, gifted, nurtured, and sustained by a divine hand. But the fact that other nations and people have less is nothing more than the successive accidents of climate, geography, and birth—are they not? The point of Thanksgiving is not to take credit for moral superiority as the source of our blessings but rather to acknowledge the source of those gifts, and then share them with others. The pharisee in us would have us take credit for our goodness as the reason for our bounty and blessing. The publican reminds us that it is the humanity we share in common with others that makes us only stewards of what we have. It can hardly be a joyful Thanksgiving for us if we only gloat over our sinlessness and good fortune while condemning others for their deserved poverty.

Without a publican's frame of mind, we will eat and drink to our condemnation this Thanksgiving Day, our blessings transformed into curses. So what will it be? Shall we go up to the temple now to pray?

Jon M. Walton, a minister of the Presbyterian Church U.S.A., in 1984 was pastor of the Setauket Presbyterian Church, Setauket, Long Island, New York.

LUKE 9:18-24

THE FIFTH SUNDAY AFTER PENTECOST
JUNE 22, 1986

Survivalists, they call them. They are the people who are absolutely intent on surviving, no matter what. We are told it is deep within us, someplace in our animal nature. The survival of the fittest, Herbert Spencer called it.

Books and articles and seminars abound telling "how to survive the coming economic catastrophe," "how to survive marriage," "how to survive retirement." Our children wear T-shirts celebrating it: "I survived growing up in Pittsburgh."

Robert Louis Stevenson has a marvelous passage about a person whose chief aim in life was to protect his health and survive everyone else through the obsessive use of raincoat and umbrella. "The man," he writes, "who never forgets his rubbers is bound to forget many things infinitely more important."

The Survivalists have now developed an exclusive underground condominium complex in the midwest for people who want to be saved in an all-out nuclear war. Dozens have already been sold at very high prices. If some unwelcomed guest should threaten to enter, the air shaft, arising out of the ground, doubles as a gun turret.

Jesus has troubling news for us who rely upon our animal instincts and are determined to be the fittest, outfitted in rubbers, hiding in our bunker. "Whoever would save his life will lose it."

Five days before William Saroyan died, he telephoned the Associated Press and among other things he reflected, "I always knew everyone has to die—but I always thought an exception would be made in my case. Now what?"

After Jesus' troubling news, now what? Maybe it's time to forget our rubbers and remember things infinitely more important: like a radical new approach to living. It was given to us by the one we have said is "the Christ of God." Deny yourself, take up a cross, follow...follow out of the bunker cave, risking the earthquake, wind and fire...listen to the voice...listen to Good News..."whoever loses his life for my sake will save it."

Few of us will be called to lose life by martyrdom, but the sense of this word "lose" in the Greek is also to "leave behind," as in a race to surpass. Thus, we are called to surpass and leave behind the punitive notion of self preservation; to move beyond saving and protecting our status based on male or female and lose ourselves in our oneness in Christ Jesus. To face and profoundly know that no matter how fit or clever, we cannot save ourselves, but we can lose ourselves for the sake of Christ! Then let God, through Grace, tend to the matters of saving. Entrusted to God, the matter of surviving no longer needs to trouble or obsess us. Given to us is the challenge of losing life.

Dr. Peter D. Weaver, a minister of the United Methodist Church, in 1986 was Senior Pastor of Smithfield United Church (United Church of Christ and United Methodist) in Pittsburgh, Pennsylvania.

I KINGS 21:1-3, 17-21; GALATIANS 6:7-18

THE SEVENTH SUNDAY AFTER PENTECOST
JULY 6, 1986

"Have you found me, O my enemy?" The bravado rings in the king's voice. There is no answer from Elijah. "What gave me away?"

"You gave yourself away," replies Yahweh's mouthpiece.

Standing between the rows of the ill-gotten vineyard, face flushed, hair tousled, finger-stained from a morning's proprietary activity, Ahab curls his lip. He is learning that you reap what you sow.

What Ahab had sown, of course, was a hybrid mix: complicity in murder, an ugly strain of greed, and the kind of self-aggrandizement peculiar to petulant monarchs. He had planted "evil in the sight of the Lord." Who knows why he ever thought he was going to harvest grapes!

According to Elijah, having sold himself to evil, Ahab never stood a chance of receiving anything in exchange but God's wrath. Not a grape. Not a summer squash. Not anything but the very thing he sought to perpetrate on the godly Jezreelite. In the end, Elijah said, the royal might that Ahab and Jezebel wielded against the little vintner would be wielded against them—by Israel's God. Ahab and Jezebel were to reap what they had sown, Elijah prophesied. And this time the harvest was going to come in with the peculiar stamp of God's justice all over it.

That's what happens, Ahab, when you tamper with the covenant between a people and their God. That's what happens, Jezebel, when you (quite literally) try to take Yahweh's turf away. That's what happens. And that's what happens whenever the privileged— thinking they are only going up against the powerless—meet God.

In the case of Ahab it happened because—as Elijah so succinctly put it—he "sold himself to do what is evil in the sight of the Lord." He sold himself to evil. He gave himself away. First, perhaps, to Jezebel. Then, a little, to her Phoenician god. Many times, probably, to his own whims and fancies. Certainly to the dream of Samarian squash replacing the Jezreelite's vines. He gave himself away. He gave himself over. He sold/sowed himself. And in doing so, he both set his own fate in motion and guaranteed his discovery: "For those who sow to their own flesh will from the flesh reap corruption" (Galatians 6:8a). Ahab was found out *because* he sold out, Elijah said. You might say the stench of his own corruption gave him away.

It's hard to mistake a grape for a summer squash and it's hard to miss the stink of the fruit of corruption. It is hard, in other words, for our sins not to find us out. Not, of course, that evil's discovery—or justice or the faithful fulfillment of God's promises—always come as swiftly as they did in Naboth's vineyard. (Who needs to be reminded of that?!) I Kings and Galatians 6 say precious little about the timetables for such things, the "in due season" reference of Galatians 6:9 being at best a slippery reassurance.

No, evil does not always give itself away as quickly as vegetables rotting under a Samarian sun. And justice is not harvested late summer by late summer with the Zinfandels. *But it does come to harvest.* In the words of Galatians, "Do not be deceived. God is not mocked...." In other words, "Don't bet against it!"

To what are you selling/sowing your life?

Jana Childers, a minister of The Presbyterian Church (USA), in 1986 was instructor of Speech Communication and Homiletics, San Francisco Theological Seminary, San Anselmo, California.

PSALM 91:1-10

THE SECOND SUNDAY AFTER PENTECOST
JUNE 21, 1987

Turn back to the psalm in your bulletin, please, for in a moment we will be repeating it again together, meditating with the psalm as our guide.

Now think about the last time you were overwhelmed...after a decent summer away, returning to Princeton to face a calculus requirement or comprehensives... overwhelmed by a particular set of responsibilities for your department...or maybe by all of your responsibilities put together, class preparation, bills to be paid, articles edited, marketing done...maybe it was something as simple as slogging through the day with a head cold or the flu.

Think for a moment about the last time you were overwhelmed...and then remember how God cared for you and calmed you.

Let us repeat the first verses of the psalm down to the word 'buckler:'
Those who dwell in the shelter of the Most high,
Abide under the shadow of the Almighty.
They shall say to the Lord, 'You are my refuge and my stronghold,
My God in whom I put my trust.'
God shall deliver you from the snare of the hunter,
and from the deadly pestilence.
God shall cover you with his pinions,
and you shall find refuge under God's wings;
God's faithfulness shall be a shield and buckler.

Now think about the last time you were afraid, really scared. For Jake Morrow it was the other night when a croup of a cough woke him out of a sound sleep. He didn't know what it was, only that it hacked awfully, and shook his little body. When was the last time you were afraid? Hearing footsteps behind you at night coming home from the library...afraid that you couldn't move off dead center...afraid there wasn't a place for you in God's grand scheme of things...another job nearly as good as this one...afraid life had nothing left to offer you. Think for a moment—then recall how God tugged you through your terror...was your shield and buckler...and as you do, I'll tell you that Jake's Dad held him in his arms in the bathroom...hot shower turned on full blast so the steam could cure the croup...held him in the middle of the night through his fear. How did God tug you through your terror, hold you? Let us repeat the next verses down to the word dwelling!

You shall not be afraid of any terror by night.
Nor of the arrow that flies by day;
Of the plague that stalks in the darkness,
Nor of the sickness that lays waste at mid-day.
A thousand shall fall at your side and ten thousand at your right hand,
But it shall not come near you.
Your eyes have only to behold
To see the reward of the wicked.
Because you have made the Lord your refuge,
And the Most High your habitation,
There shall no evil happen to you,
neither shall any plague come near your dwelling.

Think for a moment—have you felt the snare of the hunter...the deadliest pestilence? Maybe when you were in fact facing pestilence...maybe when you were facing physical death...or harder still...the death of the one you love the most in the world. Maybe when a dark night of the soul came upon you...when all hope was lost and you saw no need to carry on. When did you last feel abandoned by all? Now remember how God returned to you, how God held you in God's loving arms. Let us complete the psalm together.

For God shall give angels charge over you,
To keep you in all your ways.
They shall bear you in their hands,
Lest you dash your foot against a stone.

You shall tread upon the lion and adder;
You shall trample the young lion and the serpent under your feet.
Because they are bound to me in love, therefore will I deliver them;
I will protect them, because they know my name.
They shall call upon me, and I will answer them,
I am with those in trouble;
I will rescue them and bring them to honor.
With long life will I satisfy them,
And show them my salvation.

Sue Anne Steffey Morrow, a minister in The United Methodist Church, in 1987 was Assistant Dean of the Chapel at Princeton University.

EXODUS 16:2-15; MATTHEW 15:21-28

THE TENTH SUNDAY AFTER PENTECOST
AUGUST 16, 1987

It was one of those instruments used in psychological testing, this one an exercise in completing sentences. It is a rather interesting game in which one is given a series of introductory phrases out of which to build sentences. The idea, as with most of these tests, is to make the first, spontaneous response, without reflection or weighing this against that, pro against con, considering carefully. There were such starters as: Husbands usually.... Most wives.... Many women.... Some men.... The most important thing in the world....

Suppose we could somehow be spontaneous and just come out with a response to that: The most important thing in the world is.... Of course, what we came up with might well be different today than a year ago, maybe even from what we would have put down yesterday! There are times when an aching tooth or a lost dog fills every horizon.

But what would it be, this revealing sentence? The most important thing in the world is —security? The national budget, the decisions we make from day to day, the values we teach our children, all seem to suggest that as a possible answer. The people of Israel in the wilderness might well have put it that way, nostalgic and concerned as they were for a chicken in the pot and eating as much as they wanted. One analysis of contemporary values, both inside the church and out, suggests that the sentence might read, The most important thing in the world is security, meaning by that family, career, standard of living and health (where that is a factor). If we were honest, a similar word, *comfort,* might be the one.

Israel is in fact an exciting place; not so comfortable but exciting. Between Pharoah's slavery and the land of promise, their temple a tent, the people follow a cloud by day and fire by night. There is an easy intercourse between the people and God, mediated by inspired leaders. But the most important thing in the world is...? They seem more interested in checking the thermostat to make sure that the needle stays within the "comfort zone." This orientates them toward the past, blocks their vision of the future, and diminishes their awareness of God's presence. Have you ever been hiking on a high trail, with mountain wildflowers at your feet and the air so sweet you could live on it—at least for a day!—and your companion is worried about what's for supper or where you are going to sleep? I remember standing at a desk in the Eastside Airlines Terminal complaining whiningly about a long delay, stranding me in the city for a day. The young woman gave me an impatient smile: "Look, mister, you are in New York City!"

There is no question where the writer of Exodus comes out. The most important thing in the world is obviously God! How often would a psychologist see such an answer? But in the story of Israel, even as the manna and quails are forthcoming, it is so that the people will move toward what is really important: "At evening you shall know that it was the Lord who brought you out of the land of Egypt, and in the morning you shall see the glory of the Lord...." And just so they don't forget, this bounty comes as a daily ration.

The woman who comes to Jesus beseeching his help has sorted it out, in her necessity. The most important thing is not her being a Canaanite, Jesus a Jew. She is able, as it were, to persist in the face of a seemingly indifferent silence and to laugh off, as it were, the prejudiced rebuke. Her hunger is too great, her daughter's situation dire. She seeks the source of healing and life, and it is her single-minded passion which Jesus commends, and to which he responds. Here the longing for God wears a human face, revealing both realism about the human condition and turning toward the one who sees and loves all.

How about it: The most important thing in the world....

Charles Rice in 1987 was Professor of Homiletics in The Theological School, Drew University, Madison, New Jersey.

---

2 CORINTHIANS 5:6-10, 14-17

THE THIRD SUNDAY AFTER PENTECOST
JUNE 12, 1988

Judging and being judged—we do and we are every day of our lives. At home, at school, at work we are making judgment calls. Of course, the word "judgment" has such a forbidding sound that we now mute it by other, more neutral names that smack of shiney hi-tech: "review," "evaluation," "play-back." Whatever the "in" bureaucratic lingo, judging is what we are about.

So how do we judge? On what basis do we approach each other? For the most part, the first thing we notice about people is their appearance. Are they male or female? Physically disabled or well-bodied? Jew or Gentile? Black or white? And what is more, often we do not get beyond these identity descriptions. They are taken as decisive. If you doubt that, just ask a black person in New York City about hailing a cab; or, a clergywoman, with several years in the ministry, about finding a senior pastorate; or, a laid-off white male about rejoining the work force at age 55;—not to mention someone with a physical disability, let alone an AIDS diagnosis! Folks like these will tell you how the world sees them.

This dehumanizing situation often calls forth two strategies to counteract it. On the one hand, there is the assimilationist model which says, "Deny who you are and become what you are not." Fix your nose. Change your accent. Hide your age. But, whatever you do, fit in! On the other hand, there is the autonomous model which says, "To hell with the others, for that's what hell is!" So, the barriers go up. Our kind, your kind. Our neighborhood, our "good people," our way of life. To each his own. Birds of a feather. All others, keep out!

But Jesus Christ did not keep out.

And Jesus Christ did not fit in.

And because he did not fit in and would not keep out of the way, the world shoved him aside and on to a cross. The same gospel story which tells this horrifying tale also says that this one—weak, rejected, and fallen—this one God has raised up, anointed, and made mighty for our sakes. What is more, this one who was judged will be the judge. What a strange thing! What a strange, new world. A world in which everything obvious is rendered unsure. A world in which human judgments are dethroned from self-appointed finality. A world in which the mighty are fallen and the fallen are raised to new life.

We only see this new world, this new creation, very imperfectly in the fog of our own. We catch its sound on an Easter Sunday in an Orthodox Church in Moscow as a Communist Party member greets his companion with, "Christ is risen" (*The New York Times*, 15 April 1985); or, when an Alabama Governor who vowed, "Segregation forever!," now admits, "It's good that the Civil Rights Bill has passed. It hasn't been the evil that we thought..." (*The New York Times*, 7 January 1979); or, when a Yuppie wife, confessing, "I've always been afraid of hospitals—the smell, the people, the loneliness," answers God's call anyway, and begins regularly visiting AIDS patients at Bellevue (*Grace Church*, 22 November 1987). When these things happen—and they do—we overhear something of what Paul was getting at when he declared, "From now on, therefore, we regard no one from a human point of view..." or simply by their appearances.

So sisters and brothers, as those whose lives are entwined with Christ's, our calling is not to uphold the world's judgments, or to sanctify its common sense. Our calling is to live amid the uncommon sense of the gospel, the gospel which judge all things not simply by their appearances, but by their destiny in Jesus Christ.

James F. Kay, a minister of the Presbyterian Church (U.S.A.), in 1988 was a Ph.D. candidate, Union Theological Seminary, New York.

MARK 5:21-43

THE FIFTH SUNDAY AFTER PENTECOST
JUNE 26, 1988

Today's lessons turn us to the power of God working among us through the Holy Spirit (Acts 1:8). The power of God is often manifested in works which God alone can do such as healing.

The gospels report a number of stories of healing by Jesus. One element that appears in most of them is that he touched the sick and they sought to touch him. Healing power is conveyed in touch. We should note that the gift of the Holy Spirit and the laying on of hands often go together in the New Testament, for example, Acts 8:14-24. This is not surprising. The touch of someone we love makes us feel good while the touch of someone we do not like is repulsive. We hold a child who is sick or frightened. The holding becomes a channel. Our love flows out; the child feels our love. The child's pain flows to us; we feel the pain. Holding is just as important to us as to the child. I find that when I shake hands with people in the hospital they are reluctant to let go and we end up holding hands. Going to the hospital to hold someone's hand is no joke; it is serious business. It does more than we realize. Some months ago I was undergoing a rather painful medical test. The nurse assisting knew my pain. She put her hand on my arm and held it. I felt a power to endure that I did not have before. From that experience I realized again a truth that had become submerged since my children had outgrown the "hugging" stage (at least from parents). I have had the privilege of sitting by "the bed of pain" with people whose last consciousness was surely that those who love them were there and holding them.

Healing is much more than a mechanical process of surgery and medication as Bernie Siegel tells us. He observes that 15-20% of cancer patients wish to die, 60-70% behave as their physicians expect, 15-20% are Exceptional Patients because they refuse to play the victim (*Love, Medicine & Miracles*, pp. 22-24). He concludes, "One of the best ways to make something happen is to predict it" (*Love, Medicine & Miracles*, p. 35). Applying his observation, we could say that Uzzah believed that the ark was the locus of the awesome power of God. So when he touched it, he expected to die, and he did. Jairus and the woman believed that Jesus was the locus of healing power. So when the woman touched him, she expected to be healed, and she was.

We also have power to do God's works, but it is often sharply limited by the power of sin. Thus we need other gifts of the Holy Spirit. By faith we receive the grace of Christ so that we can trust in God's saving power. Then the limiting bonds of sin are broken. We are free to live to God, to use the power we have, to be channels through which power flows to others. But faith also needs the gift of hope. Without hope, Jairus and the woman would not have come to Jesus. The mourners had already given up hope. Siegel found that hope is essential in healing (*Love, Medicine & Miracles*, pp. 36-45). Then we must add the gift of love which enables us to reach out with the power we do have, for love is the power of God at work among us.

But what happens if our power is still weak? We have the promise that "my God will supply every need of yours according to his riches in glory in Christ Jesus" (Ph. 4:19). We may not have the gift of healing, but we surely have gifts that can help us ease the pain of those to whom we are sent.

Biblical people tended to refer the cause of events directly to God. In this age we are uncomfortable with the idea of "miracles" and attributing events to God. We generally prefer proximate answers that fit our thought patterns of rationality and science. Too often this Procrustean bed causes us to miss out on seeing the power of God at work and drawing upon it.

Paul E. Grosjean, a minister of the United Church of Christ, in 1988 served as pastor of the Meyersville Presbyterian Church, Gillette, New Jersey.

MARK 7:31-37

THE FIFTEENTH SUNDAY AFTER PENTECOST
SEPTEMBER 4, 1988

Perhaps subway cars rattle and squeak their rolling way forward beneath your busy city streets. They do in mine. Conversation takes place on them only with difficulty. We raise our voices over the din of background noise, and strain our ears to discern intelligible sounds. Sometimes we abandon the effort.

Children who attend the School for the Deaf, as it is called, board the train at my stop. Throughout the journey they converse, the grace and speed of their motions painting a sharp contrast to the slow, jarring progress of the train. Just who is deaf in this context? I hear too much and so am deaf. I speak and am not heard. Yet they who hear nothing still hear each other. They who shoulder the burden of our labels—"mute" and "dumb" we call them—still speak and are understood. It is just that theirs is a foreign language. My eyes are not yet trained to hear their words, nor are my hands prepared to speak so that they may understand.

Sarah is a character in the Mark Medoff play, *Children of A Lesser God* (New York: Dramatists Play Service Inc., 1980). She, like the children on the subway car, is deaf — a description she is prepared to use for herself, but one experience has taught her is tainted with the biases of people who have ears that hear. Throughout the play her words, spoken with her hands rather than her voice, impale the stereotypes of deafness and of the deaf. "Deafness isn't the opposite of hearing," she says. "It's a silence full of sound ... the sound of spring breaking up through the death of winter" (28). "Listen," she goes on to say:

> "For all my life I have been the creation of other people. The first thing I was ever able to understand was that everyone was supposed to hear but I couldn't and that was bad. Then they told me everyone was supposed to be smart but I was dumb. Then they said, oh no, I wasn't permanently dumb,

only temporarily, but to be smart I had to become an imitation of the people who had from birth everything a person has to have to be good: ears that hear, mouth that speaks, eyes that read, brain that understands. Well, my brain understands a lot, and my eyes are my ears; and my hands are my voice; and my language, my speech, my ability to communicate is as great as yours. Greater, maybe, because I can communicate to you in one image an idea more complex than you can speak to each other in fifty words. For example, the sign 'to connect', a simple sign—but it means so much more when it is moved between us like this. Now it means to be joined in a shared relationship, to be individual yet as one. A whole concept just like that. Well, I want to be joined to other people, but for all my life people have spoken for me. *She* says: *she* means; *she* wants. As if there were no I. As if there were no one in here who *could* understand. Until you let me be an individual, an *I*, just as you are, you will never truly be able to come inside my silence and know me. And until you do that, I will never let myself know you. Until that time...we cannot share a relationship" (65-66).

Just who is deaf? Deafness marks each of us. Spirits ossify as well as ears. We can and do steel ourselves from the sounds and emotions we dread, from the issues and people we have difficulty discussing. Sarah and James, her "hearing" husband, eventually recognize this "inner deafness" within themselves, the presence of a hardness in each other to truths they have long denied. Healing comes as they open themselves to these truths. They talk plainly, finding power in this moment of vulnerability to communicate effectively.

Long ago, a person whose ears were closed to the sound of the thrush and whose tongue was bridled by an impediment of speech, was brought to Jesus. During the encounter, the ability to hear and to speak intelligibly was restored to this person. Healing in that day involved empowering people to hear and be heard, to be equipped with what it takes to communicate and participate in relationships. In our day, God's healing power accomplishes no less.

James Ball, a minister in The United Church of Canada, in 1988 lived and worked in Caledon East, Ontario.

I KINGS 19:9-14

THE SIXTH SUNDAY AFTER PENTECOST
JUNE 25, 1989

Mood swings afflict all of us. Life does not move from one glorious high to another. Rather, like a yo-yo, we go up and down. A new job, a new opportunity for service, a victory over an obstacle or handicap, or a rare moment of religious illumination boosts our spirits and puts us in a near state of ecstasy. But we can quickly slip from the heights to the depths, from the euphoria of success to a mood of defeatism and depression. The job, we find, has its dull monotonous side; the service demands that we get our hands dirty; the obstacle persistently recurs in a different form; and the vision rubs up against the tough realities of life and fades.

Elijah, the greatest of the oral prophets, also had his mood swings. Within a twenty-four hour period he slipped from the heights to the depths, from the ecstasy of Mount Carmel to depression under a broom tree in the wilderness.

A bit of historical background gives the clue to Elijah's mood swing. On Mount Carmel he had challenged and completely routed the 450 prophets of Baal. Elated and buoyed by this victory, he was confident and in high spirits. But Elijah's moment on center stage proved to be brief and fleeting. Ahab and Jezebel quickly regrouped their forces and warned the prophet that he would soon suffer the same fate as Baal's prophets. In panic Elijah fled into the wilderness, sat down under a broom tree, and cried out in self-pity: "It is enough; now, O Lord, take away my life; for I am no better than my fathers." He was saying in effect: "I've had it, Lord! Count me out. From now on the battle is all yours!"

Elijah's recovery from his deep depression occurred in several stages: removal from the site of conflict, rest, sleep, and food. Following this therapy, Elijah traveled on to Horeb where his recovery was completed.

Horeb, known as the mount of the Lord or Sinai, was a sacred spot to the people of Israel. It was here that God had called Moses, given the Law to the people, and covenanted with them to be their God. But these sacred associations did not automatically relieve Elijah's depression. He hid himself in a cave until God called out to him: "What are you doing here, Elijah?" That is, "Why have you fled the scene of action? Why have you gone absent without leave?" Elijah replied in words that are defensive, self-serving, and shot through with self-pity, concluding: "I, even I only am left; and they seek my life to take it away."

Following Elijah's pathetic outcry, the Lord commanded him to go and stand on the mount. A mighty hurricane swept across Horeb. A rumbling earthquake shook the ground beneath his feet. A mass of flaming fire lit up the heavens. But God was not in these natural phenomena. It was not until God spoke to Elijah through "a still small voice" that he was cured o his despondency and equipped to get back to his work.

How does God's "silent voice" become audible to us? Martin Luther frequently spoke of "the masks of God." By this phrase he did not mean that God is silent or inaccessible but that God most often speaks to us through commonplace people and events. God's "silent voice" may be a word of encouragement or the simple handclasp of a friend or even a stranger, an inner confirmation of some task that we have undertaken, the sensing of a "Presence" that reassures and communicates love, a moment of quiet silence when our frenzied, hurried lives find focus and wholeness. But supremely, this "silent voice" comes to us through Jesus Christ. The Word made flesh is always "a sound of gentle stillness", for the Incarnate Word is never coercive or overwhelming but one that woos and beckons, saying: "Come to me, all who labor and are heavy laden, and I will give you rest."

Robert G. Hall, a minister of the Presbyterian Church, USA, in 1989 was Professor of Preaching and Worship at Erskine Theological Seminary, Due West, SC.

2 SAMUEL 11:1-15

THE NINTH SUNDAY AFTER PENTECOST
JULY 21, 1991

My father-in law had as the chairperson of his church board a man who was more committed to the church than he was to reading his Bible. One Sunday when the reader of scripture forgot where the Old Testament lesson was to end, she kept on reading the entire story of David! The chairperson was furious and said afterwards, in private, "I didn't know all those things were in the Bible, did you? I didn't know that David did all of those things! And what's more, I didn't want to know!" That is how many of us may feel when we hear this text. Why is this included in Scripture? What is there about this story that can be edifying for the community of faith?

Perhaps the question can be approached from the other direction. What would Scripture look like if people like David, and Saul and Jezebel and Herodias, John the Baptist's wife, were not included? What if people had been left out who, no matter how great, after all was said and done, were ordinary sinners? David is the one chosen by God to unite Israel and Judah and to establish a reign of justice. Yet this same David is the one we find in our lesson who commits adultery with Bathsheba, taking advantage of his power as king. He is moreover unable to extract himself from his sin but commits more sin in the killing of Uriah, to cover it up and to obtain his desires.

If David and people like him were not in the Bible there would be little hope for people like us. No matter how important or unimportant we may be in the eyes of the world, we are all quite common in the eyes of God in at least two respects. First, we are all common sinners. And all of our own attempts to make our sin better, to cover it up, to get rid of it in the waste basket, are miserable failures. All our attempts cannot remove it from our hearts or from the sight of God.

The second way we are common is that we are all loved in common, all bathed in the uncommon love of God, It is God alone who can remove our sin. We cannot be perfect, though we may try, to the great expense of others, and though we may convince ourselves that we are, to the great expense of ourselves. But God can make us perfect, and does. David, though a sinner, was loved. And while God could not tolerate the sin, God also could not tolerate the separation from the sinner.

In the outposts of Newfoundland, for many years Protestant Christians have been taught not to take communion unless they were pure. I will call her Ruth. She had never taken the elements except at confirmation. One day, when her husband seemed lost at sea (he was later found safe) and she was desperate, she took the bread and wine as they were passed to her. "I thought it was for people who were without sin. I was just ordinary, no different from anyone else. I wasn't going to take it. Even when I received the tray. But then I knew I needed it. I didn't know why, I just needed it. That's when I learned it is for sinners, just ordinary sinners like me. It is for anyone who badly needs God."

Deanna Wilson in 1991 was the Associate Minister of St. George's United Church, Toronto.

———————————

LUKE 12:13-21

THE EIGHTH SUNDAY AFTER PENTECOST
AUGUST 2, 1992

When Joseph Broadmore Stockton died, friends, neighbors and relatives filled the white board church at Lady Springs with its green shingles and pointed bell tower.

The church yard, on that summer afternoon, was filled with cars and pickup trucks and the black hearse from Plummers Funeral Home which took him for the last time to the old home place three miles away, where he was buried in the family plot alongside Momma and Poppa, as he had always called his parents.

J.B., as his friends had called him, was a down-home dairy farmer who inherited 2,500 acres from his daddy; and with—
   hard work,
      and marrying into money,
         and some slick dealings that folks in those parts still talked about,

he had managed in his 63 years of living to make himself a medium sized fortune for a South Carolina country boy.
   When he died, he was—
      past president of the Holstein Breeders Association,
         a member of the board of directors of the Farmersand Merchants Bank
            and a charter member of Kiwanis.

Well, the list goes on, and it's all history now, and J.B. Stockton has gone the way of all flesh. Even though the granite marker over his grave is larger than most, it took the same amount of earth to bury him as any other departed soul.

There is a story they tell about J.B.; it may be apocryphal, maybe not, but it seems that back in '79 he went to Clemson's homecoming,
   partied harder than usual...
      that is, he drank too much,
         and had one nightmare of a dream in which he found himself at the gates of hell with the ole' boy himself reading from the list of the shady business deals he had pulled off

   ... to the way he had treated his aged mother the last two years of her life,
      ... to his lip service to church and paltry giving record,
         ... to his philandering on his wife and the list of a dozen other things he couldn't remember doing, but was sure he did.

   The dream was terrifying ... he said he could
      feel the heat,
         smell the burning sulfur
            and see the hungry look on the devil's face with eyes of fire.

His friends kiddingly said the reason he felt heat was he had the electric blanket on high that night, while one of his closest friends, Charlie Tagart, said—

"Anybody that goes to Clemson games is bound to have nightmares."

At any rate, after that awful or fateful night in the Holiday Inn, back in the fall of '79, J.B. Stockton returned home a changed man.

He started going to church regularly...something he had not done since his mother dragged him to Sunday School as a boy.

... He seemed to stay at home more, spending time with Betty Lou, his wife, and visiting the grandchildren.

... He gave $30,000 to a small church college and paid for nine stained glass windows in the little church at Lady Springs.

... He even cleaned up his language and shied away from hard liquor...with the exception of a glass or two of homemade muscadine wine.

Some of J.B.'s closest friends said he "got religion" because the doctor told him he had a bad heart.

Others said he was just like his father...he didn't come to his senses "til six years before he died. J.B. insisted, however, that it was the scary dream he had; as he said—

"It was the Lord's way of giving me a second chance."

Well, if the story of J.B. Stockton seems like a thinly disguised and embellished version of Jesus' parable with a southern accent, it is.

And in keeping with our North American penchant for stories with happy endings, the rich farmer in the Dixie version came to his senses and changed his ways. We like stories where people are given a second chance and turn their life around. It gives us all hope.

However, in Jesus' story, there is no second chance or little hope for the well-to-do farmer to mend his ways, so that he can

increase his pledge,

or be a better husband

or give a lump sum to the college of his choice. It is, in fact, curtains for him with God, not the devil, closing the final scene and offering this stern epitaph—

"This is how it is with those who pile up riches for themselves but are not rich in God's sight."

Where is the good news? The good news is that grace not greed has the final word in the Realm of God; and we like J.B. Stockton by the Word of the Spirit can see the world with different eyes. Oh, the work of grace and greed will continue existing side by side; and on more occasions than we care to admit we will pay the fool, but the Kingdom of Grace is enduring and eternal. For the younger brother, who came to Jesus asking for help with division of money, and went away with a parable ringing in his head, the Realm of God was just beginning.

Richard A. Cushman in 1992 was minister of Dorchester Presbyterian Church in Summerville, South Carolina.

GENESIS 21:8-21

THE THIRD SUNDAY AFTER PENTECOST
JUNE 20, 1993

I was settling down to an evening of "mindless activity" just a few nights ago. My daughter was comfortably in bed, fed and bathed, and tucked in between her "Garfield" sheets with her favorite blanket and stuffed animal. She was comfortable and secure and dreaming, no doubt, pleasant dreams. How could she have any other kind?

With all my parental duties completed, I sat down to watch the news. A television program caught my eye. It was a program about the drought in Somalia; it captivated me. The first picture was of a small child (probably about the same age as my daughter), dark skinned, with large brown eyes. His bones were protruding. He was lying in his mother's arms, motionless. He wasn't crying, perhaps he had long lost the energy for such things. He was breathing, but only breathing, not moving, not making a sound.

I remember thinking how "colorless" the world was around him. Faded in the background were the silhouettes of dirt colored huts that I suppose provided some protection from the sun. The earth was parched and brown. The clothing was brown. Even the sky seemed to be a grayish color, though not the color of rain clouds. The sky just seemed to be one with the land, no difference between what was above or beneath the horizon. The commentator was describing the African community. "This community will have water for about three more days," he said. "Only three more days and their water will be gone."

We have seen these scenes so many times. You would think that we would be immune to them. Yet, they still bring tears of sadness and exasperation. A child lying out in the desert. The water is gone and the threat of death fills the hot, stale air.

"I can't bear to see the child die," Hagar said. She spoke knowing that no one would hear. No one was near, and she began to cry. She had been robbed of her future, robbed of her home, but no one could rob her of her grief. And she sat in the wilderness and she cried.

"Why are you troubled, Hagar?" Mysteriously the unannounced voice came from nowhere. Someone was there. The absent God was present in her misery. "Do not be afraid." "Not be afraid?" she thought. The child was about to die. "Do not be afraid? Do not be afraid?"

I sat there staring at that child from Somalia, wishing I could erase his image from my mind - put him under a bush, far away, out of sight. But he was there silently looking at me, staring eye to eye. Why was I troubled? There was no way I could reach him, no way I could touch him, comfort him, give him a glass of water to drink. Why was I troubled? Why was I suddenly afraid?

"Open your eyes," the voice said to Hagar. "I have heard the child, and I know the child's sufferings. Open your arms to the child. Pick him up and comfort him. Open your eyes. There is water for him. There is enough water in the world for him. Open your arms. Open your eyes."

Was there enough in the world for that thirsty child, ready to die? Was there enough water for my child and for that child, too? That's what Sarah asked. Is there enough for both these children? Yes, is the answer. There is. There is enough in the world for all of its children. There is enough food. There is enough water. "I hear the African child silently crying," God says. God is hoping that we will allow our eyes to be opened to the well of water we have to share.

Mary Donovan Turner is an ordained minister of the Christian Church (Disciples of Christ). She has a Ph.D. in Old Testament studies from Emory University and in 1993 was an Asst. Professor of Homiletics at the Pacific School of Religion in Berkeley, California.

DEUTERONOMY 34:1-12

THE TWENTY-FIRST SUNDAY AFTER PENTECOST
OCTOBER 24, 1993

In small towns in the South one frequently encounters older women who have an enormous interest in the past. They are the dynamos behind local preservation efforts. They are the ones who work to see that the local library has a genealogy research room. They write the town histories and tend the flowers around the statues on the courthouse lawn. Many are members of the D.A.R. (Daughters of the American Revolution) or The U.D.C. (United Daughters of the Confederacy). When you are introduced to one of these ladies, they may politely inquire about "who your people were". If you are a Southerner, you know they are not checking pedigrees as much as looking for distant cousins. To be able to answer their question and explain who "your people" are, you must minimally know the maiden names of all your foremothers back to your great great grandmothers.

One of my favorite local historians was Ola Grace. (Southern women often have double first names. Southerners take the time to use both. We are in no great hurry.) Ola Grace was the historian of our local church, which had a lot of history since it had been established before Alabama became a state. It even had in its steeple a bronze bell cast by Paul Revere and Sons. Ola Grace was also on the Methodist Conference Commission on Archives and History. I distinctly remember the year she traveled to Annual Conference sessions to exhort the assembled delegates to go home and ignite an "Archival Revival". She urged churches to videotape oral histories with their senior members, to buy acid free storage boxes for church records, and to preserve their past.

What made Ola Grace, a person of grace, however, was not her love of the past. It was the way she leaned into the future. When a senior citizens exercise class was organized at the church, Ola Grace, then in her late seventies, was one of the first to sign up. She planned to get a lot more use out of her body. And a year later, when a prayer group for peace and nuclear disarmament was started in the congregation, Ola Grace was a charter member. She typed letters to her senators, filled with hope for a future without the terror of war and the costs of preparing for it. At one meeting someone suggested we needed to establish a lending library of books and pamphlets on peace for our church. So in a few months Ola Grace's dining room table was covered not only with acid free cardboard storage boxes of church records. She had made room for file boxes of literature on peacemaking.

It was in exercise class that Ola Grace slipped and fractured her hip. Senior adults fear such an injury. They all have had friends who went into a steep decline after such a break.

But a few days after her new hip joint was installed, Ola Grace had her sister bring some things from the dining room table to her room at the rehab center. And before too many more days Ola Grace had make herself known to the doctors and the nurses and the orderlies and the other patients as, "that lady who gives away those books on peace." Ola Grace figured as long as she had to be cooped up in that hospital, she might as well get these people thinking about how we can work for a more peaceful future. Down the hall rolled Ola Grace in her wheelchair, in and out of the solarium. Always looking for someone who needed to have one of those books on peace that she carried right beside her brand new hip.

When Moses, age one hundred and twenty, stood on Mt. Nebo, he had a storehouse of memories to savor. Incredible memories of a burning bush...a Pharaoh's throne room...a walk across the sea bed...an encounter with the Holy One of Israel on a cloudy mountain top. But as Moses stood looking out toward the west from Mt. Nebo, his daydreams were not about the great and good things God had done in the past. Moses was squinting into the sunset, shading his eyes with his hand, looking over into the Promised Land; trying to catch a glimpse of the wonderful tomorrow God was stirring up for his people.

Michael M. Stewart in 1993 was a United Methodist pastor in Fayette, Alabama.

II CORINTHIANS 5:6-10, 14-17

THE THIRD SUNDAY AFTER PENTECOST
JUNE 12, 1994

Today Andre Stein is a professor at the University of Toronto and a Canadian citizen. But he was born in Hungary and when he was eight years' old, the Nazis marched into Budapest. Stein is a Jew and before the war was ended, sixty members of his extended family were killed, including his mother. He was tortured by members of the Arrow Cross, the Hungarian fascist party, and left for dead in a ghetto alley. Thanks only to the cunning of his sister and an aunt did he survive. After liberation, his father returned from a forced-labor camp, blind and broken in spirit.

For the next forty years Stein endured an ongoing confusion about what had happened. Then he gave utterance to his grief and rage in a book titled, *Broken Silence*. After its appearance, he was invited to a conference led by Elie Wiesel in Washington, D.C., the first ever held on the theme of "the righteous gentile." There, for the first time also, Stein met the people he calls "rescuers" - Christians who had hidden Jews and helped them escape deportation to the extermination camps. It was these rescuers who were the guests of the Holocaust Memorial Council of the State Department of the United States.

Honored though they were, these rescuers felt mostly lost and ill at ease. For them, the celebration of their heroism was overstated and misplaced. "Since when does a man deserve praise from the highest human sources for being just that, a man?" asked one. Another vigorously resisted the phrase "righteous gentile": "As for being righteous, that is the exclusive domain of the Lord."

Stein discovered that most of these self-effacing people with time-worn faces were Frisians, from the north-eastern province of The Netherlands. Many had emigrated to Ontario, Canada, after the war. Before the war, there were 140,000 Jews living in The Netherlands. Through the efforts of the rescuers, some 15,000 were saved; the others perished.
Perhaps it is necessary to emphasize that the great majority of Christians in Europe stood by and did nothing. The father-in-law of one of the rescuers rebuked him for risking the lives of his wife and newborn child: "You can't get involved in the life of every little Jew. What are those people to us anyway?"

To take an overview of the Holocaust of European Jewry is to view a very dark prospect indeed. By and large people co-operated, whether actively or passively, with grotesque evil. The view "from above" might lead us to despair about humanity and about the power of evil in the world.

But there is another view, the view from below—from garden level!—a view that takes into account the individuals who refused to co-operate and who were willing to die so that others would not. The young pastor rebuked by his father-in-law made this response: "What if Christ himself came knocking on your door, Father? Would you send him away too? Do you recall that Jesus was nothing more than a little Jew?"

Meeting the rescuers was a transforming experience for Stein. For the first time since he was eight he found a reason to begin to take hope seriously. Out of this growing tendency to hope came his second book, *Quiet Heroes* (Lester & Orpen Dennys). In it he says: "These quiet heroes did not respond to an overwhelming situation in either of the two extreme ways which are so prevalent now. On the one hand, they did not take upon themselves the impossible burden of their times. They did not feel responsible for everything and everyone. On the other hand, they did not choose to do nothing. They chose, instead, a way of response which was as effective as it was humble. They did not do everything but they did do something."

The mystery of evil is formidable. But there is another mystery as worthy of our attention: the mystery of goodness. As Mary Jo Leddy (a Roman Catholic activist sister) has said, "Although we know something about why people are cruel and violent, we need to learn more about why human beings are good and merciful." What enables people to march to the sound of a different drummer in the face of apathy and self-protection on the part of the majority?

Bill Bouwma is one of the rescuers in Stein's book. One day he was challenged by Edith Cohen, whom he was hiding, to explain why he was doing it when it meant

, life. Finally, he gave this answer: "I am involved in hiding Jews because a ‸side me told me that I had to do it. Regardless of anything else, that's all there ‸ it. If I had disobeyed that voice in me, I would no longer be me." That's all there , to it! As if in that mustard seed of unbreakable conviction there were not already a tree leafing out to shade many! As if in that recognition of an inescapable imperative there were not the mysterious working of the providence of God!

Archbishop Desmond Tutu attended the General Council of our denomination in August of 1990, before the big breakthroughs in South Africa. His address was an enrapturing, mountain-top experience. What comes across when he speaks is a confidence and hope that bubbles up, like effervescence.

When Tutu and other South African church people speak to their enemies about apartheid, there is a constant, ringing theme. "We must assert, and assert confidently, that God is in charge. You are not God, you are mortals. It is God whom we worship and God cannot be mocked. You have already lost. Come and join the winning side."

The Reverend Peter Wyatt in 1994 served in a pastoral team with his wife, Joan, at Trinity-St.Paul's United Church, Toronto.

MARK 4:35-41

THE FOURTH SUNDAY AFTER PENTECOST
JUNE 19, 1994

[handwritten: 6-21-97 "Faith"]

It had been one of those incredibly long and tiring days. The sun's rays were hot, hot enough to scorch the bottoms of their feet. From the very start of day until dusk, the people had been clamoring after him. He hadn't had time to take a break. He'd had no chance to rest or get a bite to eat. People were anxious to learn from him—to hear what this new teacher had to say. So, he taught them all kinds of precious things. Using stories of their lives and experiences, he explained great truths. But when evening finally came, the teacher had had enough. It was time to go. He looked at his dearest friends and urged them to give the crowd the slip so they could go someplace else. Mark says the teacher was so tired his disciples took him "just as he was"—tired, hungry, talked out.

Jesus got on board the boat for two reasons. First, like that infamous old chicken crossing the road, he was simply trying to get to the other side! There were more people to reach, other lessons to teach—his mission and ministry were expanding. But also, and maybe even more so, Jesus was taking that little boat ride for much the same reason you and I take them when we go out on Sebago or one of the other area lakes or ponds—he was going off to get away from it all. There on that Sea of Galilee, Jesus was taking a break. Leaving everything in the able hands of the boaters, Jesus snuck into the back of the boat and dozed off with his head on a cushion....

It wasn't long before his rest was interrupted. Soon the disciples came looking for him. They figured somehow he might at least calm them since their boat was sinking. But before he calmed them, Jesus said to his sea: "Be still." To the wind, he uttered, "Peace." And a calm overcame them. The disciples hadn't figured on this. They had been angry about his apparent indifference and evidently had no idea about his extraordinary powers. They had scolded him for not caring, but surely it would have been fair for him to scold them for not believing. Yet his only rebuke was of the wind and waves; to these he had said, "Peace! Be still!" To his disciples he simply said, "Why?" He asked why they were afraid, he wondered at their lack of faith.

After such a long day of teaching, Jesus' stories must have been ringing in their ears. Still, that was not enough to give them confidence that they would be safe in the storm. They knew enough to turn to Jesus, but it stopped there—their faith was yet as small as the tiny mustard seeds he'd spoken of earlier in the day. The disciples had only the first inklings of faith—they knew to call on him—but they weren't quite sure what it was all about, they weren't too sure what he would do when they called....

Far removed from us as is this stormy night's boat ride, within its detail rests a truth as accurate now as it was then. The reality is we aren't so very different from the fisherfolk who followed Jesus as he went about teaching and healing. We too have witnessed some signs. We have heard stories that stir us deep inside—yet however faithful and devoted we seem to be, our faith is not all it could be. There aren't many storms of life that we get through without crying out to God, "Don't you care?" Whatever words or actions we use to say it, we are very much like those disciples caught in a storm wondering why God doesn't care enough to help. While we know Jesus is with us, yet for one reason or another, in a moment's panic or disappointment or fear, we have a hard time knowing that it matters. We need to be told again—we need to know in the depths of our souls that all will be well because of Jesus' presence. All will be well no matter what the storm, no matter how hard the gales blow against us. The One whose voice wind and waves obey—Jesus—is with us. He's with us always. What's more, he's calmed the sea of death that ultimately would swallow us up. Because of his death and resurrection, we really don't need to be afraid. In his tender compassion, he has made sure of that. And instead of railing against us for doubting, Jesus puts his arms around us—and even gives of his own body and blood to seal his promise to be near to us.

My friends, with your doubts and fears you are in good company—all the way down the line from Jesus' closest companions to the person sitting beside you and the one standing before you now. For each and all of us, our faith has a ways to go—a ways to grow. But we must know that the seas of our souls respond to his voice as did the wind and waves in Galilee. To us, Jesus will keep on coming with reminders of his presence and his power. He comes as Master of the wind and waves and Lord of your life. He comes to you again this day and says, "Peace. Be still." There is no need to be afraid. You are not at the mercy of nature or anything else—you are safe in the mercy of a God who sent Jesus to save you. Jesus is here and he will keep you safe. Don't be afraid.

Joanne Engquist in 1994 was a pastor of Faith Lutheran Church (E.L.C.A.), Windham, ME.

EPHESIANS 2:11-22

THE EIGHTH SUNDAY AFTER PENTECOST
JULY 17, 1994

Xenophobia: the fear of the alien, the fear of strangers. It's a virtual epidemic in our society and world! We protect our residences with dead bolts, our airports with metal detectors, our farms with dogs and make sure we've got ammunition for the Smith and Wesson Strangers are welcome so long as they hold our majority's opinions and abide by our parochial rules. But watch out if they undermine our political convictions or threaten our standard of living! So in Central Europe, they call strangers "inassimilable," "culturally incompatible." But we can't "point the finger"; *xenophobia* knows no bounds; and it's not always so dramatic. African American and Anglo American students sit at separate tables on my campus. Faculty departments are suspicious of each other. Even the institutions explicitly created to make space for "the stranger within our gates" have become so dominated by this insidious mix of fear and contempt that they are unable to fulfill their original purposes.

But Christians are called to offer hospitality to strangers. It's the grunt work of peacemaking! Throughout scripture, the treatment of strangers is used as a test of faithfulness to God who identifies with the alien in our midst. Protectionist postures are soundly condemned: "When a foreigner resides with you in your land, you shall not oppress the alien. The stranger who resides with you shall be to you as the citizen among you; you shall love the stranger as yourself!" Those are the Old Testament prohibitions. And the New Testament commands *philoxenia,* hospitality to strangers; "Practice hospitality." "Do not neglect to show hospitality to strangers." Matthew 25, Jesus' metaphor of the judgment of the world, presents one question upon which eternal destiny depends: "Did you or did you not extend hospitality to strangers?" This is our essential gift and call as Christians, the hallmark of our counter-culture community: extending hospitality to strangers.

So how do we convert our fear of strangers to hospitality? The conversion process is called "reframing" (a concept from John Patton, Pastoral Care, Candler School of Theology). We "reframe" the stranger in our perception of him or her. We see the stranger not as someone who is different from us but one who is essentially like us. Really, it is an ancient idea. The Levites heard the Lord saying to them, "You shall love the stranger as yourself, for you too were once strangers in the land of Egypt." The alien is not essentially different from us; the stranger is essentially like us. That's Old Testament; now the New. Ephesians calls upon Gentile converts to Christianity to take a look at themselves and Jewish persons (Christians and non-Christian alike) in the same light! "Remember, you were in the same dire straits as they were: you were hopeless, without God, strangers to the covenant of promise. You are more like them than different from them." Before they could realize the peace that Jesus Christ had established for them, Ephesian Christians had to "reframe" those from whom they had been divided by a wall of hostility!

Now what is the result of this conversion? We are able to offer them a hospitable space where strangers can cast off their strangeness and be free to be fellow human beings. In essence, hospitality is the creation of a free, receptive place where the stranger becomes a guest. Henri Nouwen reminds us (in *Reaching Out*) that the Dutch word for hospitality is *gastfrijheid* which means "freedom of the guest." Hospitality offers friendship without binding the guest and freedom without leaving the guest alone. Hospitality does not intend to force change upon people but to offer them space where change can take place. Hospitality does not bring people over to our side, but fosters freedom where dividing walls can dissolve. Hospitality is a friendly emptiness where strangers can enter in and discover themselves, can be free to sing their own songs, speak their own languages, sing their own songs, find their vocations. These are the results of our "reframing": the creation of a hospitable space where strangers can cast off that strangeness and be free to be fellow human beings.

What then does hospitality look like? David and Ruth Rupprecht open their home to care for the needy, troubled and homeless on a short term basis. Virginia was a woman who needed such a place one cold winter morning. "Meeting Virginia for the first time," say Dave and Ruth, "was something like discovering a scared rabbit. Extremely thin and pale, she would glance nervously around, checking to see, as it were, if she were being watched or followed.... Speaking only when spoken to, she was afraid to share her ideas with others, lest she say the wrong thing." Virginia and her son, Bobby, were suffering under an abusive husband and father, who was addicted to alcohol. But their home was already "full" with three other "guests" (aliens). The Rupprechts agonized: could they provide hospitality to two more strangers who, for all they imagined, might draw yet another who brandished a gun and desired his son! Under a tearful prayer, they decided to welcome the terrorized mother and child anyway, risk and all. Almost immediately, Virginia and Bobby made great progress. The Rupprechts walked with them through a long, roller-coaster court case with the husband and father over custody rights for Bobby. Bobby became a regular school attender and improved his grades. Virginia became a confident, self-directed woman. The Rupprechts now say that, "Virginia is not the same today as she was that cold winter morning. She smiles when you first greet her, she initiates conversation, and she openly shares what God has done.... Our home in many ways has been a gift.... To draw our walls around us would be selfish and sinful, while to open to those outside who need to come in is to know firsthand the transforming power of Christ" (in *Radical Hospitality*, by the Rupprechts).

Jeff Kisner in 1994 was Assistant Professor of Religion at Waynesburg College, Waynesburg, PA, and Interim Pastor of the West Greene (PA) Presbyterian Parish. He holds the Ph.D. in Homiletics from The Southern Baptist Theological Seminary in Louisville, KY.

JOHN 6:24-35

THE TENTH SUNDAY AFTER PENTECOST
JULY 31, 1994

You have probably heard the story about the man who died and was greeted in heaven by his wife. She had predeceased him by several years. She said, "Honey, heaven is wonderful! I am so glad you are here now to enjoy it with me!" He said, "I would have been here sooner, but you made me eat all that oat bran."

With our Nautilus fitness machines, our video exercise tapes, and our low fat, high fiber diets, many of us have made a major commitment to doing our part to insure a long life and good health.

And we are wise to do so. Stewardship of our bodies is an important part of discipleship. I recently heard about a senior pastor of a large church who assembled his staff and presented each one of them with a pair of running shoes. He explained that part of their job description, as leaders in the Christian community, was to exercise regularly.

And yet we all know folks who have done everything right healthwise and died too young. And we can all point to people like Helen Keller or Flannery O'Connor whose physical lives were limited by illness and yet they radiated power and vitality.

In the sixth chapter of John, Jesus feeds a crowd of hungry people gathered by the Sea of Galilee. All the gospels tell this story, in fact. While the gospels may suggest that John the Baptist was ascetic in lifestyle, Jesus is not. Many of the most endearing gospel scenes portray Jesus sharing a meal with people. Similarly, Jesus loved spinning parables about banquets and wedding parties. I once saw a kitchen apron emblazoned with the words, "NEVER TRUST A SKINNY COOK." The Incarnation means that we ought to trust no savior who does not embrace human eating and human friendships and human loving.

But when the crowd decides to crown Jesus king on the basis of giving away free bread, he runs away. And when the crowd, still hungry for those lovely warm loaves of rye and pumpernickel, pursue him to Capernaum, Jesus offers them no bread.

But he addresses an even more profound human hunger pain than food: the craving we have to be connected to something that is eternal and holy. As the manna in the wilderness pointed to a God whose breadmaking capacity far exceeded the granaries and ovens of the Pharaoh, just so the bread Jesus gives points to the presence of One who can satisfy the deepest cravings of the human heart.

The male teenager at our house has passed his father by two shoe sizes. Now, barely fourteen, he has only a half inch to grow to pass me in height. In spite of dire warnings by grandmother about what the lining of his colon will look like when he is fifty, he disdains fruits and vegetables. Many years have passed since he has been compliant enough to let us play airplane with spoonfuls of squash and broccoli. His growth spurts today are mostly fueled by pizza, cheeseburgers, and mixing bowls full of cereal and milk (not the cheap generic cereals either; he prefers the $4.50 a box stuff).

Actually food is not a big priority with our teenager. And when we had a party for him and his friends of both sexes we discovered that they actually ate very little of the snacks we had spread out on the table. He later explained that the girls are afraid of getting fat, and the guys don't want to leave the girls long enough to go load their plates. What is more important than food is acceptance by others. The threat of "no candy today" may have worked when he was three to produce desired behavior. Now the only threat that seems to work is "no telephone tonight"—so great is his need to be in touch with others and maintain his connections.

The gospel is this: God not only provides wonderful morsels for the taste buds. God also feeds our heart by connecting us with the eternal. Though our appetite may come and go, and though there comes a time when we will taste death, we are still mysteriously nourished and sustained by God. We cannot and do not live by bread alone. We thrive by the hearty welcome God gives us. We grow up nourished by God's acceptance. And fortified with that love, we can go a long way.

Michael M. Stewart in 1994 was a United Methodist pastor in Fayette, Alabama.

I KINGS 8:22-30, 41-43

THE THIRTEENTH SUNDAY AFTER PENTECOST
AUGUST 21, 1994

On the edge of the city where I live, they're building a development of new houses. I enjoy poking around construction sites, so I've stopped by a couple of times to check on how they're doing. The houses are big: I guess this is going to be an up-scale neighborhood. They all have three-car garages—a requirement. None of that, actually, has surprised me. What has surprised me is that when I visit these new places, I get pangs of longing. I hear sounds and smell smells and almost dream dreams that seem to come over me from somewhere far away—Minnesota, maybe, or Illinois—where I grew up.

I think it's the porches. These brand new, never-lived-in houses have great big porches—something you don't see much, here in the Bay area. White, wooden railings, and plenty of room for a swing. Some even have those upstairs porches where you go to shake out your rugs and dustmops. Gingerbread trim and screen doors. And they hum the old songs, and they whisper stories about Grandpa, and they smell of roasting turkey.

The developers know full well what they're doing. My reaction is exactly what they're hoping for. Nostalgia sells houses. Maybe especially here, in this urban sprawl, people feel rootless: we long for a real neighborhood that feels like something we dimly remember. And so the architects and designers offer us buildings complete with all the most modern conveniences, but decorated, so to speak, with touches that are supposed to communicate a sense of "home" to us rootless westerners—porches and balconies and turrets and gingerbread and big yards.

So the person who builds the house is in a kind of dialogue with the person who will eventually live there. Each is saying, "This is what home is—hope you agree!" And when they do agree, they have a sale.

I know it's a bit whimsical, but I've been imagining Solomon as one of those builders. He puts together this magnificent, monumental house for the Lord, and then when he's dedicating it, he asks, "Will God really live on the earth?" What has been the kind of communication, here, between the builder and the dweller? What are the touches—pillars, treasuries, cherubim—that Solomon hopes will say "home" to God? Just what kind of Being does Solomon think that he is dealing with, who will see this awesome Temple and recognize it, right away, as "home?"

We can ask the same kind of question, can't we, of any of the houses we know that have been designed for God. Think of the multitude of styles, the multitude of shapes, of sizes, and degrees of magnificence you've seen. All labeled, one way or another, "God's House." And each time, try asking, "Who is the God that this house should appeal to? What kind of God might call this place 'home?' "

But of course, Solomon himself seemed to understand that God doesn't live in any Temple, grand as it might be; and certainly, with our thousands of churches and synagogues and other places of worship around the world, we don't believe that God lives in any single house. Maybe the very multiplicity of forms and styles and sizes already says something about who we think God is. Or maybe, like the generations after Solomon who meditated on what the Temple really was, maybe we understand that the house itself isn't really where God lives, but is really a place where we go to worship together. Then the same question asks itself once again: if, in a sense, this house is a dwelling-place for our *worship,* what kind of worship, or what kind of worshiper, will look at it and recognize it as "home?"

And if God can't be contained by a Temple, or a multitude of houses of worship; indeed, if God can't be contained by earth or even the highest heaven, yet the miracle remains that God *can* dwell in a human heart, a human soul. In fear and trembling, and with a critical eye, we might look anew at the layout of that soul and the decorations that adorn it: what is it communicating? What is its style? Can we tell what kind of God it is inviting to come and stay?

And yet the truth is more awesome still. Jesus proclaims to us that God has already made a dwelling in us and among us, just as we are. And we look honestly at ourselves—our violence, and our frailty, and our silliness, and our occasional nobility—and we ask in amazement: what kind of God can this possibly be, who has looked upon us, awkwardly decorated as we are, and said, "That looks like home?"

Linda L. Clader is a priest in the Episcopal Church and in 1994 was Associate Professor of Homiletics at the Church Divinity School of the Pacific, Berkeley, California.

MARK 9:30-37

THE SEVENTEENTH SUNDAY AFTER PENTECOST
SEPTEMBER 18, 1994

In the 1920's an American named Bruce Barton wrote a book about Jesus entitled, *The Man Nobody Knows.* Barton, an advertising executive, portrayed Jesus as the founder of modern business. According to Barton, Jesus was a regular he-man, a go-getter type. Jesus had picked up twelve ordinary men from the bottom ranks of business and forged them into an organization that conquered the world. Jesus was virile, youthful, successful, a back slapping man of affairs. Jesus the businessman. Barton's Jesus looks at you with gleam in his eye and says, go for it. A Jesus who stands to bless our quest for success.

Bruce Barton's book is now more than sixty years old, but his Jesus seems very much up to date. In fact, modern North American Christians often appear to behave as if they were following Bruce Barton's Jesus. Success and the pursuit of happiness often seems to be the first thing on our minds. Many of us are in hot pursuit. We pursue success through education. Late nights, multiple coffees, all in hot pursuit of the happiness that good grades and a good education can bring. Later we pursue success through our careers and professions. We pour in our time and energy still in hot pursuit, of money and status that successful people expect. And so we like the Bruce Barton-type Jesus, a Jesus who looks our way and nods his head with approval, go for it. Success.

But in Mark 9:30, Jesus isn't talking success. There Jesus shocks his disciples with the news that he is going to die. Jesus talks about betrayal, suffering, and death. Now how is a person supposed to square suffering and death with kicking out the Romans and ruling as one of Jesus' chief deputies? For Jesus' disciples, suffering and death didn't fit in with the way they envisioned the future. A basic incompatibility between a gold card and a cross. Designer clothes and a crown of thorns. Wing tips and nails through the feet. Suffering and death just don't fit with happiness and success. So when Jesus started to talk about suffering and death, the disciples do not understand. And they are afraid to ask for clarification. No wonder. When a leader speaks of his suffering and death, anyone can see that it hardly bodes well for those who follow him. Perhaps it's better not to ask.

So in Mark 9, Jesus' disciples won't touch the topic of what Jesus' suffering and death might have to do with them. Instead they launch rather easily into a heated discussion about which of them is the greatest. The perfect topic for people who want to find out how they are doing in the race for success and the pursuit of happiness.

Today a "who is the greatest" discussion might begin with such casual questions as: so where did you go on holidays this summer? Or so where do you work? Or where did you go to university? Are you still on your diet? Or how old was Colin when he was potty-trained? Or perhaps, what kind of computer do you have now. Modern disciples are as accomplished as the original twelve in avoiding the topic of what suffering has to do with following Jesus. We too would rather talk about who is the greatest.

So what does Jesus do? You might expect him to get rid of people like us, people so fixated upon success and the pursuit of happiness, half-hearted in our following him, and to find a few more people like Mother Teresa, or Billy Graham for his team of disciples. You might expect Jesus to do something like that, but he doesn't.

Instead Jesus quietly hauls his disciples aside and patiently explains to them what they did not understand and were afraid to ask. If anyone wants to be first, Jesus explained, he or she must be the very last, the servant of all. He calls over one of the small children that happened to be in the house where they were staying. As he picks her up, he gives her a hug. Whoever welcomes a little child like this welcomes me, Jesus tells his disciples.

Well not just little children. Jesus uses that little child as an example. A child is a good example of someone who needs things. Think of all the things that a little baby or young child needs. He needs to be washed, cuddled, changed, carried, clothed, cooed to, and fed. Children especially at the time of Jesus had almost no standing. The rabbis classified children with the deaf, the dumb, and the weak minded, persons low on the totem pole. So by pointing to that little child, Jesus invites his disciples to focus their attention, not upon those who can help them the most in their drive for success, but upon the lowly and the needy. Welcome them and you are welcoming me he tells them.

What an incredible privilege. As we meet the needs of the lowliest, Jesus dignifies us with the pleasure of his company. Jesus meets us in them and empowers us to serve. Jesus goes with us even as we follow him toward the cross.

As we get set this morning to go back into the work a day world of the coming week, we know how easy it is to get all caught up in the quest for success. We know how easily we are sucked into discussions about who has the most bedrooms, megabytes, or youngest potty trained child. Don't be afraid, Jesus assures us. I'm not going to cut you from my team of disciples. But focus your attention upon helping those people with little status and great need. I will be there. I will be so pleased to accept your hospitality.

John Rottman in 1994 was a doctoral candidate in homiletics at Emmanuel College of the University of Toronto and an ordained minister in the Christian Reformed Church

---

MARK 12:28-34

THE TWENTY-THIRD SUNDAY AFTER PENTECOST
OCTOBER 30, 1994

He had just finished cleaning up around the corn crib and stepped out of the wind and into the late November sunlight when he heard a strange high pitched sound. He listened carefully as he sat back on his heels leaning on the crib. Then he heard the sound again and his heart stopped momentarily and suddenly raced wildly. In fear he was in a panicked run almost instantly. He started the old pickup truck and bounced the vehicle wildly over a quarter mile of corn field toward the corn picker that sat at the far edge of the field.

His worst nightmare appeared before his eyes as he neared the far side of the picker. There his brother, Dave, lay across the corn head screaming and kicking. The corn picker's engine was still running and the corn head kept pulling at his 17 year old brother.

Over the next couple of hours Dave never lost consciousness, but minutes seemed like an eternity as the picker engine was stopped, rescue squad called, corn picker disassembled to remove Dave, a rush to the hospital and finally surgery to remove the mangled remains of his right arm. Later he would relate that he had relatively little pain until the days following the accident.

Two weeks after the horror had happened Dave returned to high school, his right arm replaced by a bandage that ended only inches from his shoulder. A strong and formerly outspoken farm boy told his story softly and timidly. He tried hard to remain unnoticed in our small school where everyone knew each other. Everyone wanted to hear, first hand, all the gruesome details and express genuine concern and support.

For three years I sang bass with Dave in the high school choir. Half of the time was before and half after the life changing incident. Over the months following the accident Dave privately shared with a few of us the personal side of his experience. He was from a strong Northern European family ancestry. His parents taught and lived hard work, strong personal and spiritual values, and a close adherence to life's rules.

Following the shock, fear, pain and realization that for the rest of his life he would live without his dominate right arm, an equal horror plagued this young man. What would his Dad and Mom have to say to him? He had been carefully taught every aspect of life and that included the rules of safety. His mind went over the happenings of the day again and again. He knew he should have turned off the picker before getting off. He had done so literally hundreds of times in the past couple of weeks. Yet there was so much downed corn because of an early ice storm. He had only been feeding in the downed and lodged mess that kept slowing an important harvest.

When his parents entered the hospital room Dave had searched for the verbal and non-verbal messages that would say, "I taught you not to take any risks around machinery. Why didn't you follow the rules!" Yet, all he heard and all his mother or father said was, "We love You!" He expected it from his Mom, but although he knew how his Dad felt he could never remember hearing the actual words spoken before. Yes, and they were so easy and genuinely said.

The rules of farming, the rules of life, and the moral rules of God, even the commandments, are not merely to keep us in line. The commandments are for our and our society's protection and fullness of life. God loves us and wants the best for all of us. A parent's love for a child leads him or her to teach the child to not touch a hot stove, or play in the street. The same concern causes the parents to teach the child to brush his or her teeth regularly. Breaking some rules have immediate and painful consequences, while others have consequences that are harder to identify and slower in coming. Disobeying the limits that God has set forth for us often do not have such immediate or clear consequences. Dave was loved and forgiven for his bad judgment around the corn picker, before he could even ask, but he will live with the consequences of his actions for a life time.

"Which commandment is the first of all?" asked the scribe. Jesus responds with a good news, Gospel, message. Love God, love your neighbor, will not prevent the loss of an arm, the burning of a hand, or the breaking of all relationships, but it focuses the intent and character of all of God's rules and dealings with us. We are God's beloved children.

Dr. Norman E. Wall in 1994 was senior pastor of Covenant Lutheran Church of Stoughton, Wisconsin. He is an ordained minister of the Evangelical Lutheran Church in America.

LUKE 8:26-39

THE THIRD SUNDAY AFTER PENTECOST
JUNE 25, 1995

A SWINEHERD: Listen. My buddy and I were just lying around in the shade that day, watching the pigs. Down the shore a ways, a bunch of folks from the other side of the lake came ashore out of two boats. Suddenly there's this scream, and the crazy man jumped out at them from behind one of the tombs. Yeah, we knew him; we used to throw rocks at him for fun. Anyway, we could hear him screaming over there. We could see five or six of those guys struggling to hold him, keep him from attacking their leader. Then he and the crazy man talked for a couple of minutes. Then the crazy man pointed toward us, and then so did the leader he was talking to. Then it was quiet for a bit. All of a sudden some of the pigs started acting crazy. They reared up and lashed out at the others. They ran and butted. They stood and frothed at the mouth and squealed to make your hair stand up. Me and Jerry stood up. We were scared. The squealing and screaming got louder and louder, and they began to move, and suddenly they were running toward the lake. We yelled and started to chase them, but it was too late. They just piled over the edge, down into the water. We stood and watched. They churned it into foam, and then slowly it all got still. We took off for town to tell the mayor and them.

MAYOR: As Mayor of Gerasa, I am proud to say that the police chief and I have seen to the restoration of order in the area out around the Tombs. Of course we are shocked at the wanton disregard for safety and property which has been exhibited by those Jews from across the lake. And while we do not believe that their leader, a man named Jesus, has terrifying supernatural powers, we nevertheless ordered him and his motley crew to re-embark and leave immediately; naturally, they complied. We are gratified that the town demoniac seems to have returned to his senses. We cannot explain this, but we doubt that the stranger named Jesus "made the crazy man's devils go into the pigs," as one of the swineherds has been saying. As to the pigs themselves, as Mayor I'm sure the Town Council will reject the claims of their owners that the township ought to reimburse them; the pigs were grazing illegally on public land anyway. That's all for now; no questions, please.

DOCTOR: You all know me; I've been the doctor here for over thirty years. I've examined the—the former demoniac. (Like us, he long ago forgot his name, and we'll have to search the records for it.) He's in good health, considering his long exposure to the elements. There are very many old and more recent scars on his head and body; apparently he would throw himself on the ground or beat himself with rocks when these fits came on him. But he's very strong, and his constitution is sound; now that he has recovered his wits, his future looks good. I remember his mother and father, and his brothers and his sister. They moved away from town long ago, of course; no doubt it was the shame of having a "demoniac" in the family. It all started when he was about seven or eight. He began having fits, rolling on the ground, making strange sounds. Sometimes it seemed a dozen or more different people were inside him trying to get out. His family tied him down when a fit began, but as he got older, he broke any bonds used on him. Several times the police tried to manacle his hands and feet, to restrain him so he wouldn't hurt someone; but he would break the chains and escape, howling, into the Tombs. As to his recovery, I am quite at a loss. While I don't hold with the idea of demon possession, of course, it does look as if something that had him in his grip has gone. I know of no adequate explanation.

THE FORMER DEMONIAC: It was Jesus. I saw him, even through the dark clouds in my mind. I saw him! I hadn't seen anything for so long. The clouds were so dark. But I saw him, like light through all those clouds. And I yelled at him, and ran to him. Oh, how the Bad Ones inside me struggled to stop me! They didn't want to be near Jesus. But I took them by surprise. They hadn't heard from me for so many years, they had forgotten I was in there. I rushed at Jesus before they could stop my legs from moving. They tried to stop my voice, but I told them, "What do you have to do with me?" Then I shouted at him, "Jesus! Son of the Most High God! I beg you! *Don't let them torment me!*"

But by then they had taken back control of my voice, and they made me say, "Don't torment me!" But Jesus knew! He wasn't fooled! Helpless as I was, I was thrilled when he said to them, "What's your name?" Because they had to answer. They'd never had to answer anyone before. They tried to frighten him; "Legion," they growled. His eyes flashed, and they were afraid. "Don't send us back into the pit again!" they cried. Jesus stood there looking at my eyes, and suddenly I knew: he could see me! The real me! The Bad Ones lost their grip that instant. I looked around. I saw those swine over in the field. I lifted my arm—I could do it!—and pointed at the pigs. Jesus smiled. He gave me a little nod. Then he lifted his own arm and pointed. Something broke, and I felt a long, terrible ripping right down the center of me, and then they were gone! And then the pigs ran down into the water and drowned.

I could see! hear! smell! I could feel again! How wonderful it was, the breeze on my skin, the light on the water, the gentle sound of the waves on the pebbles. How wonderful the sound of his voice. I could have sat at his feet and listened forever. I wanted to go with him when they made him leave. But he stopped at the water's edge, and put his hand on my shoulder, and said, "I will be with you always, to the end of the age. Go back home, and tell them all what great things God has done for you."

So I'm telling you. Jesus has done great things for me. He is the son of the Most High God. He will do great things for you, too. Call out to him, and let him look through all your clouds, deep into your eyes. Let Jesus see the real you.

Thanks be to God!

Donald F. Chatfield in 1995 was professor of preaching at Garrett-Evangelical Theological Seminary in Evanston, IL, and is an ordained minister in the Presbyterian Church (U.S.A.).

LUKE 10:1-11, 16-20

THE FIFTH SUNDAY AFTER PENTECOST
JULY 9, 1995

God's way in the world is absurd! Is that your experience with the way of the Lord? That's what Naaman discovered when he met the God of Elisha.

Naaman knew life with things in order and under control. Naaman was a lot like us. Reasonable. Sensible. Serious. Settled and secure. Enjoying the good life. But there was a chink in Naaman's carefully designed armor. Naaman suffered from the dreaded skin disease—leprosy.

It doesn't take much to remind us of how shaky our world can be. An apparently successful businessman files Chapter 11. Our best friends have separated and are contemplating divorce. A lump, or a chronic cough, or the sudden death of a daily jogger of a heart attack while he's mowing the yard. Shaky.

But Naaman was in luck. He found out about a faith healer in Samaria. Still, notice the spiraling absurdity of God's way:

A little slave girl knows more about health than the empire.

The king in charge of security is totally insecure and helpless.

Elisha is too busy to meet personally with an important man carrying a million dollars in cash!

Naaman is commanded to wash his perfumed skin in the mucky Jordan River seven times. Absurd! No wonder Naaman threw a fit.

After the healing, Elisha refuses a thank you gift. There's no question of payment for healing here. Just a thank you. But Elisha says, "No!"

Can you imagine turning down a million dollar gift from one whose life was changed? Gehazi couldn't imagine it either. The root of deceit twisted the grace that gives into a race to grasp. Gehazi misunderstood God's timing! "Is this a time to accept money and to accept clothing, olive orchards and vineyards, sheep and oxen, and male and female slaves?" Elisha asks. "Therefore the leprosy of Naaman shall cling to you and to your descendants forever."

This upside-down value system is not unlike the recent jolting experience in an exclusive jewelry shop. They opened for business-as-usual one Monday morning, unaware of a break-in over the weekend. Nothing had been taken. Not one sale item had been broken, scratched, or so much as touched. But the first customers were amused to discover that all the price tags had been changed. Discontinued, inexpensive watches now sold for $20,000. $20,000 diamond bracelets were marked $10. God's grace has similarly changed all values. We are possessed not by the leprosy of greed but by the grace of God.

Many of us are encouraged by Naaman's story. We, like Elisha, have made commitments that our world can't understand. Sometimes the results are so small. And yet God calls us to values that are upside-down when compared with those of our world. But doesn't Naaman's experience show that it is more complicated than that? Can one continue to offer an arm to masters who traffic in the temple of Mammon?

The good news of the story of Naaman, Elisha, and Gehazi is that God's grace can free us, too. As Naaman's cleansing in Jordan, our immersion into the company of faith marks a turn-around.

Chuck Colson tells about the conversion of Jack Eckerd, founder of Eckerd Drug Stores, the second largest chain in America. When he committed himself to Christ during a phone call, Chuck said, "You're born again." Eckerd replied, "No, I'm not; I haven't felt anything." But the first thing he did was walk into one of his drug stores and saw *Playboy* and *Penthouse*. He'd seen them many times before, but it had never bothered him. Now he saw them with new eyes. He'd become a Christian.

He went back to his office. He called in the president. He said, "Take *Playboy* and *Penthouse* out of my stores." The president said, "You can't mean that, Mr. Eckerd. We make three million dollars a year on those magazines." Eckerd said, "Take 'em out of my stores." And in 1700 stores across America, those magazines were gone because a man had made an absurd cleansing commitment to God. When Colson called Eckerd about the incident, he asked, "Did you do that because of your commitment to Christ?" "Of course! Why else would I give away three million dollars?" And Jack Eckerd was free. Free!

God invites us to a clean start, too. Our shaky moments can be reversed by God's free gift. Let God change the price tags and set you free. Really free.

Franklyn Jost in 1995 was studying homiletics at Vanderbilt University in Nashville, TN, on leave from his position as assistant professor of biblical studies at Tabor College, Hillsboro, KS, and is an ordained minister of the Mennonite Brethren Church.

LUKE 10:25-37

THE SIXTH SUNDAY AFTER PENTECOST
JULY 16, 1995

A man traveling between Jericho and Jerusalem was beat up by robbers. That is how the story begins. Of his clothes, they stripped him, then proceeded to beat on him. Street violence. You can see for yourself. Sores—black and blue; swelling; blood oozing from lips and nose. They left him Lying there half dead.

Now by chance a priest came along. He saw what was there—the tragedy, and swerved himself to the other side of the road and kept right on toward Jerusalem.

Then along came a Levite, a man of the synagogue. Religious. He too, when he saw this man Lying—took the other side bf the road. Out of sight, out of mind.

But then along came a Samaritan. When he saw what was there—a motionless body covered with dust and blood—he was moved with pity. Bandaging his wounds, he poured oil and wine on them. Putting him on his animal, he brought him to an inn, and took care of him. The next morning, he gave two denarii to the innkeeper, and said, 'Take care of him, and when I come back I will repay you whatever you spend.'

Then, Jesus—turning to those who were listening said, 'which of these three, do you suppose, was a neighbor to the man who fell into the hands of the robbers?' Neighbor. Which one was neighbor?

The telephone rang Wednesday evening, about 6:30. Just came home from church. Our family finished the evening meal. I was about to read the newspaper. A voice on the other end of the phone said, "You the preacher there at the church?" "Yes," I said, "What can I help you with?" "I'm out of money. Need to get to Kewaunee. How can you help me out?" "Well," I said, "I just got home. I've been gone all day. I, ah...." The words weren't coming out too well. I knew he was a transient. I knew I would never see him again.

He spoke some more, "I could use a place to stay or how 'bout a ride to Kewaunee. That's all I need. Tried hitchhiking, but no one's picking up today. Stood for four hours on the side of the road. What can ya do for me?" he said rather forcefully on the other end of the phone. What's a neighbor to do?

"You shall love the Lord your God with all your heart, and with all your soul, and with all your strength, and with all your mind; and your neighbor as yourself." Who is my neighbor? What's a neighbor to do?

A man fell upon robbers. Beat up. Scratched up. Pummeled unconscious. Dropped half-dead on the side of the road. A priest comes that way, then a Levite. They both walk by. That's the irony of the story, the 'shock'—if you will. The priest and the Levite are supposedly in the people business. The priest and the Levite are supposed to know better. By profession, they were to have been the compassionate ones—yet they walk by, ON THE OTHER SIDE.

Were they tired? Were they late for a meeting? Did they have families to get home to? 8 hour day? 10 hour day? 12 hour day? Just exhausted? Did they forget who they were?

It's so easy to forget 'who we are.' A carpenter builds a home. The sun is beating upon him. Sawdust gets in his eyes. A blister on his hand, until finally he takes his hammer and gives the house one solid 'whack'. Did he forget—his love for wood? The artistry of being a carpenter? Did he forget?

Or the school teacher. She stays up late correcting yesterday's test. Of course, it's the same test she gave last year's class. It's pretty well canned. The kids walk into her classroom looking tire. She gives the same lecture she used last year. In the back of her mind she's thinking, 'Only 12 more years until retirement.' Did she forget 'her love for educating'? Did she forget the enthusiasm she once had? Did she forget?

The priest and the Levite walk by on the "other side of the road." Did they forget that they were in the business of compassion?

I've got a bird nest in the tree outside my office window. A morning dove—like a helicopter—lowers herself into this big overgrown bush outside my window. She has a beautiful voice. I love to hear her sing.

About a month ago, she had baby birds. One of them, right after birth, was pushed out of the nest. It landed on the ground, next to the bush, chirping. The mother never came down. Perhaps this baby was deformed. Perhaps sickly. A couple days later, it was dead. In the animal kingdom, the rule of thumb is 'survival of the fittest.' The weak are left to die.

But not with us. "Be compassionate as your Father is compassionate," Jesus spoke to his disciples. "As you have done it onto the least of these, you have done it onto me." Ever since God's heart was undone/broken by the suffering of those Hebrew slaves — ever since then, 'compassion' has been company policy for people of faith.

As Jesus tells that parable, compassion may not be done best by religious professionals. Remember, the priest passes by. The Levite passes by. The professionals are gone. The one whose heart is strangely moved, the one who becomes 'as neighbor' is the Samaritan. The laity.

And the parable lets us know how costly compassion is. The Samaritan interrupts his journey. He too, like the priest, like the Levite was going somewhere. He too had places to go, meetings to attend. But he allowed his journey to be interrupted because the journey was less important than the person he met along the way. Compassion sees the hurt of another and cannot walk away. Yet, more than seeing, he was willing to touch! The Samaritan washed his wounds, put ointment on the wounds, bandages the wounds. Compassion sees, and compassion touches.

But more than that, compassion costs money. After giving himself, after interrupting his journey, the Samaritan gives the innkeeper two denarii and a promise for more if the cost exceeds that. I didn't think this was going to be a stewardship sermon, but that's how the parable ends. Compassion is a willingness to offer money for the care of another. Our money will say as much about us as just about anything else we say or do.

I would like to close with this. To come back to my earliest illustration—there was a time when I felt 'put out' by transients and others who would stop by the church looking for a hand-out. The church never received a thank you note, not even a card or a phone call saying they arrived at their destination. $10 here. $15 there. At first, I was put out by that, but now I understand—that many unchurched who have never been inside a place like this. At least they know, on the outside, that compassion is spoken and lived here. By the grace of Jesus Christ if they ever find their way home to God, let it be by compassion.

Kim M. Henning in 1995 was pastor of Grace Congregational United Church of Christ in Two Rivers, Wisconsin.

LUKE 10:38-42

THE SEVENTH SUNDAY AFTER PENTECOST
JULY 23, 1995

In a recent book, Will Willimon describes the gospel as an intrusive word (*The Intrusive Word: Preaching to the Unbaptized,* Grand Rapids: William B. Eerdmans Publishing Company, 1994). As a matter of fact, he uses the definite article, which heightens the issue; to Willimon, the gospel is the intrusive word. I'm not sure that I like the sound of that. Intrusive? Intrusive! Intrusive means annoying, bothersome, disturbing, even irritating. How can those words describe the gospel. The gospel is good news, isn't it? I've been taught that it's characterized by faith, hope, and love. I've preached that the gospel liberates, sets free those who are oppressed. Remember the words of Jesus' sermon in Nazareth: "The Spirit of the Lord is upon me, because he has anointed me to preach good news to the poor. He has sent me to proclaim release to the captives and recovery of sight to the blind, to let the oppressed go free" (Luke 4:18). Jesus is talking about freedom and liberation, words that offer hope and a future. I like to think about the gospel as being helpful and supportive, but intrusive? How can the gospel of Jesus Christ be intrusive?

I remember my first preaching course when I was a seminary student. The professor said that one way to define preaching was "Preaching comforts the afflicted and afflicts the comfortable." Like most twentieth-century Christians, I've spent an inordinate amount of time "comforting the afflicted" with the gospel. Now that's okay, mind you, if the people are really afflicted. But as I reflect on it, I wonder if my preaching, and if much of Christianity, isn't focusing on *comforting the comfortable!* If we're not careful, we make Jesus' message sound an awful lot like our way of thinking, our value system, even our way of doing theology. Both conservative and liberal wings of the Church have made Jesus a product of their own image — Jesus becomes the thundering fundamentalist or the reflective activist. But the gospel, the good news of Jesus Christ, this intrusive word, more often than not calls our world view, our way of thinking into question. I wonder if that's why the apostle Paul referred to the gospel as scandalous?

You can only imagine why Luke's readers would have been a bit scandalized when they read about Jesus entering Martha's house. "He should have known better!" they mumble under their breath. "After all, he's trying to be a religious leader. He has his reputation to maintain. Doesn't he know that?" And then they probably went ballistic when they found out that Mary, Martha's sister was sitting at Jesus' feet listening to what he was saying. "She shouldn't be doing that," they thought, with upturned eyes, "Doesn't she know how that looks. People will talk. They'll begin to say that Jesus allows women to be disciples. There'll be a scandal!" Exactly!

When Martha comes tearing into the room, you can almost hear Luke's audience cheer. "Get her to help you Martha. Ask Jesus for advice. He'll tell Mary what he told that lawyer: 'Go and do likewise!'" That's often how we want Jesus to act. That's often how we want the gospel to operate. We think the gospel is a helpful tool for our agendas, like the gospel is a theological marionette attached to the strings of our world view, our way of thinking, at our command. Have we deluded ourselves! This intrusive gospel has no intention of upholding our oppressive theologies. This irritating word, more often than not, rubs us the wrong way because it will not coddle our dogmatism, whether that dogmatism be conservative or liberal. This gospel is disturbing because it isn't under our control.

Martha wants Mary to come and give her a hand. Jesus says that Mary is doing the right thing by sitting and listening, and that maybe Martha should come and do likewise.

When we first come across this story in Luke's gospel, it almost seems like an intrusion. Jesus has been doing so many more *important* things. Why does Luke waste time and space dealing with such an *insignificant* scene. Two grown sisters arguing over who's doing the most work seems so trivial in light of the gospel. That's how we've been conditioned to think. But this so called textual intrusion characterizes the very nature of Jesus' gospel. It turns the world upside down. It makes Mary the hero because she has chosen "the better part." It makes us the villains because if Mary is right and Martha is wrong, we have a real problem. Willimon is right. This is an intrusive word!

Craig Loscalzo in 1995 was the Vicar and Louise Lester associate professor of Christian Preaching at The Southern Baptist Theological Seminary, Louisville, Kentucky.

LUKE 12:32-40

THE TENTH SUNDAY AFTER PENTECOST
AUGUST 13, 1995

Every June our church has a Strawberry Festival that is a wonderful time of camaraderie and fun. Like so many church fairs, we have a white elephant table, a book table and a silent auction. These give each person in the parish a chance to go through their attics, closets, basements, and barns and weed out all the stuff that has been accumulating over the years. Some people relish the opportunity to weed out, to simplify. Others struggle with letting go of anything. One man in our parish was renown for bringing things in for the fair and leaving with more, much more than he brought.

Perhaps because I am into middle age, I find myself thinking about what I own and my deep desire to simplify my own life, not just externally but internally as well. But I am realizing more and more that simplifying means letting go and for most of us, that is not easy, not easy at all. I am finding this year that preparing for the fair has raised in me a new and profound sense of what I own, what I want to give away and what I don't, and why. Many, many questions flood my mind as do wonderings. "If I let go of this book, this game, this knickknack, will anybody buy it?" "Will it be important to anyone else?" "Why am I holding onto this?" "Why can't I let go of that?" "When I die, what will happen to all of this stuff?" "Will anyone care about it?"

Many of my possessions are important to me not because of their monetary worth but because of the emotional attachments. Books, records, knickknacks and even my college and seminary notebooks and papers are so much a part of me that I can't let them go. Some of these possessions are gifts that people have given me that I simply don't use but "what if they should come for a visit and their present is nowhere to be seen?" Things become a part of me, of us but so do attitudes and beliefs. Recently there was a fire in a nearby town that destroyed seven businesses. Reading about it was sad but I felt distant from it all until I realized that I knew one of the people and then I suddenly was aware at a more personal level what that loss must have been like. One minute everything in the office stands in its proper place, and without warning, everything is destroyed by fire, smoke, water and falling debris. It is one of the greatest fears many of us have—fire destroying our business or our home. In light of this fear we have of losing our possessions, Jesus' words are haunting. "Sell your possessions, and give alms. Make purses for yourselves that do not wear out, an unfailing treasure in heaven, where no thief comes near and no moth destroys. For where your treasure is, there your heart will be also" (Luke 12:33-34). In a consumption driven economy where we are taught culturally that more is better, newer is important, up-grading is necessary, Jesus' words can ring loudly with truth or can be drowned out by the roar of advertisements and by our own insecurity with keeping things simple, with being content with what we have because our greatest possession is our relationship with God. That is a truth that only God can enable us to grow into. One commentator has written, "Perhaps the deepest fallacy in the seeking of security through possessing things lies in the belief that possessing things is simply a matter of having them in our hands. Actually, things possess us, unless we are possessed by God. If God possesses us, we are possessed by nothing else, and therefore possess all things in the only way we can truly possess anything" (*The Interpreter's Bible*, volume 8, Abingdon Press, N.Y., 1952, p.231). God possesses us only if that is our desire and if there is a willingness on our part to be possessed by God. It is a strong word, possessed. We usually think of it in evil terms but if one can be possessed by evil, one can surely be possessed by God and by God's love. What possesses us is up to us. It is always our choice. God never forces us to accept God's love, forgiveness or transforming power. Revelation reminds us that Jesus stands at the door and knocks. If we will let him in he will come in and eat with us and we with him. If we will open the door, the door being our hearts, our minds, our lives. God's deepest desire is to possess us so we may be wholly the people we were created to be.

The Rev. Charlotte Dudley Cleghorn in 1995 was Rector of St. Ann's Episcopal Church in Windham, Maine.

LUKE 14:1, 7-14

THE THIRTEENTH SUNDAY AFTER PENTECOST
SEPTEMBER 3, 1995

When I was in university a dynamic speaker for Campus Crusade for Christ moved me deeply when he said that Jesus was my friend. At that point in my life I really needed to make at least as great a commitment to Jesus as I had already made to the friends I'd grown up with. I wasn't sure how to love Jesus as the second person of the Trinity, but I had some idea of how to love him as I would love a friend.

Jesus isn't less of a friend to me now; he's just more of a stranger. Ironically, this hasn't happened because I've been neglecting scripture, but because I've been reading it more carefully than I used to. I once only saw, and identified with, Simon Peter's vociferous devotion to Jesus. Now I see his persistent misunderstanding and fearful denial of Jesus. I was once sure that I loved Jesus as if we had grown up together in the same home town. Then I read how those in his home town received him with hostility.

As much as any of us want Jesus to be an intimate friend, Luke insists that he is a stranger. The refugee baby born in a manger grows to be a man without a hole or a nest to call home. Jesus is an enigma to his parents, a hard-to-understand teacher to his students, and a troubling puzzle to those in authority whose job it is to put everyone in the proper category. John the Baptist's disciples are sent to ask, "Are you the one who is to come...?" (Lk.7:19) His own disciples ask, "Who then is this, that even the wind and sea obey him?" (Lk.8:25) Herod perplexes, "John I beheaded; but who is this...?" (Lk.9:9) and Pilate takes a guess, "Are you the king of the Jews?" (Lk.23:3)

It is infuriating the way Jesus just shrugs Pilate off by saying, "You say so," when any answer with even the smallest clue in it would likely have stopped his execution. Yet, his refusal to identify himself before Pilate is but the final echo of his much earlier admonition to the disciples not to tell anyone that he is the Christ (Lk.9:21).

Jesus moved through the world as a stranger, and that's the way he wanted it. He ensured that he was crucified as a stranger, and when he appeared for the first time as the risen Christ it was as a stranger on the Emmaus road. We know that Jesus is the Christ, and we know that he is a stranger.

It's not so easy, then, for us to talk glibly about welcoming Jesus into our lives and setting a place for him at our tables and loving him; for, we are suspicious of strangers and we feel threatened by them. We install fences and video cameras to keep track of strangers. We blame strangers when something unaccountable happens, and point fingers at them for our problems like unemployment and crime. In so fearing the stranger, how can we love Jesus who said, "Truly I tell you, just as you did it to the least of these, you did it to me." Were he to come knocking at our door one night, seeking entrance, would we pull up the welcome mat, or pull out a gun?

To move from hostility to hospitality (which means, "love of the stranger," in the New Testament) requires a conversion of our hearts, our minds, and our communities away from socially sanctioned hatreds and prejudices. As with all things having to do with God's in-breaking Kingdom, the way things are is already being challenged by signs of the way things could be.

Not long ago I heard a community chaplain in my area of the city speak about his ministry with men who had recently been released from prison. His job is to help them make the transition back into the mainstream of society by offering them pastoral care and personal support. All of us in attendance agreed that this was, indeed, a noble undertaking. There was an uncomfortable silence, however, when he went on to say that he was most recently working with a man who is one of this city's most notorious sex-offenders. We were informed that every Tuesday evening, in the very room in which we were now sitting, a small group of men meet with this fellow to encourage him to stay in his treatment program, and to offer him a supportive community that will also hold him accountable on a weekly basis. For months he had no permanent residence. The group went from one church to another with an appeal for assistance in helping this man find an apartment, but there was no response whatsoever. Nobody wanted him in their backyard, and they frankly didn't care where he went or what happened to him. Finally, through a contact in an Alcoholics Anonymous group, they were able to rent an apartment. They could have stopped there, having already done more than anyone would have expected for such a disreputable person. But they didn't stop, because there was one last thing to do: they threw him a house-warming party! Hospitality is never complete until there is food and laughter.

This party was a remarkable sign of God's gracious Kingdom precisely because it took place against the backdrop of a society's loathing for its honored guest. A man with a history of being a sexual predator of children is currently the lowest of the low, and public permission to hate and ostracize him is freely given. But, instead, a group of Christian men committed not to personal gain and glory but to restorative justice gathered him up. They don't condone what he did. They don't make any guarantees that he won't offend again. They are convinced, however, that he is less likely to harm someone again if he has a community that will embrace him as a redeemable fellow-sinner rather than dispatch him like a damaged animal.

Were we disquieted and a little shocked to hear about this radical hospitality? We were probably no less shocked than those around the Pharisee's table who heard the honored guest, Jesus, say that an appropriate list of dinner guests ought to replace friends with the poor, the crippled, the lame, the blind, and other outcasts and strangers just like him.

Steve Willey is an ordained minister of the United Church of Canada and in 1995 was serving Humbercrest United Church in Toronto.

LUKE 14:25-33

THE FOURTEENTH SUNDAY AFTER PENTECOST
SEPTEMBER 10, 1995

From every quarter we have been hearing about values. We hear about values from the media, from social science experts, even from politicians. The more I hear, the more I feel that some of them wouldn't know a value if it bit 'em on the leg. Since I was a little boy, one of the things that was drilled into me was the good old fashioned American value that says: pay as you go.

I remember standing in line at the little Mom and Pop grocery store. It was the old days. Mom picked out the groceries. Dad wrote the check. I had tried my best to beg some gum, but no luck. I was told, "We don't have money to waste on candy." I was trying to come up with a new angle of approach when I noticed that the customer ahead of us had not paid for his groceries. He just signed a little book, and the clerk gave him a slip of paper.

Later, in the car, the new angle came to me. I suggested that we buy candy like the fellow had bought groceries. Dad made it clear that the groceries were on credit and that eventually the bill would be paid. Dad said, "Never buy food or gasoline on credit, 'cause you still have to pay even if it is gone. Always pay as you go."

Dad ran a little electric motor repair shop in the basement under the barber shop. I remember the long nights he put in rewiring, or installing in new bearings in a motor so that an essential water pump or a furnace blower or a feed auger would be fixed as quickly as possible. I remember how many times customers didn't pay. Dad would shake his head and say, "Well, that's one for the 'thank you' box". The imaginary thank you box was for all the work he did and got just a thank you, and sometimes not even that. He said that when the box got full he was going to trade it in for groceries.

Times change, but every time I use a credit card at a gas station I think about what Dad said. Pay as you go.

This text hits right at the heart of that value that says pay as you go. We take pride in knowing that we pay as we go.

Until Jesus comes along.

Jesus comes walking along on his way to Jerusalem, walking toward the cross. Though he has tried to tell the crowd about the consequences of following him on to Jerusalem, he realizes that they have no idea what is ahead. He asks them to count the cost of what they are doing.

Every time I read this text I stumble over that hard word in verse 26: "Whoever does not HATE ... cannot be a disciple." It is so tempting to try to explain it away, to make it all right, but the text says. Hate. Deny, Despise, Disdain.

Disdain your father, your mother. Despise spouse, and children, brothers, sisters. Deny yourself.

I love my wife and kids, my friends and family. I just can't do this. But there is more!

Carry the cross. Take it up. Not a little gold cross on a chain but a real heavy wooden cross of death. If you want to become a disciple, go out and get yourself killed.

This is even worse! I am not going to be able to do this either.

Give up all your possessions. Get rid of everything. No money, no land, no house, no clothes on your back. Get rid of it all, tennis racquets to toothpicks. It has to go.

I'll tell you what, I will...if you will! Neither one of us will. Will we? Brothers and sisters, we have a problem. Have you ever arrived at the check out counter and discovered that you can not pay?

I have to tell you that when I estimate the cost, there is no way that I can become a disciple of Jesus Christ no matter how I try. That good old time value of pay as you go is stabbed in the heart. It dies hard and it hurts to admit it.

I can't become a disciple of the Lord Jesus Christ. Neither can you. How do we dare to call ourselves Christians? We have done nothing to deserve the privilege. What are we going to do?

It is time to wave the white flag and ask for peace terms. It is time to surrender. Surrender is a powerful word, and has such potential for abuse that we don't use it much anymore. But what else can we do in the face of this text? Surrender. It is time to repent, admit the truth that we know all too well. The cost is too high. We can't pay as we go. Maybe we better try to sneak out? Wait! Listen! *Someone else has paid for us.*

Someone went against the wishes of his father and mother. Someone defied his brothers and sisters. Someone. Jesus gave them up.

Someone carried the cross. Someone bore the shame and pain and horror of the cross. It wasn't me! Jesus took it up.

Someone gave up possessions. Someone had nowhere to lay his head, nothing but the robe on his back. Though he was God, Jesus emptied himself...for me.

While we were yet sinners Jesus died for us. The cost has been paid. The joy and wonder and miracle of the gospel is the news that *we don't make ourselves disciples. Jesus makes us disciples!*

How did Peter and James and John become disciples? They were fishing. Jesus called them and they followed. Matthew was sitting at the tax office. Jesus called and he followed. They didn't make themselves disciples. JESUS made them disciples. Now Jesus' call makes YOU a disciple.

The old way dies hard. We want so much to pay something. It is time to repent, surrender and believe. It is time to quit working to earn the name disciple and start following to live the gift that we are given. It is time to stop trying to pay a debt that can never be repaid. It is time to surrender. Surrender to love. Surrender to peace. Surrender to service and joy and life in Jesus Christ. Our journey lies ahead, across this whole wide world. So disciples, it is time to hit the road.

Rev. Eric C. Kutzli in 1995 was Pastor of Mamrelund Lutheran Church, Evangelical Lutheran Church in America.

LUKE 15:1-10

THE FIFTEENTH SUNDAY AFTER PENTECOST
SEPTEMBER 17, 1995

I know a woman who has wandered away. When she was a little girl of 10, her mother was diagnosed with cancer, within a few months her mother died and she was left alone. When she was a young woman of 24, she grew to love her mother in-law like her mom. Yet, within a few terrible seconds on a busy highway, her mother-in-law was killed and again loneliness touched her and she swore she would never be touched this way again. Today, this woman continues to mourn and she continues to wander. God, for her, is not real because God would not allow such pain to exist. When invited to come to church and to hear of the love of God, all she can say is: "I lost my mom. I lost my mother in-law and along the way I lost God."

Being lost and being found, like alternating beats of a heart, define much of our life. All of us know what it is like to feel lost, to feel cut off from each other and from God. There are times in our lives when we feel as if the alley into which we have wandered is so dark, so forbidding, so far off the beaten path that we think no one can find us. And the question that arises out of the darkness is: "Does anyone care? Is there anyone who cares enough to come into the alley and get me?"

This is the question addressed in our text for today. In Jesus' day, tax collectors were among the most despised people in Israel. They were the people who had aligned themselves with the enemy. Their allegiance was to Rome. They had exchanged the God of Abraham for the gods of those who ruled over them. But these are the same people who are now drawn to Jesus. We know that there were other sinners there. Jesus had that effect upon people who felt cut off from God. Maybe it was because Jesus didn't push them away. Maybe it was because they sensed in him one who listened, one who cared, one who really knew God. So they listened when Jesus talked about God, faith and the lives they were living. And when Jesus came into their homes to share a meal with them they knew that this love, God's love, was more than just words.

This is what upset the religious leaders of the day. Its what caused them to mumble under their breath: "This man welcomes sinners and eats with them." Jesus heard their mumbling. It seems as if they were always upset with him. They had often made it clear that, in their opinion, this was not the way a follower of God would act.

That didn't stop Jesus. If anything it made him more bold. Jesus goes on to tell those who had gathered, the stories of the lost sheep and the lost coin. He tells them about how God leaves the ninety-nine in order to find the one that had wandered away. He tells them about how God frantically searches for the one that has no awareness that its even been lost. Yet, the result in each case is the same. God rejoices in finding the one who was lost. God rejoices so exuberantly, so freely, that heaven itself joins in a song of praise.

The picture of God searching frantically for those that are lost is not a very God-like picture to see. There's something strangely disturbing about seeing God leave the ninety-nine to go after one, or to hustle and bustle about the house so desperately for an object of seemingly little worth.

It's not a normal way for us to think about God. But it is comforting. Jesus teaches us that God loves us so much that God refuses to let us go and that when we are lost in the dark alleys of life, God comes in to find us.

I know a young man who is in love. He loves this woman with all his heart and has loved her for several years now. But it is difficult for his beloved to believe him, she has been lied to by others so many times before. So, every time he tells her of his love for her, she hides behind the words that, 'they should just continue to be good friends.' When he offers to leave, she urges him to not give up on her. He stays. Hoping to show her that his love is real, praying that one day she will come to love and trust him. Jesus tells us that this is similar to the way of God. God loves us and pursues us, and when we are fearful and push God away, God loves and pursues us some more.

What does this say to those of us who are gathered here? With one heartbeat, it is a word of warning. It's a word which reminds us to continue to gather, to listen and to pray. Like a child who takes a mother's love for granted and then neglects to hold on to her mother's hand; we need to stay close to God and remain attentive to God's presence in our lives. With the other heartbeat this is a word of comfort. It assures us that God comes to us with love and the promise of a continuing relationship. God comes into the dark alleys of our lives and assures us we have not been abandoned. Like a healthy heart, this is a word of encouragement. God, in Christ, empowers us to love and care for one another. This is what it means to be a church. It means that we are to be a caring and loving place; a place where people can encounter God; a place where trust can grow and new life can be nurtured. Today we are encouraged to embody Christ's persistence, compassion and joy in reaching out to others.

Rev. Dr. Earl E. Vorpagel III in 1995 was the Senior Pastor at Calvary Lutheran Church in Green Bay, Wisconsin and is an ordained minister in the Evangelical Lutheran Church in America.

LUKE 18:1-8

THE TWENTIETH SUNDAY AFTER PENTECOST
OCTOBER 22, 1995

An article in the *Presbyterian Survey* last year (Lee C. Barrett, "What Can We Hope For?" June 1994) noted that contemporary Christians tend either to hope for too much or too little. When you ask Christians what their faith leads them to expect in terms of God's plans for the distant horizon of history, you may well get one of two quite different responses. Some believe staunchly in eye-popping descriptions of endtime cosmic disaster, complete with probable dates and locations. Others, more cautious, express a pale hopefulness about better personal adjustment and a general trend toward societal improvement.

Only a few will probably express with conviction and clarity what has been a traditional Christian view: that God is still working to make all things new, and that ever since the events of Good Friday and Easter, something has been going on behind the scenes. While the Church faithfully watches and works and prays, God's plans to overcome sin, evil, and injustice and to renew heaven and earth continue to unfold.

We say we *believe* that's so. But what does it look like to *live* as if that were so? In other words, what does active faith in God's gracious future look like?

Last spring I found myself witness to a drama of such faith. Early one damp morning as I left my townhouse to drive to church, I was all but bowled over by a small boy racing past me toward the back of our building. I recognized in the blur of t-shirt and red sneakers my next-door neighbor, Matthew, age four. "Where's the fire?" I called after him. The small feet just kept pounding, but Matthew shouted half over his shoulder, half into the air, "Gotta go see my vegetables!!" Vegetables? I knew there was a small fenced garden patch in the back yard, but this was only late April, too early for much of anything in eastern Pennsylvania. Curious, I followed him.

Matthew stood at the edge of the garden enclosure, staring intently. "Where?" I asked (sounding, I suppose, like the disciples at the end of Luke 17 who wonder where in the world to look for any sign of divine activity). "There! My vegetables!! See? They're growing!" Matt pointed to the flat soil. I did not see. Not a sprig of green showed that morning, or for quite a few mornings after that. But Matt would tear out to the garden anyway and happily stare and stare at the perfectly bare earth.

Faith. Being confident that something's happening when there's nothing to see yet.

Some months ago, the congregation I serve held a capital funds campaign with hopes to build a new Christian education complex. At the point when pledges to the project totaled less than half of what would be needed, the board and pastoral staff decided to hold a big celebration service on our wide green front lawn on a spring morning.

A few leaders were reluctant. "Isn't this rather premature? What's to celebrate? We're miles away from even breaking ground!!" Others in the congregation got wind of it, and a few of them, too, raised an eyebrow. But we went ahead. We had discovered that over the years, this congregation had been confronted again and again with visions of ministry that were, practically speaking, "too big" for them. And yet they had plunged ahead with startling persistence, trusting God for outcomes that nothing less than divine intervention could bring about.

So one June morning, more than a thousand of us gathered on the lawn and celebrated—what?? Not a completed campaign; *that* still teetered on the edge of feasibility. We celebrated a God who has plans in the making too big for us to achieve through mere ingenuity. We celebrated the God who calls us to live by faith. Banners flapped in a strong breeze and hymns rose to God, even though we all knew it was too early in the game to so much as turn a spadeful of dirt on the field where we dreamed of building.

The Church, in fact, is in the habit of holding such "premature" celebrations. We baptize startled infants sucking on their fists and say words about the disciples they will be. We stand by gravesides and sing about resurrection. We sing about freedom for captives though sons and fathers still disappear in Central America. We point to the lion and lamb asleep in the shade while ethnic groups still pledge to eliminate one another from the face of the earth.

We celebrate because we are convinced that the cross and resurrection of Jesus Christ have changed the balance of things, despite appearances. Evil has been dealt the telling blow.

We live in a culture that tempts us to play the part, not of the persistent widow, but of the jaded judge of Luke's parable. Notions of irresistible divine justice seem a little silly in a system where it seems as if justice is only for those who can afford good lawyers. Too much compassion, too much idealism is a liability in this world. The fact is that life is unfair, and those who learn that, and learn to live with it, survive.

In such an atmosphere, we Christians are tempted to adapt ourselves to injustice. Especially when we ourselves are comfortable, we find ways to turn down the volume on the cries of life's victims. Some say that all victims are at least partly responsible for their own suffering, after all. Only fools take up every poor widow's petty case.

Enter God, a fool if you will, for those who can't save themselves. With God, the widow matters. The day of the Lord, the day of vindication has already started. We pray in the shadow of the cross. We work for the deliverance of captives in the light of Easter morning. We pray and act with our eye on the horizon, because in the cross and resurrection of Jesus, we believe we have seen the outline of God's future plans. The risen Christ gathers us to the table and points to a new heaven and a new earth.

Faith is premature parties, caring for victims, praying for God's justice and grace. Faith is the conviction that God is up to something when and where nothing seems to be happening. Living in faith, praying in faith is like trips to the garden: we know the underground story.

Sally A. Brown in 1995 was a doctoral student at Princeton Seminary in Homiletics and was Associate Pastor for Adult Ministries at First Presbyterian Church, Bethlehem, Pennsylvania.

LUKE 19:1-10

THE TWENTY-SECOND SUNDAY AFTER PENTECOST
NOVEMBER 5, 1995

Luke's relation of the story of the chief tax collector of Jericho contains something unexpected. An apparently inconsequential detail is reported in such a way as to point up its importance. Luke tells us that Zaccheus is short. Many people who are short can recall painful moments growing up—getting chosen near last for sports teams on the school-ground; being left out of social circles; becoming targets for bullies. Sometimes short people get a reputation for being aggressive, coming at life with their gloves on. Do you remember Randy Newman's scurrilous song of some years ago?

We could go to extremes here, of course. There are many people claiming the mantle of victim today and sometimes one wonders whether the category is in danger of being trivialized. (Did you know they changed the title of the fairy tale to "Snow White and the Seven Vertically Challenged Persons"?) As well, there's a story to tell about growing up tall. If you're tall, people expect you to be more mature and responsible than other kids; also, if there's a scuffle, it's the big boy who gets blamed. More significantly, there are vitally important stories about growing up colored, growing up female, growing up homosexual, growing up aboriginal....

But Zaccheus was short. Maybe he'd had to battle for everything he'd ever achieved. Maybe he'd always been the sawed-off butt of stories and pranks, and even now was the target of malicious gossip and unfair exclusion. Is that why Zaccheus comes into the street to watch the parade? Does he come because he is trapped by such circumstance and needs some event, some thing, some one, to break the gridlock and give him the opening he needs?

Before Jesus enters the town, word of his life-changing influence has spread, spread sufficiently for an apparently infamous inhabitant to undertake such high-risk exposure along a parade route. Ironically, it is his liability that pushes him into taking the step that catches Jesus' eye.

Some of the Biblical commentators have made an interesting suggestion about the Zaccheus story. We have been accustomed to reading it as the case of a notorious sinner repenting and turning to a new life. But what if the statements which Zaccheus makes— "I give half of my income to the poor" and "If I have defrauded anyone, I restore it fourfold"—are not promises about future conduct but indignant claims about his present behavior? What if Zaccheus has been given a "bum rap" and unfairly ostracized? What if, according to this reading of the text, he has all along been one of the most conscientious and generous of the citizens of Jericho, though anonymously? Then this encounter with Jesus is the moment of his vindication!

As Habakkuk and his generation waited for deliverance from the bloody violence of the neo-Babylonian Empire, and vindication of their integrity; as the congregation at Thessalonica was later to await deliverance from the heel of state persecution, and vindication of their status as children of God; so Zaccheus as an individual was waiting for deliverance from unfair calumny, and for vindication as a son of Abraham, one who belongs in the household of faith.

Few people get to enjoy unqualified moments of vindication in the face of criticism and condemnation. (Like Reggie Jackson!) And in an era when society relegates religion to the private sphere of personal taste or treats it as a matter of indifference or contempt, we who are disciples of Jesus can expect little public validation or vindication. The story of a friend of mine illustrates the difficulty of discipleship in a post-Christian context. Pirie is a high-school teacher who serves as pulpit supply in a small rural/suburban congregation. He was also a member of the Lion's Club whose leadership recommended a benefit entertainment night. They were planning to sell alcoholic beverages, have gaming tables and—*piece de resistance*—finish with three strippers. It was the last item that got Pirie on his feet to protest. He tried to avoid moralistic priggery and asked his fellow members simply to agree that bare body parts on public display is *passe*. His position was resisted at first with jocular ripostes, but when he continued to object at subsequent meetings the mood turned ugly. "Just shut up!" Pirie resigned and was badmouthed to his church board and to anyone else in the community who would listen. One of the ironies was that the benefit was for the Scout group committee which Pirie chairs! He has a fellow teacher who still refuses to talk to him, and as far as I know the strippers appeared at the benefit. The lion-tamer was mauled!

A moving story is reported of the return of missionary H. C. Morrison to the United States following a life-time of service in China. It happened that he was returning on the same ship that was carrying the President Teddy Roosevelt back from a safari in Africa. As the ship passed into New York harbor, barges came out with bands on board. Flags and banners were unfurled; firefighting ships sprayed their welcome aloft. Morrison confessed that the recognition that this display was all for a man returning home from big-game hunting plunged him into bitter self-pity. He remembered his labors in China and how isolated and alone he had felt. The work of a life-time for God was nothing; was without recognition or reward. Where was the justice in this home-coming? He said that it was later that day, as he leaned upon the deck rail, when a voice came to him "like the voice of many waters": "But you are not home yet."

The Rev. Peter Wyatt in 1995 was General Secretary, Theology, Faith and Ecumenism for the United Church of Canada.

MATTHEW 18:21-35

THE SIXTEENTH SUNDAY AFTER PENTECOST
SEPTEMBER 15, 1996

Several years ago a *Peanuts* comic strip appeared in the Sunday paper, on Father's Day. "Have you ever played hearts?" asks Charlie Brown.

"You mean the card game?" replies Linus.

"Uh huh..." Charlie continues. "My dad was telling me, before he was married, he and his friends used to play hearts, all the time. He said they used to go over to this one friend's house whose mother always baked hot rolls or biscuits or homemade bread or something. She used to play hearts with them, too, because she loved the game. They played around the dining room table, and because there were always about twelve of them playing, they had to use two decks of cards."

Linus knowledgeably interrupts, "that meant there would be two queens of spades."

"Right," answers Charlie, continuing, "And the whole idea is to slip someone the black queen. Well, on this particular night, my dad said he gave the mother both black queens on the same hand. That was twenty-six points against her. Everybody laughed so hard they got hysterical, but she still gave them hot rolls and bread. And now, when he thinks about it, my dad says it makes him feel kind of sad. And that was ten years ago."

"Your dad is very sensitive, Charlie Brown" says Linus as he turns to walk away, "Wish him a happy Father's Day for me."

"Thank you," says Charlie, half musing to himself, "I'll do that...(sigh). ...Twenty-six points, and she still gave them hot rolls!"

Rather like a little modern parable, this story echoes Paul's letter to the Romans and Matthew's gospel today. All of them tell of forgiveness.

For most of us, forgiveness implies a setting aside of injury or wrong-doing; to overlook a wrong or hurt. Yet we are told that the forgiveness of God is far more than simply a setting aside. Thus our definition of forgiveness is inadequate. For if one merely sets a grievance aside, one can just as easily take it up again. It is only when a grievance is completely eradicated, loosed and let go, that forgiveness is complete. So the incredible strength of God's forgiveness lies in a kind of forgiving that is a profound forgetting. When God forgives, it as though the slate is wiped clean and life begins anew.

This is where our forgiveness falls short of the truly divine forgiveness. It is not until our forgiving embraces a complementary forgetting that we begin to forgive as God forgives. As Paul reminds a Roman congregation factionalized by grievances and as Jesus responded to Peter, there can be no place among us for grudges, those semi-conscious animosities we keep alive against the time when we might use them to advantage.

Throughout scripture we read of God's grace, God's limitless forgiveness. Our hymns abound with gratitude to a God of amazing grace. Week after week we confess our wrong-doings, hear the pronouncement of absolution and assurance of pardon for a whole world gone awry. Yet we arise and return to our daily living unable to forgive ourselves, much less forget the the many ways in which we have been wronged by others. Do we realize the arrogance of the common confession, "I can't forgive myself?"

When we come to the altar, we come before the God who played a cosmic game of hearts. it was a costly match. When the heat was on, we slipped the black queen. But the stakes were higher than we knew. In the cosmic games of hearts, the blood which flowed from the heart of God's only son shattered and ripped the very heart of God.

Yet when we come to the altar, we do not have that tragedy thrown back in our faces. We find no wrathful, vengeful, antagonist awaiting us with displeasure in hand. No, instead, we find a table spread with refreshment. In place of a bloody sacrifice, we find a bountiful sustenance. it is as though God has forgotten our evil. It is perhaps the greatest mystery of all: not that wine and wafer become blood and body, but rather that blood and body became and yet become wine and bread, holy food and drink—that our misdeed be met with such overwhelming munificence in such a meal.

The Sunday comics may seem an unlikely place to hear the word of God, but then, God has chosen stranger means. The simple truth of the good news of Jesus Christ finds voice in every age. And the commonwealth of heaven is like unto Charlie Brown's simple amazement: "Twenty-six points, and she still gave them hot rolls!"

Sam Portaro in 1996 was the Episcopal Chaplain to the University of Chicago.

All Saints Day

REVELATION 7:9-17

ALL SAINTS DAY
NOVEMBER 1, 1978

From the standpoint of almost any reasonably intelligent, aware, modern person, All Saints' Day in its traditional guise must seem rather an embarrassment. Revelation 7 gives us the picture with all the trimmings—a vast heavenly host, dazzling white robes, palm branches, hymn singing. But doesn't Christianity have to do, not with "Jerusalem, my happy home," but with the here and now of real everyday existence? Isn't it necessary to alter the nature of the Feast of All Saints, to make it a kind of ecclesiastical Memorial Day? We remember the saints as good men, good women, fine people, moral examples to be emulated, living on in the hearts and minds of those who follow them.

Are we restricted to these two options—Memorial Day on the one hand, or seventh heaven with harps and halos on the other? What are we to do about the fact that the church continues to read this flamboyant passage from Revelation every year on All Saints' Day? WHO ARE THESE, CLOTHED IN WHITE ROBES, AND WHENCE HAVE THEY COME? Who are the saints? And the elder answered, THESE ARE THEY WHO HAVE COME THROUGH THE GREAT TRIBULATION. What is the great tribulation? Does it mean that they have all died? Does it mean that they've crossed over Jordan— "Michael, Row the Boat Ashore" and all that?

"The great tribulation" does not refer to plain ordinary suffering and death. Wouldn't it be nice if it were so? How comforting it would be to say that the great reward comes to all who have been stricken by disease or grief or loss!

The New Testament teaching about suffering is far tougher than that. Revelation holds no sentimental message about harps and halos, but one of drastic and terrible and final import. Those white robes were not always so white. They were stained with the bloody sand of the Colosseum and burned by the Saracens and shot through with holes by the Nazis and dragged in the dust of Selma, Alabama. The Saints are those who follow Jesus Christ into the valley of the shadow of death, suffering the same humiliation and rejection that he did. *It is the nature of the Christian gospel to attract murderous enmity.* We in America forget that, because we have gotten the gospel mixed up with something else far more comfortable and far less threatening.

WHO ARE THESE, CLOTHED IN WHITE ROBES? They are the faithful Christians who have endured to the end, who have suffered contempt and loneliness and abuse because they would not deny the Lord. Some of the saints died dramatic and glorious deaths with great words on their lips. Other saints, the great majority, have led ordinary lives and died conventional deaths, but they played their part in the great drama of salvation by showing unswerving loyalty to Christ whatever their circumstances.

In the middle of the great tribulation, the church sings the song of victory. That is the meaning of the Book of Revelation. Revelation is not a Fielding's guide to heaven, nor was it ever meant to be. It was written for the encouragement and strengthening of the Christians who were facing terrible persecution. *In the endurance of the saints* God causes the world to *know even now* that the power of death has been vanquished forever in the cross of Christ.

The church's liturgy on earth is an anticipation of the triumph song of heaven. When we gather here we join hands and combine forces with all those who have fought the good fight and gone before. "The communion of saints"—that little phrase in the Apostles' Creed is one of the most tremendous articles of our faith. Just as we Christians comfort, strengthen, and encourage each other in our daily lives, so the faithful departed join with us in our prayers and praises and, especially, in our struggles, for it is the church that knows it will have trouble that sings the triumph song.

An American Episcopalian tells of visiting with Jana-ni Luwum, Anglican Archbishop of Uganda, not long before Luwum was murdered by Idi Amin in February 1977. "Aren't you afraid for your life?" asked the American, knowing that the Archbishop's fearless proclamation of the gospel was causing political opposition. "Sam," replied Luwum, "I don't worry about that. My life is in the hands of the Lord."

Fleming Rutledge in 1978 was a priest of the Episcopal Church in the Diocese of New York and curate at Christ's Church, Rye, New York.

MATTHEW 5:1-12

ALL SAINTS DAY
NOVEMBER 1, 1984

Who else are the saints we are called to remember on this day, and indeed, who else are the saints we are most likely to remember than those, in one sense, unexceptional people in our lives and in our particular pasts, who have come through for us? They are saints not because they were capable of anything of which you or I are not also capable, but because through them we glimpsed our own deepest hope for our lives and our world, indeed, God's hope for us. Tell the stories of such saints, from your own particular life, or from other's lives of which you are aware, from our common life together.

I think of Will Campbell's biographical book, *Brother to a Dragonfly.* Among others, Campbell tells of his Grandpa Bunt, who "never raised his voice, lost his temper, lost a fight." " 'Have chairs,' he said to guests on the day of his death." And there was his wife, Grandma Bettye: "Grunting every breath, sometimes twice, with neuralgia and lumbago. But smiling, too. Because her lover (for sixty-six years her lover) never once forgot to say: 'Mighty fine supper, Mrs. Campbell.' No matter what the fare." Grandma Bettye had worn a "flannel bathrobe to church the very first Sunday after Christmas. Because it was the prettiest thing she had ever seen, and the Lord deserved the best. And because it was 1933 and she didn't have a bathroom." And then there was his Grandma Bertha on the other side who said: "Be kind to the Lillys. Lice don't make folks trash. They may be angels unaware. Some folks say I oughten to dip snuff." On another occasion, Grandma Bertha said: "I don't care if he's a darkie. And I don't care if he stole Albert Carroll's old truck. He's fourteen years old, and they ain't gonna beat him." Campbell tells of his Uncle Jessie, who he describes as "a man of great courage." Uncle Jessie had gotten up and walked out of church one night when the Ku Klux Klan had come in and presented a Bible and some money to the congregation. "Only a brave and strong man would walk out on the Ku Klux Klan in 1925" (Will D. Campbell, *Brother to a Dragonfly,* Continuum, 1980).

Can remembering people such as these become for us an affirmation of faith in the God of all futures? Can such remembering be for us a call to lives which express the hope of Revelation and Matthew and Isaiah?

I recently heard Robert Coles tell a story about a little six year old girl named Ruby. She was one of three black children who were the first to be sent to previously white schools when integration was begun in New Orleans. Every day for months, escorted by a Federal Marshall, Ruby would walk past a screaming mob of people yelling all kinds of names at her and telling her they were going to kill her. They were there when she went to school and there waiting for her when she left. During these months Coles would ask Ruby the same questions over and over, and always receive the same answers. "How are you doing Ruby?" "Fine." "How are you making out in all of this?" "Okay." And then one day Ruby's teacher noticed something as Ruby was walking past the mob that morning. It appeared that Ruby was talking to the people in the mob. Coles questioned her. "Ruby, what were you saying to those people out there?" "I didn't say anything to them." "But, Ruby, your teacher saw you, you were talking to those people." "I wasn't talking to them. I was praying for them." Coles was astonished. "Why," he asked, "why would you pray for those people?" "Because I should," said Ruby. "Do you always pray for them?" "Oh yes, I pray for them every morning and I try to remember to, every afternoon and when I say my prayers at night, too." And when he asked her *what* she prayed, Ruby replied, "I pray, 'Father forgive them, for they know not what they do.'" Ruby knows in which communion she stands, doesn't she. The communion of saints.

David T. Reynolds, a minister of the United Methodist Church, in 1984 was the associate pastor of Fairlington United Methodist in Alexandria, Virginia.

COLOSSIANS 1:9-14

ALL SAINTS
NOVEMBER 1, 1985

Professor Steimle asked, as October waned, what festival of the church was approaching, to which one of the less liturgical in the class answered "Halloween." Dr. Steimle then suggested— it was a course on doctrinal preaching—that it would be good to be in chapel on November 1.

I connected saints with medieval piety, and the notion of a day for the commemoration of all of them seemed remote, if not both "catholic" and spooky. The preacher that day was John Knox, the eminent professor of New Testament who, I knew, prayed earnestly at the beginning of each class and sometimes spent afternoons in his office with the door open, available to students struggling with his course on christology.

The story on which he preached told of Jesus washing their feet. Dr. Knox reminded us who this was who stripped himself, took a towel and did the dirty work. Then he called on us to recollect the persons in our own lives who had, as it were, stripped themselves down and taken a towel to our feet. "Take a few moments of silence and just remember the saints who have, in the name of God, blessed your own life." He finished the sermon by giving thanks out loud for some of his own saints and leading us in singing, to the great tune of Vaughan Williams, "For All the Saints."

That was the day that saint found a place in my vocabulary, that the church year became real time, and a new link was forged between discipleship and christology. Halloween opened, like the worst of self-concerned fears turning into self-giving compassion, toward All Saints. Years ago, in an article in *The Christian Century* titled "How the Jack-O-Lantern Lost Its Teeth," the writer (whose name has receded into the dim past like many a nameless saint!) observed that the dark forebodings and haunting fears of Halloween become, on All Saints Day, a pumpkin pie! On this day we give thanks for all those who have belonged to God, not as plaster saints spared the world, but as men and women of flesh and blood who, by some grace have come through the muck of being human, have endured the darkness and now shine as the stars.

If Professor Knox asked me today to name in my heart my own saints I should need more time. But on the list for sure would be Melissa. She was white-haired and by all appearances frail when I got to know her. But she kept her own house, and the flowers from her garden supplied not only her own airy living room but the neighbors as well. When I took time out from being a graduate student to walk across the street for a visit, it was as if she had thought of no one but me since the last time we talked. I would have to say that she was, for a year or two, a pastor to me, this small lady in plain dresses as fresh as the flowers in her sunny rooms.

I saw things change for Melissa, a problem with her stomach which made eating difficult and kept her from going to church altogether. But, as difficult as life became, some things did not change. She always cared, for the people who knew her, for beauty, and for the world which stretched so far beyond her sitting room and that front porch and tidy garden.

And there were the pearls. They were real, splendid, obviously cost plenty. Her children had given them to her on the condition that she would wear them every single day. And that is the way it was: Melissa, in her garden, cleaning her house, sometimes able only to sit in her rocking chair and listen to the young man from across the street, falling so terribly ill, was always wearing those softly lustrous pearls.

Charles Rice, a minister of The United Church of Christ, in 1985 was professor of homiletics in the theological and graduate schools of Drew University, Madison, New Jersey.

REVELATION 7:9-17

ALL SAINTS DAY
NOVEMBER 1, 1990

Joseph Campbell in a recent PBS TV series with Bill Moyers noted that we could trace the spirituality of a people by observing what their buildings were like and where they were located. In the middle ages, the cathedral stood proud and tall, full of sculpture and stained-glass depicting the lives and deeds of the heroes of the faith. Then, secular government began to dominate and great capitol buildings were erected. Finally, in today's world, the office building for commerce overshadows the city scape. He pointed out Salt Lake City as the "perfect example" where the Temple was once the largest building in town; then the capitol, built next to it to govern those who worshiped in the Temple. And now, there exists an enormous skyscraper over-shadowing both, the church's own commercial center in which the business affairs of the worshipping-governed are handled!

All Saints Day is a day to recall our past and to look forward into the future. We remember our forbearers in the faith, those teachers of the way, who have passed on their tradition, have preserved the "story" and incorporated us into it. Since commercial buildings dominate our skylines, those once familiar figures of salvation, now may seem like distant, irrelevant, and foreign persons—men and women of extraordinary, if not quaint, strength and faith relegated to a dusty past, antiques lining the shelves of a shop visited only by those who, in a frenzy of nostalgia, want to "buy a relative" in the guise of an old portrait. Or is there something else involved in the current wave of nostalgia for things ancient and storied? Is this a hidden desire for "connectedness" to a meaningful and hope-filled past for which, perhaps, those irrelevant saints of old might provide the link?

In the aspe of Canterbury Cathedral there is a modernized chapel dedicated to twentieth-century martyrs. A strange hush falls over the crowds of modern-day "pilgrims" as they approach the small area in that impressive and ancient place to look at the list of names, among them Dietrich Bonhoeffer, Oscar Romero, Martin Luther King, Jr., the six Jesuits killed in El Salvador. Ancient history becomes poignantly modern when, standing in the place of Becket's martyrdom, these noble people of faith, these "salvation figures," as Bishop Marshall would deem them, stand starkly throbbing with the flesh and blood of contemporaneity.

Memory will draw the centuries close when the great figures are recalled such as Gregory the Great, Francis of Assisi, Martin Luther, Julian of Norwich, St. John of the Cross; or teachers and writers such as Augustine, Aquinas, Anselm, Catherine of Siena, Lancelot Andrews, Jeremy Taylor. We all can recall "famous" names of people who deepened the understanding of the faith and its implications for living as Christian men and women. It is when we lose our self-consciousness that we begin to realize that "saints" are flesh and blood people "just like me;" they are the vast company of ordinary Christians struggling to be free, breaking out of bondage in places as far flung as China and Czechoslovakia, living dedicated lives in city, suburb or farmland. The realization must dawn that all the baptized are embraced in the company of saints in the kingdom of God, for sainthood is a gift of grace, the birthright of the baptized, and not something earned by superhuman piety, violent death or ecclesiastical honor. The saints were and are people whose lives included Christ as their companion and guide, whose faith exemplifies the beatitudes—the merciful, the peacemakers, those who hungered and thirsted after righteousness; those who embodied the spirit of the beatitudes and thus owned their discipleship of worship, witness and service. They are people who have helped create our past, who have formed our story, who have been brought out of stained-glass and are on the stained sidewalks of the cities of our country. The saints of the past were not alone; the saints of today are not alone. Look again and Christ will be there; wherever a saint is noted, there is Christ as the constant companion in the struggle. Sainthood is indelibly associated with the crucified one; just as our baptism is not something we do, but is something Christ did, namely the baptism of the cross, so is our sainthood characterized.

To make the connection between saints past and saint at sixty-miles per hour is to bridge the ages. To read the lives of the saints, those who continued the struggle against wickedness and evil and remembered the vision of John, who grasped their son or daughtership as of God, is to realize they were real people struggling to be faithful in confusing times. To live today the life the Beatitudes describe, is to live in no more nor any less confusing time than those whose names we know are recorded in heaven, known only to God. When we gather at the altar or around the Lord's Table, we gather in faith and are reminded that we are a small group surrounded by "that multitude which no one could number, from every nation, tribe and peoples and tongues, angels and archangels and the whole company of heaven." People of the beatitudes encourage us to be people of the beatitudes in our own time and place, knowing that Christ, crucified and risen is always with us. What a connection of time and place. What a force for prayer!

Alan K. Salmon in 1990 was Rector of Christ Episcopal Church, Riverton, N.J.

Reign of Christ

MATTHEW 6:24-34

CHRIST THE KING
NOVEMBER 26, 1978

How can we get ready for Doomsday? Doomsday conjures differing images but for most people they are negative and frightening. The purpose would be to reduce the fear of the end of things and to enhance anticipation of them because Christ is King.

I recall two childhood stories about doomsday. One involved an older cousin who frequently visited our home. He would often get into apocalyptic material and have us all terrified at the prospects of impending disaster from Gods' angry hand. The other experience was positive. My pal's grandfather visited him every summer. A tradition grew up. There would always be one day during the visit, we were never sure when, that "doomsday" would take place. It meant that his grandfather would take all of the neighborhood kids who happened to be in the backyard that afternoon to the ice cream parlor where we could order as much of anything we wanted at his expense. We were never far from Johnny's backyard during Grandpa's visits. Half the fun was getting ready for it. We couldn't wait for the treats of "doomsday."

Knowing what we do from Christ about God, and what God has in store for us we can also anticipate the real "doomsday." The Day of the Lord is not something to be afraid of or to run from. We want to be there. We gladly accept God's invitation.

As we await that exciting day we want to stay close to the Lord's back yard, listening to Christ's stories, seeing the smiles and tears in his eyes. We respond to his signs of love with acts of caring for everyone else in the back yard. We don't want anyone to be left out. Even Ronnie, the pimply kid, is caught up in the contagion of being with the Father.

It is more than a silly picture that is to be painted. The Christian's life with God is more than chocolate ripple. The whole of Christian life is more than mere charity to the naked and hungry. But such charity and such simple joy springing from the love made known in Christ is essential, and without it faith languishes and dies. And it is not just individual charity. It must get to the iniquitous systems so that they no longer maim our brothers and sisters. But this wider sense of justice begins with the spontaneous personal kindnesses. The righteousness of the Kingdom is many sided but this love experience is the fruit of genuine religion and by this fruit our true relation to God is known.

I would try to further sensitize the hearers' senses to the ways in which God may be nudging them to respond to the basic needs of those close to us. In our church it might be the members of our Laotian refugee family who are still in the Thailand camps waiting for a sponsor. Or it might be baking bread for the jail ministry program.

J. Paul Seltzer, a minister of the Lutheran Church in America, in 1978 was pastor of Atonement Lutheran Church, Syracuse, New York.

DANIEL 7:13-14; REVELATION 1:4-8

CHRIST THE KING
NOVEMBER 25, 1979

"It was the best of times, and the worst of times," Dickens begins his *Tale of Two Cities*. In Europe, an old world was passing and a new world was in the agonizing, revolutionary, uncertain process of birth. Such times are inevitably the worst of times, for the passing of the old and the advent of the new are invariably chaotic, violent, painful times. But the worst of times, history shows, are paradoxically, the best of times, times when some new and better age is breaking forth.

Such are the times of the texts we read today from Daniel and Revelation. One would be hard-pressed to find stranger, more confusing books than Daniel and Revelation. Their strange dreams, visions, beasts and battles tend to overpower the modern reader. In Daniel, Israel is suffering terrible persecutions at the hands of the Roman Empire, many are falling away into apostasy, many are paying for their faith with their lives. In Revelation, the Church, the "New Israel," is suffering persecution at the hands of the Emperor, many Christians are falling away into apostasy, many are paying for their faith with their lives. "Is there any hope in such a terrible time?" many asked.

These were desperate times. And desperate times tend to lead people to ask desperate questions: What will our end be like? When will it come? Who is in charge?

There is much to suggest that we may be living in similar desperate times. Must I catalog for you the indications that many in our own time look upon our age as the end of time? When there are movies like *Star Wars* and *The Late, Great Planet Earth*, when there are Jonestown suicides, when prophets of doom prophesy my end due to food additives in my breakfast cereal or the very air I breath, in this age of wars and rumors of wars and life in the shadow of the mushroom cloud; who can deny that our age is also a desperate time? In such times, many are trapped between wild utopian visions for the future or dismal doomsday visions of an imminent end. People do strange things in such desperate times.

But lest we too easily read ourselves into Daniel and Revelation, let us be reminded that these books were written, not to a contented, successful, affluent, mildly discomforted church like ours, but to an Israel and to a church suffering under great persecution. Persecution is not a problem for the American, established church. But it is a very real problem for the church in many parts of the world. So perhaps we should let these suffering, persecuted churches read today's text and take hope, not us. Apostasy—that vast, disinterested, disheartened falling away from the faith—may be more our church's problem than forbearance under persecution.

But I remind you, there were apostates in Israel and in the church during Daniel and Revelation. Difficult times produce not only Christians who are glorious martyrs but also Christians who are unfaithful cowards. And *these texts address both groups of Christians.* To the one is promised judgment and reckoning. In other words, to both groups of Christians is promised the *coming* and *near presence of God.*

Desperate times demand the most desperate of actions. The texts today proclaim that bold, decisive, transforming action has been, is being, and will be taken—not by us, not by political powers, not by the oppressed or the oppressors—but by *God Almighty*. Out of the chaos and confusion of Daniel and Revelation's worst of times. On this last Sunday of a dying Church Year, the Advent of Christ's coming among us. There comes a confident, expectant word that God yet rules, God's purposes will yet be fulfilled, the difficult present is but a prelude to the glorious coming of God. There is, even in these times, hope for us; not hope based upon our goodness, or optimistic views of future progress for the world, or the success of some political program, or even hope based upon the good works or faithfulness of the church. It is hope based solely upon God— the one who is the Beginning and End of all our hope, the one who holds us martyrs and apostates in the palm of his hand, the one whose "dominion is an everlasting dominion," the one "who is and who was and who is to come." The King is coming, and may he come quickly. Amen.

William H. Willimon, a minister of the United Methodist Church, in 1979 was Assistant Professor of Liturgy and Worship, The Divinity School, Duke University, Durham, North Carolina.

LUKE 23:35-43

CHRIST THE KING
NOVEMBER 20, 1983

In a sermon preached and recorded at Princeton on August 2, 1953, George Buttrick told about the night he stumbled in the dark. He was staying in a hotel in western New York and had retired for the night, when he remembered a telegram that had to be sent. Lying in bed in the darkness of an unfamiliar room, he first had to put on a light. "But where was the light switch? I stumbled over my own shoes. I banged my nose on the open closet door. I was quickly in a minor frenzy…when I saw glowing on the wall, in this new iridescent material, the light switch. And I touched it. Now what had happened? I had re-established contact: not merely with the hotel cable, because that would have been to no purpose. What had happened was that I had re-established contact with nearby Niagara Falls—with the whole Falls; that is to say, with the whole universe, because it is the economy of the whole universe that keeps Niagara Falls in motion. I touched the light switch and instantly I was in communication with the whole universe."*

So what spared the preacher further harm, what delivered him from darkness into glorious light, was not the kindness of some maintenance person who used flourescent orange tape to mark the switches, nor was it the wisdom of Thomas Edison to invent the light bulb. It was the grace of God, who ordered the universe to bundle energy and water and gravity together for the blessing of God's creatures.

Is that too large a leap of fancy? Surely we are more comfortable with narrow slices of history and with tinier pieces of the cosmos. We are tempted daily to reduce the Word to smallness, including this day. For as a purely practical matter, this Festival of Christ the King will also be, in many congregations, the only service of the week to pay homage to America's national day of Thanksgiving. In some others, it will also be the day when a harvest of commitment cards will be collected to support the church budget for the coming year. In our own community as a tiny piece of the cosmos, in our few hundred years of American history as a small slice of history, in our own little congregations, we can distort the day of Christ the King into a procession of pledge cards and Pilgrims.

"As I read the Old and New Testaments," wrote Madeleine L'Engle, "I am struck by the awareness therein of our lives being connected with cosmic powers, angels and archangels, heavenly principalities and powers, and the groaning of creation. It's too radical, too uncontrolled for many of us, so we build churches which are the safest possible places in which to escape God. We pin him down, far more painfully than he was nailed to the cross, so that he is rational and comprehensible and like us, and even more unreal" (*The Irrational Season*, New York: Seabury Press, 1977, p. 171).

So we celebrate our own efforts to handle the cosmos—a piece of glow-in-the-dark tape here, a tithe there. But in truth our only hope lies in a gift from the creator of the cosmos, to transfer us from a realm of our mere efforts to a realm whose King surpasses all his foes. And he did it from a cross, in what Christian theology calls the Atonement.

Analogies to this happened in other ages, of course, when a victorious king transferred to his control those who had been subject to the one he vanquished. But it happens in our time, too. Only now we call it a corporate take-over: one day, someone goes to the office, dictates correspondence and makes decisions, in the employ of Bendix; the next day she sits at the same desk, works with the same clients, and makes decisions for Allied. So Christ's subjects remain in the same world but become subject to a new King.

And yet, we have difficulty in celebrating Christ as King. For we have democratized everything. Corporation maneuvers and political enterprises are two of the devices which we human beings have engineered to deceive ourselves into thinking that we are in control. We even choose our royalty in the entertainment world—choose them, use them, and dispose of them or let them dispose of themselves. The pulp magazines at supermarket check-outs are cluttered with our fallen kings—Belushi, Lennon, and the one they still call "king," Elvis. Each enjoyed a narrow slice of history and, with a peep of glory, brought doses of temporary joy to a world that proved horribly mightier than they.

We cherish so much our own little glories. We are so easily deceived by the glitter of it all. But by His atoning death, Christ has transferred us to His realm: now we witness to a cosmic triumph; now we celebrate a matchless victory. Each narrow slice of history bows in His service. Each tiny piece of the universe moves in his honor. With the eyes of faith we need not strain at all to glimpse His grace, given to us in falling water and on a cross.

*Transcribed from recording purchased from Princeton Theological Seminary.

William B. Lawrence, a minister of the United Methodist Church, in 1983 was writing a Ph.D. dissertation at Drew University and was pastor of the First United Methodist Church, West Pittston, Pennsylvania.

MATTHEW 25:31-46

CHRIST THE KING
NOVEMBER 25, 1984

11/24/96

There is nothing like forgetting yourself into forever. That seems to be at the heart of Matthew's scene of the final judgment. When those called blessed asked in surprise just when they did all of the things mentioned, evidently they had taken them so much into the stride of their living and loving that they had to be reminded. By contrast those on the left, those cursed, were also surprised. It was not the surprise of discovery but the surprise of hurt arrogance. They asked, "When did we see you and not give, visit and clothe?" What's striking here is that there were some deeds to their credit. Let's admit that because it may be an acknowledgment that we ourselves will want on the record, for, after all, there is so much in this group that applies to us.

It appears that those on the left side were pretty sure about their doings or their deeds. They hint at some kept records. If they did not have the statistics, they hint further that they were pretty sure that they always knew what they were doing. Well, what's wrong with that? Don't we all tend to keep a pretty good account of our ethical actions? Isn't that what we are exhorted to do time and time again in our worship service, especially in the preaching we hear? So why shouldn't we protest being put on the left side?

So many of us can claim a fairly good batting average when it comes to omissions or what we haven't done or left undone. The problem is that we tend to take pride in these omissions. More than we imagine, we all have a tendency to live our lives highlighting more of what we haven't done than that which we have done. Remember the time when our parents asked what we were doing, and usually got our angelic reply, "nothing?" The question is, have we put away such childish things? Matthew's word is that such a lifelong habit of stressing omissions will find Heaven putting us on the "left side, the cursed side."

Perhaps we need this view of final judgment to see that what we need for abundant living and serving is not so much a formula but a forgiveness. The general prayer of confession points to the contrition we need in the words: "We have done those things we ought not to have done and we have left undone those things we ought to have done." Such a confession is appropriate to Matthew's overall emphasis, an ethic rooted in God's grace and forgiveness.

Think of this final judgment as asking about what counts as "neighborly." Whether we encounter the "least" as those who surrender all to Jesus as disciples and Apostles, or whether we encounter the "least" as the hungry, sick, naked and imprisoned, it is our response, our reception, our welcome that is the difference between God's forever or God's kingdom judgment. Our norms, as valuable and necessary as they are, are not enough. It is our neighbor that channels our God. We are called to be found doing what is neighborly. Let the blessings already given as our heritage abound in our hearts.

Evans E. Crawford, a minister of the United Methodist Church, in 1984 was Dean of the Chapel at Howard University and professor of social ethics and preaching at its Divinity School.

LUKE 23:33-43

CHRIST THE KING
NOVEMBER 26, 1995

Proclaiming "the kingdom of God" was the linch-pin in Jesus' public ministry. He told parables about the kingdom, invited people into the kingdom, told people the kingdom was at hand. But always the kingdom was something different than what people expected. In a day when many Jews wanted a militarily powerful kingdom with which to challenge Rome, Jesus said, "The kingdom is like a tiny seed... the kingdom is like yeast hidden in the dough... the kingdom is like a hidden pearl." The kingdom, while the most precious reality on earth, was never quite what people thought.

The kingdom gets mentioned one last time in Jesus' ministry when the thief on the cross asks Jesus, "Remember me when you come into your kingdom." Considering the shape Jesus was in when this request was made of him, the words seem the height of folly. Cross-eyed in pain and looking more like a street accident than a Savior, Jesus did not appear to be heading anywhere worth following. Certainly the disciples had concluded this as they had all fled in disillusionment (even Peter, "The Rock" had crumbled). Yet in reply to the thief, Jesus does not say, "Forget it, buddy. It's over—can't you see I'm washed up, finished, through!?" No, he says, "Okay, today you will be with me in paradise."

Somehow the thief recognized a central gospel truth: In his apparent weakness, Jesus was strong. Through the humble path of service and the dreadful way of the cross, Jesus accomplished salvation and established his kingdom. Jesus reconciled the world to himself and is, therefore, both King and Lord over all Creation.

Now he is also Lord of the Church, which proclaims our theme for today: The Reign of Christ. So what should this Lord's Church look like? Well, some now suggest that the road to success for churches is through political power mongering or through retrofitted worship services designed to attract media-oriented people who desire a jolt of religious entertainment each week.

But we should not be surprised if the church actually does not look very impressive or powerful as the world reckons those things. For while the Church truly is in touch with the one who has "the supremacy over all," it often witnesses to that Supreme One in humility and in apparent weakness.

But while the apparent weakness of the Church may not be surprising, it can make life difficult for believers. For we must somehow confess our faith in the reality of Jesus' Lordship directly into the teeth of a world which does not appear to be ruled over by anyone, let alone a loving God. We must confess our belief that the church is connected to the universe's true source of power even though the church is often not much to look at. How can we do this? How can we gain the eyes of the thief to see past the trouble and apparent defeat of the moment?

One key way to do so is by a faith which is regularly nourished by the confirming signs of our weekly liturgy and our daily acts of devotion. For during most weeks while we are out in the world, the smog of sin dirties the lenses of our faith. So every week we return to the Body of Christ so that, by our acts of faith and liturgy, God can clean off our spiritual lenses to see clearly once again the Christ who rules this entire world. Through worship and devotion we perceive, and then also incarnate, "the Reality underneath the reality" (from Douglas John Hall, *The Lord's Prayer*, ed. Daniel Migliore. Eerdmans, 1993, p.136). For "reality" is not just what Tom Brokaw reports or what Time magazine lays out in glossy photos and snappy prose.

We Christians believe that Reality is God's power at work in the Creation—the Creation which he made in Christ and which he has now redeemed through the blood of the Lamb. Reality is God's hand at work, moving and shaping all events toward the consummation of his kingdom.

"Reality" is not just reports on Bosnia but the news that God is working to end all warfare and rescue all those held hostage by evil conflicts. "Reality" is not just reports of racism in Los Angeles or Toronto but the truth that God in Christ is stamping out all injustice and will release all those held captive by the chains of prejudice. "Reality" is not just news footage of starving children in Africa but the fact that God wills that all hungers be sated and all thirsts be slaked through the coming of the one who fed the multitudes.

Before Advent again focuses us on the beginning of Jesus' life, we do well to think back to the end. We do well to remember that Jesus came to forgive sins and bring God's kingdom. He does have the supremacy over all things. But seeing that truth is no easier today than it was on the day of the crucifixion. For a crucified man to promise the paradise of his kingdom looked almost as foolish back then as when Christians today huddle in their sanctuaries to proclaim that this chaotic world is still ruled by a loving Lord of Life.

Surely the powerful of our world do not and cannot see this—they can only wag their heads and scoff at the church and at the Lord it proclaims. Yet some, like the thief, manage to see it and grab hold of it. For all such as this, the way to paradise is opened—and not just at the end of history, but already today.

For once we see our Lord, we can then live for him in kingdom ways. But to feel his power and to participate in his kingdom takes faith—a faith nourished through worship and liturgy. For through the formal liturgy of worship, but also through the informal liturgy ("service") of the everyday, we can see and proclaim and make plain to all people that grand truth first declared by the early church: "Jesus is Lord!"

Rev. Scott Hoezee in 1995 was Pastor of Preaching and Administration at the Calvin Christian Reformed Church in Grand Rapids, Michigan.

LUKE 23:33-43

CHRIST THE KING
NOVEMBER 26, 1995

Proclaiming "the kingdom of God" was the linch-pin in Jesus' public ministry. He told parables about the kingdom, invited people into the kingdom, told people the kingdom was at hand. But always the kingdom was something different than what people expected. In a day when many Jews wanted a militarily powerful kingdom with which to challenge Rome, Jesus said, "The kingdom is like a tiny seed... the kingdom is like yeast hidden in the dough... the kingdom is like a hidden pearl." The kingdom, while the most precious reality on earth, was never quite what people thought.

The kingdom gets mentioned one last time in Jesus' ministry when the thief on the cross asks Jesus, "Remember me when you come into your kingdom." Considering the shape Jesus was in when this request was made of him, the words seem the height of folly. Cross-eyed in pain and looking more like a street accident than a Savior, Jesus did not appear to be heading anywhere worth following. Certainly the disciples had concluded this as they had all fled in disillusionment (even Peter, "The Rock" had crumbled). Yet in reply to the thief, Jesus does not say, "Forget it, buddy. It's over— can't you see I'm washed up, finished, through!?" No, he says, "Okay, today you will be with me in paradise."

Somehow the thief recognized a central gospel truth: In his apparent weakness, Jesus was strong. Through the humble path of service and the dreadful way of the cross, Jesus accomplished salvation and established his kingdom. Jesus reconciled the world to himself and is, therefore, both King and Lord over all Creation.

Now he is also Lord of the Church, which proclaims our theme for today: The Reign of Christ. So what should this Lord's Church look like? Well, some now suggest that the road to success for churches is through political power mongering or through retrofitted worship services designed to attract media-oriented people who desire a jolt of religious entertainment each week.

But we should not be surprised if the church actually does not look very impressive or powerful as the world reckons those things. For while the Church truly is in touch with the one who has "the supremacy over all," it often witnesses to that Supreme One in humility and in apparent weakness.

But while the apparent weakness of the Church may not be surprising, it can make life difficult for believers. For we must somehow confess our faith in the reality of Jesus' Lordship directly into the teeth of a world which does not appear to be ruled over by anyone, let alone a loving God. We must confess our belief that the church is connected to the universe's true source of power even though the church is often not much to look at. How can we do this? How can we gain the eyes of the thief to see past the trouble and apparent defeat of the moment?

One key way to do so is by a faith which is regularly nourished by the confirming signs of our weekly liturgy and our daily acts of devotion. For during most weeks while we are out in the world, the smog of sin dirties the lenses of our faith. So every week we return to the Body of Christ so that, by our acts of faith and liturgy, God can clean off our spiritual lenses to see clearly once again the Christ who rules this entire world. Through worship and devotion we perceive, and then also incarnate, "the Reality underneath the reality" (from Douglas John Hall, *The Lord's Prayer*, ed. Daniel Migliore. Eerdmans, 1993, p.136). For "reality" is not just what Tom Brokaw reports or what Time magazine lays out in glossy photos and snappy prose.

We Christians believe that Reality is God's power at work in the Creation—the Creation which he made in Christ and which he has now redeemed through the blood of the Lamb. Reality is God's hand at work, moving and shaping all events toward the consummation of his kingdom.

"Reality" is not just reports on Bosnia but the news that God is working to end all warfare and rescue all those held hostage by evil conflicts. "Reality" is not just reports of racism in Los Angeles or Toronto but the truth that God in Christ is stamping out all injustice and will release all those held captive by the chains of prejudice. "Reality" is not just news footage of starving children in Africa but the fact that God wills that all hungers be sated and all thirsts be slaked through the coming of the one who fed the multitudes.

Before Advent again focuses us on the beginning of Jesus' life, we do well to think back to the end. We do well to remember that Jesus came to forgive sins and bring God's kingdom. He does have the supremacy over all things. But seeing that truth is no easier today than it was on the day of the crucifixion. For a crucified man to promise the paradise of his kingdom looked almost as foolish back then as when Christians today huddle in their sanctuaries to proclaim that this chaotic world is still ruled by a loving Lord of Life.

Surely the powerful of our world do not and cannot see this—they can only wag their heads and scoff at the church and at the Lord it proclaims. Yet some, like the thief, manage to see it and grab hold of it. For all such as this, the way to paradise is opened—and not just at the end of history, but already today.

For once we see our Lord, we can then live for him in kingdom ways. But to feel his power and to participate in his kingdom takes faith—a faith nourished through worship and liturgy. For through the formal liturgy of worship, but also through the informal liturgy ("service") of the everyday, we can see and proclaim and make plain to all people that grand truth first declared by the early church: "Jesus is Lord!"

Rev. Scott Hoezee in 1995 was Pastor of Preaching and Administration at the Calvin Christian Reformed Church in Grand Rapids, Michigan.

LUKE 23:33-43

CHRIST THE KING
NOVEMBER 26, 1995

Proclaiming "the kingdom of God" was the linch-pin in Jesus' public ministry. He told parables about the kingdom, invited people into the kingdom, told people the kingdom was at hand. But always the kingdom was something different than what people expected. In a day when many Jews wanted a militarily powerful kingdom with which to challenge Rome, Jesus said, "The kingdom is like a tiny seed... the kingdom is like yeast hidden in the dough... the kingdom is like a hidden pearl." The kingdom, while the most precious reality on earth, was never quite what people thought.

The kingdom gets mentioned one last time in Jesus' ministry when the thief on the cross asks Jesus, "Remember me when you come into your kingdom." Considering the shape Jesus was in when this request was made of him, the words seem the height of folly. Cross-eyed in pain and looking more like a street accident than a Savior, Jesus did not appear to be heading anywhere worth following. Certainly the disciples had concluded this as they had all fled in disillusionment (even Peter, "The Rock" had crumbled). Yet in reply to the thief, Jesus does not say, "Forget it, buddy. It's over— can't you see I'm washed up, finished, through!?" No, he says, "Okay, today you will be with me in paradise."

Somehow the thief recognized a central gospel truth: In his apparent weakness, Jesus was strong. Through the humble path of service and the dreadful way of the cross, Jesus accomplished salvation and established his kingdom. Jesus reconciled the world to himself and is, therefore, both King and Lord over all Creation.

Now he is also Lord of the Church, which proclaims our theme for today: The Reign of Christ. So what should this Lord's Church look like? Well, some now suggest that the road to success for churches is through political power mongering or through retrofitted worship services designed to attract media-oriented people who desire a jolt of religious entertainment each week.

But we should not be surprised if the church actually does not look very impressive or powerful as the world reckons those things. For while the Church truly is in touch with the one who has "the supremacy over all," it often witnesses to that Supreme One in humility and in apparent weakness.

But while the apparent weakness of the Church may not be surprising, it can make life difficult for believers. For we must somehow confess our faith in the reality of Jesus' Lordship directly into the teeth of a world which does not appear to be ruled over by anyone, let alone a loving God. We must confess our belief that the church is connected to the universe's true source of power even though the church is often not much to look at. How can we do this? How can we gain the eyes of the thief to see past the trouble and apparent defeat of the moment?

One key way to do so is by a faith which is regularly nourished by the confirming signs of our weekly liturgy and our daily acts of devotion. For during most weeks while we are out in the world, the smog of sin dirties the lenses of our faith. So every week we return to the Body of Christ so that, by our acts of faith and liturgy, God can clean off our spiritual lenses to see clearly once again the Christ who rules this entire world. Through worship and devotion we perceive, and then also incarnate, "the Reality underneath the reality" (from Douglas John Hall, *The Lord's Prayer*, ed. Daniel Migliore. Eerdmans, 1993, p.136). For "reality" is not just what Tom Brokaw reports or what Time magazine lays out in glossy photos and snappy prose.

We Christians believe that Reality is God's power at work in the Creation—the Creation which he made in Christ and which he has now redeemed through the blood of the Lamb. Reality is God's hand at work, moving and shaping all events toward the consummation of his kingdom.

"Reality" is not just reports on Bosnia but the news that God is working to end all warfare and rescue all those held hostage by evil conflicts. "Reality" is not just reports of racism in Los Angeles or Toronto but the truth that God in Christ is stamping out all injustice and will release all those held captive by the chains of prejudice. "Reality" is not just news footage of starving children in Africa but the fact that God wills that all hungers be sated and all thirsts be slaked through the coming of the one who fed the multitudes.

Before Advent again focuses us on the beginning of Jesus' life, we do well to think back to the end. We do well to remember that Jesus came to forgive sins and bring God's kingdom. He does have the supremacy over all things. But seeing that truth is no easier today than it was on the day of the crucifixion. For a crucified man to promise the paradise of his kingdom looked almost as foolish back then as when Christians today huddle in their sanctuaries to proclaim that this chaotic world is still ruled by a loving Lord of Life.

Surely the powerful of our world do not and cannot see this—they can only wag their heads and scoff at the church and at the Lord it proclaims. Yet some, like the thief, manage to see it and grab hold of it. For all such as this, the way to paradise is opened—and not just at the end of history, but already today.

For once we see our Lord, we can then live for him in kingdom ways. But to feel his power and to participate in his kingdom takes faith—a faith nourished through worship and liturgy. For through the formal liturgy of worship, but also through the informal liturgy ("service") of the everyday, we can see and proclaim and make plain to all people that grand truth first declared by the early church: "Jesus is Lord!"

Rev. Scott Hoezee in 1995 was Pastor of Preaching and Administration at the Calvin Christian Reformed Church in Grand Rapids, Michigan.

MATTHEW 25:31-46

CHRIST THE KING
NOVEMBER 24, 1996

"When the Son of Man comes in glory...."

Any funeral is sad, but the service for a 31 year-old quadriplegic was particularly heartbreaking. He hadn't been feeling well, but when his caregivers went to bed he was with friends and everything seemed normal. A popular and intelligent young man, he had many friends who frequently visited him during the 13 years following his diving accident. Just before sunrise, his caregivers were awakened by the arrival of an ambulance. Something was very wrong. First reports were that his unfeeling body had deteriorated from the strains of being a quadriplegic. Later reports said he abused alcohol. A couple weeks later, a newspaper reported what only insiders knew: death was attributed to a heroin overdose. How does a quadriplegic abuse heroin? Apparently a friend—one with a long police record—thought it was a nice favor to inject the young man when he couldn't do it himself. Only something went wrong. He died.[1]

"When the Son of Man comes in glory... he will separate people one from another...." Come, Lord Jesus. We just can't wait.

The trial of Susan Smith had just ended. She had confessed to drowning her two sons in a South Carolina lake, and had been sentenced to life in prison. Much of the western world was closely following the case, arguing over whether she should receive the death sentence, life in prison, or be found mentally incompetent to stand trial. Then the extenuating circumstances began to come out. Abuse. Affairs. A broken home. Suicide attempts. Her step father, who admitted having sex with her from her teen years until shortly before the murders, resigned his prominent positions in the republican party and the Christian Coalition.

Come, Lord Jesus. Separation time has got to be near.

In Bosnia, a mortar shell hits a market where women are shopping, men are relaxing, and children are playing. Serbian guerrillas hiding in positions around the city are blamed for yet another act of cruelty against innocent civilians.

In Jerusalem, a crowded bus explodes, killing fifteen and injuring many. The victims were on their way to work, school, and the market. They didn't realize they were in a war zone. A terrorist on a suicide mission wearing a body bomb was "credited" with the attack.

In Detroit, three men are charged with attacking, beating and chasing Dorthea Word until she plunged from a bridge to her death in the Detroit River. The kicker: an estimated fifty people watched, and some even cheered and goaded on the attackers. No one offered help.

Come, Lord Jesus. Judge between the sheep and the goats.

There are those moments, aren't there, when we just can't wait for the Son of Man to intervene and get things straightened out once and for all. There seems to be trouble everywhere, and we aren't getting anywhere trying to make it better all by ourselves. The fundamentalists have the right idea: we need a good, hot hell where all those misbehaven' folk can go when it's time for them to get their just desserts.

And here we have it. At the end of history, "When the Son of Man comes in his glory... he will separate people one from another." Nice, fluffy, docile lambs who do what they are told over here. Mean old Billy Goat Gruffs over there. Good folks this way, bad folks that way. This is not rocket science. We all know who gets it and who doesn't. Those headline-makers might bring misery to our peaceful planet for a time, but sooner or later, Judge Jesus is going to get them all good. And Matthew's report of the great judgment says so.

So here's the picture: the Judge is on the bench, gavel in hand, with angelic bailiffs and tipstaffs tending to his every need. After ages and aeons of watching evil and sin running rampant across the globe, the Judge will see to it that justice is served.

There's only one problem. This is the same judge who preached, "Judge not, that you be not judged." He also instructed us to love our enemies and do good to those who would hurt us. He died on the cross rather than calling lightning from the sky, and is the heart and center of a theology of grace. That's not exactly an open invitation to gleeful vengeance, and certainly not a suggestion that any of us should enjoy the thought of bad people getting punished. Movie-goers may have laughed when Arnold Schwartznegger's wife in *True Lies,* discovered his secret agent identity and asked "Have you ever killed anyone?" His lame attempt at justification, "Yes, but they were all bad." This judge doesn't want to kill the bad people and damn the evil doers; this judge wants to convert them and bring them over to the other side. Judgment will happen. The sheep and goats, as well as the wheat and the tares will be separated in the end. In both cases, however, it's all in the hands of the judge. None of us get to do the separating, and there will be more than a few surprises in store for everyone.

As much as we might desire to gloat over judgment, the Reign of Christ Sunday is an invitation to celebrate the joy of enthronement. God is victorious at the end of history. "When the Son of Man comes in glory..." is an affirmation of certainty that does not invite equivocation and evasion. There are not ifs, maybes, or mights in the promise. The Son will come. Count on it.

What adds to the confusion of the Reign of Christ is that when the Son of Man comes in glory, the basis for his judgments will befuddle both the innocent and the guilty. The ones invited to "come" and "inherit a kingdom" won't realize they did anything so special. Those told to "depart from me into eternal fire" won't know they missed the chance to serve the Lord. These standards for judgment should prevent gloating and cause us all to take a real close look at our spiritual lives, while we flip frantically through the pages of the Bible for assurance that salvation is ultimately received as a gracious gift through faith.

On this the final Sunday of our Christian liturgical year, joy and faith are found in the certainty of Christ's final and ultimate victory. The God who saw that all was "good" in the beginning of creation will assure goodness and justice at the end.

Scriptural confidence oozes forth. Faith steps forward with power. Regardless of our kind acceptance of doubt and evasion during other Sunday worship hours, and our occasional anger over the evil that seems to pervade the cosmos, today we are offered the best of all hopes. "When the Son of God comes in Glory..." chimes an eschatological reality that peals from the page, echoing a hymn of God's justice persevering to the end of histoly. This isn't empty triumphalism, for we wish no harm on anyone and bring no praise to ourselves. In fact, this isn't about us. We celebrate God's act in Jesus Christ, who will sit *at the right hand of God the Father Almighty, from whence he will come to judge...."*

Come, Lord Jesus. Quickly come.

Duane Morford in 1996 was the senior pastor of The Holiday Park United Methodist Church in Pittsburgh, PA

INDEX OF AUTHORS

INDEX OF BIBLICAL TEXTS

Thanksgiving 1996

Please send **Seasons of Preaching: 160 Best Sermons**

_____ copies at US$20.00 each = $_____

Shipping & Handling = $_____

Total Enclosed = $_____

Shipping Charges
❑ In USA, $3.95 for 1st book; $1.00 for each additional book.
❑ In Canada, US$5.00 for 1st book; $1.00 for each additional book.

❑ Check enclosed. Or if paying by credit card, please check from the following:
❑ Visa ❑ MasterCard ❑ American Express ❑ Discover Card

Card No._____ Exp. Date_____

Signature_____

Ship to: _____

_____
(street address please, UPS will not deliver to P.O. Box)

_____

_____

Liturgical Publications Inc
Publications Division
PO Box 432
Milwaukee, WI 53201-0432

96BOOK   Or call toll-free: **800-876-4574** or **email: lpi@execpc.com** to place your order today!

Give _Seasons of Preaching_ to a Friend!

Call to order
1-800-876-4574

email: lpi@execpc. com

Seasons of Preaching

160 Best Sermons from the Preaching Resource Word & Witness

Edited by
John Michael Rottman &
Paul Scott Wilson

For a Subscription to **Word & Witness**

❑ 1-Year Subscription: US$ 54.95
❑ 2-Year Subscription: US$104.95
❑ 3-Year Subscription: US$153.95

Subscriptions to Canada, add US$14.00 per year; Foreign subscriptions also available, please write or call for prices.

❑ Check enclosed. Or if paying by credit card, please check from the following:
❑ Visa ❑ MasterCard ❑ American Express ❑ Discover Card

Card No._____ Exp. Date_____

Signature_____

Send to:_____

_____

_____

_____

Liturgical Publications Inc
Publications Division
PO Box 432
Milwaukee, WI 53201-0432

96BOOK   Or call toll-free: **800-876-4574** or **email: lpi@execpc.com** to place your order today!